A GUIDE FOR CO-OPS, INTERNS AND FULL-TIME JOB SEEKERS

FIND YOUR FIRST PROFESSIONAL JOB

Scott Weighart

This textbook is dedicated to Tim Hall and Jan Wohlberg, the two mentors who were the most helpful and influential in beginning my career in experiential learning.

Fourth Edition
Copyright © 2013 by Scott Weighart

ISBN: 978-0-9621264-9-9

Printed in the United States of America

CONTENTS

ACKNOWLEDGEMENTS

Much has changed since the third edition of this book was published six years ago, so I first want to acknowledge the constants that have remained in place in that time. As I no longer work in higher education, I am especially grateful to the former colleagues who have both stayed in touch and kept me in touch with the world of co-ops and internships from the university perspective. As a result, this book is stronger than ever: It reflects my more recent experiences from the recruiter and employer side of experiential learning as well as an ongoing appreciation of the perspectives of students and career professionals in higher ed. Thanks to Susan Bacher, Charlie Bognanni, Erin Doyon, and Deb Hunt for their ongoing friendship and professional perspectives. This new edition would have been impossible without their ability and willingness to contribute exciting new material to the book.

For this new edition, I also am extremely grateful to the co-op and career services team at UMass Lowell. On very short notice, Diane Hewitt, Erin Doyon, Anne Apigian, Rae Perry, and Martina Witts were able to meet with Susan Bacher and me in May 2013. They generously shared their perspectives on how the book could be improved, and you'll see considerable evidence of their insights, perspectives, and tools within these pages. They also reached out to their employers and students to broaden the range of sidebar boxes that you'll find here. The book is far better for it.

In my role now as the first-ever Director of Learning and Development for Bates Communications, I am grateful to our great team and our leaders, Suzanne Bates and Dave Casullo, for providing me with a dream job: Every day is an opportunity to create, and the work I'm doing in instructional design has only strengthened my belief in the power and relevance of experiential learning in professional development.

Given that this book has been a work-in-progress since 1995, many others have played important roles in its ongoing development, including students, employers, and colleagues. I am grateful for the opportunity to work with so many terrific people over the years—too many to name here—who contributed to the collective wisdom found in this book. For this new edition, my former student Rebecca Harkess provided some great new material. Additionally, I should thank Nancy Johnston from Simon Fraser University, a true expert on learning theory, for her ongoing perspectives as well as her friendship.

Thanks also to those who have brought this book a long way in terms of its appearance. Over the years, Victoria Arico continually refines the professionalism of the book with her cover design. Lastly, my wife Ellie, as always, contributed significantly in ways I can't begin to enumerate. Thanks to everyone.

Scott Weighart
July 2013

INTRODUCTION

In May 2013, Adecco Group—a company that provides talent management support to organizations across the country—announced the results of a new survey of roughly 500 employers of young professionals. These employers were asked to weigh in on their perceptions and experiences with hiring and managing young professionals from ages 18 to 24. Here are a few highlights—or maybe we should call them lowlights:

- Two-thirds (66%) believe that students are not ready for the workforce when they graduate college.

- Over half (54%) have ruled out candidates because of weak resumes.

- Half of them said dressing inappropriately for an interview is a big issue.

- Almost half (44%) said that showing up late—or on the wrong day altogether—is one of the biggest mistakes of job seekers.

- Another 36% percent were put off by candidates' overly aggressive expectations about pay, vacation, and benefits.

In a sign of the times in our Digital Age, I should note that 30 percent of those surveyed also complained about young interviewees checking their phone or texting during a job interview.

What's your reaction to this information? My goal here is not to rant about unprofessionalism or go off on some sort of "kids these days" lecture. I actually see these results as mostly good news for those reading this book. Sure, there are negatives here: If you're in that 18-24 age range, you may be treated as guilty until proven innocent because of employers' preconceived notions about how ready you are to find—and succeed at—your first professional job.

But here's the silver lining: The bar is really low out there. And not just for your age range: A few years ago, I provided independent recruiting services to many employers, and I was amazed at the poor quality of the resumes, cover letters, and interviewing skills for *all ages* of job seekers. For every 100 applicants I reviewed, I can say that about 80 of them made it really easy for me to hit the delete button because their resumes and cover letters were of such poor quality. If 10 of the 100 qualified for the phone interview stage, more than half of them were easy to eliminate at that point due to their poor preparation and judgment on the phone.

So if employers have fairly low expectations, imagine what a great impression you can make by being *good* at this stuff! When an employer or recruiter is going through a pile of resumes, you can't blame them for eliminating people based on an especially bad spelling error, the lack of a cover letter, or because of submitting documents that simply look bad aesthetically. On the other hand, it's downright refreshing for a recruiter to come across a carefully crafted cover letter and a beautifully formatted resume with clear, compelling language. It's a thrill to have someone interview who actually has researched the job and the job description and who has put some thought into how they might do a great job for the employer. Because that just doesn't happen very often.

You might think that most hiring managers are dying to find fault with you. In my experience, nothing could be further than the truth for most employers. I know that I am *always* rooting for an interviewee to be fantastic. I want to have options! So with that in mind, I'd like you to think about some positives as we launch into this book:

- You can't always be the ideal candidate for a job... but you can always outwork all or most of the people you're competing against for a position.

- If you can master the content of this book, you'll have a competitive advantage now and for the rest of your career... because most people don't do the things that I say to do in this book—even people twice your age.

- For example, that Adecco survey also said that "lack of relevant work experience" is the most common reason young adults struggle in interviews. That is indeed a challenge, but it's one that we will address directly in this book.

- The Adecco survey also said that new grads don't need a ton of experience to get hired. Actually, 84% of managers said that one or two internships is sufficient. So the time and energy you put into getting experience sooner rather than later will really pay off for you.

Here's another way to look at it: Being successful in your first professional job is not magic. It requires a positive attitude and the willingness to keep taking small steps toward self-improvement in your career. Whether you are planning for your first co-op job, internship, or first full-time job out of college, this guidebook was written to show you exactly what separates the extraordinary new professional from those who are ordinary or mediocre. Follow these steps carefully, and you can transform yourself into a great job candidate and performer... a little at a time.

Universities across the country are embracing multiple forms of practice-oriented education, including co-op, internships, practicum assignments, volunteer work/community service learning, work abroad, and clinical rotations to name a few. Basically, the rising cost of higher education has resulted in students and parents asking, "What return will I get on my investment in higher education?" As a direct result, schools ranging from small community colleges to big-name Ivy League institutions have found it necessary to give their students more opportunities to get real-world experience.

This is a terrific development for the 21st-century student: Working in your field gives you a chance to test a career, build a resume and references, make connections between the classroom and the real world, create connections with post-graduation employers, and—often but not always—earn money.

While this represents a great opportunity, it also creates challenges for students. Some of these challenges relate to planning your co-op or internship: What can you do right now to increase your chances of getting the best possible job—even if you don't intend to look for your first job for a year or more? How will the job market affect your search? What are your job search options? The first chapter of this guidebook, "Planning For Your First Professional Job," tackles these questions.

Other challenges arise during the preparation stage—the weeks and months immediately preceding your co-op job, internship, or other work-related endeavor. How can you write an effective resume when your best job was working as a Burger King cashier or as a babysitter for families in your neighborhood? What should you include and emphasize on your resume, and what is best to leave off? How can you overcome your jitters about interviewing and present yourself positively but honestly? How can you deal with fuzzy open-ended questions, interviewers who are "nonstop talkers," and the fact that you can't possibly anticipate all questions that may be asked. How do you deal with a phone interview? What do you do if you get an offer from Company A when you're waiting for Company B to get back to you? Chapter Two ("Writing an Effective Resume") and Chapter Three ("Strategic Interviewing") of the guidebook cover this terrain and much more.

Once you have lined up your work experience, the real work begins. What is at stake when you are working as a co-op? How can you live up to your interview and make the most of your co-op opportunity? How can you balance a part-time internship with full-time classes? What should you do if problems arise? How can you get the best possible evaluation and reference? Chapter Four reviews "Keys to On-The-Job Success" and handling these concerns among others.

You also may wonder about how to make sense out of what happened during your co-op or internship when you return to campus for classes. What steps might be required of you when you return to school? What might you need to do to get credit for your work experience? What are some options to consider as you process the experience? Chapter Five goes over "Making Sense of Your Experience" and considers the reflection steps that are required at many institutions.

The appendices include many other potentially useful resources. I've separated them into this final segment of the book because some of them will be more relevant than others depending on where you're at in your career. Among other things, you'll find resources on how to conduct informational interviews, how to identify skills that are relevant to employers, how to write a cover letter, and a new section on success factors for international students. There are many tools and exercises that may be helpful to both students and educators; my advice is to browse the back of the book carefully and see what most applies to you.

This book has been through numerous editions and has been used by tens of thousands of students across the US and Canada. As such, the material here is tested by experience— just as you will be as you go through your first professional job experiences. While this is certainly serious business, I have tried to write the book in a light and conversational way, including many real-life anecdotes and quotes to make the book as fun to read as it is informative. I also will give you my perspective from both sides of the hiring process: While I worked for several years preparing students for co-op jobs and interns, I also have been a recruiter and interviewer. In the past two years, I've had the chance to manage several interns, too.

But you'll hear much more than my own opinions and experiences. It's really exciting for me to have the voices of some great co-op students and interns included in the guidebook. You'll find these thoughtful perspectives in sidebar boxes. Here's an example:

> **A Student's Perspective On This Guidebook**
> *by Keith Laughman*
>
> The co-op guidebook is a student's Bible to landing that great job during co-op semesters and even upon graduation. It's the only book that I've used for all five years of college! The information contained in this guidebook may be overwhelming at first, but believe me when I say that it will greatly influence your resume skills, interview skills, and job searching skills.
>
> *Keith Laughman was an MIS/Marketing student at Northeastern University, Class of 2002.*

This guidebook also includes the perspectives of employers and co-op or career professionals from Northeastern University and beyond. Another new feature in this fourth edition is the "Employer Roundtables" and "Student Roundtables" at the end of the first four chapters. We asked employers and students questions about the main topics of this book and captured their answers here. As a result, these sections are just like an employer panel or student panel on campus: You can hear many different opinions about the keys to job seeking and success. By a wide margin, there are now more "voices" in this textbook than ever before, and you might be surprised at how much a student in ANY major can learn by reading and reflecting on advice from a wide variety of perspectives. There is a considerable amount of wisdom in this field that proves to be universal.

Like most aspects of being a first-time professional in the workplace, what you get out of this guidebook will depend heavily on the amount of effort you spend in truly understanding the material that we present to you here. If you just skim through the chapters, you will find that this text is no more useful than giving a menu to a starving man.

If, however, you really put some energy into thinking about how this material applies to you and incorporating these concepts into how you approach resume-writing, interviewing, and your actual co-op job, you will find that these principles will help you in your career long after you have graduated.

I hope that this book helps you gain confidence as you approach your first co-op job, internship, clinical experience, practicum, or full-time job after graduation. Good luck in your preparation activities and in all of your efforts to professionalize yourself in the weeks and months to come. You might just amaze yourself with the results!

Scott Weighart
July 2013

CHAPTER ONE

Planning For Your First Professional Job

Whether you opt for a co-op or internship, a clinical assignment, or simply your first full-time job after graduation, you have a great deal at stake. Yet even though many students now realize how important some form of practical job experience is these days, not all students really understand everything that they're going to get out of the experience. Additionally, many students fail to realize that there is a great deal that can be done to get ready for a co-op or internship—even if their first professional job is months and months away.

Congratulations! You have the information to help you to prepare yourself right here in your hands. This chapter is intended to get you thinking about your first professional job *now* so you will have a better understanding of the benefits of getting practical job experience and what you can do to give yourself a head start on the process.

BENEFITS OF PROFESSIONAL EXPERIENCE

For all undergraduates getting real-world experience, there are still many common themes when we consider the benefits of doing a co-op job, internship, clinical assignment, or practicum before graduation.

Career Testing

In any form of experiential learning, getting practical work experience as an undergrad helps you test out different careers. This will help you determine whether you are on the right career path. It's one thing to be in a finance class for three or four hours per week: It's a whole different ballgame working in a finance job 40 hours per week for a summer or six months. You really wouldn't want to spend $150,000 or more on your education over four or five years, only to find out six months into your first "real job" that you actually *dislike* working in that field as a full-time professional. What do you do then? Go back to school?

It's not at all uncommon to see the following scenario with co-op students: John Schlobotnik

1

goes to see his co-op or internship coordinator right after completing his first job experience in accounting (or psychology or engineering or any other major). The coordinator welcomes John back and asks how the job went. "What did you *learn* on your job, John?" John blushes, looks at the ground, and sheepishly says, "Uhhh, I think I learned that I don't want to *be* in accounting."

It's almost as if John thinks that his coordinator will criticize or condemn him for such rebellious thinking! Hardly. We remind the student that this is a primary purpose of internships and co-op, and then we can begin a dialogue about what other concentration or major may be more appropriate.

Career Testing – A Co-op Professional's Perspective
by Bob Tillman

Most of the students I have coming in want fieldwork. And then when they do it, they don't want it anymore. Okay, well, tell me what that means: What changed? How hard was it? What does it feel like when people scream and yell at you? You know, you're only as good as your last mistake—and that's big in engineering, especially civil. And when you're the engineer or the super some day, how are you going to handle it differently? Remember what it felt like to be a beginner.

Bob Tillman is an Associate Professor and cooperative education faculty coordinator in Civil and Environmental Engineering at Northeastern University.

In my days at Northeastern, I knew more than a few physical therapy students who absolutely loved the subject in the classroom. During their first field experience, however, a few found out that they felt amazingly uncomfortable having to touch people in their role as a physical therapist in training. For most, this was a startling and upsetting realization—but also an absolutely critical discovery that led them to make a necessary change very early in their college careers.

See another example in the sidebar box coming up shortly.

Experience Building

You may not begin your first internship or co-op with much directly relevant job experience on your resume, but you can change that fact dramatically over the course of a few real-world experiences. How this happens will vary depending on a few different factors.

If you begin your undergraduate years with a very clear sense of your career goals—and if your real-world experience merely confirms those goals for you—you will graduate with great depth of experience. Student A may know before she even meets with her coordinator that she wants to be a Network Administrator. Even if she has no direct experience, she can be assured that she will end up with in-depth knowledge of the field after completing two or three six-month co-op jobs. Maybe her first job is a rather light Help Desk job. With that on her resume, she is able to get a substantial PC/LAN position next time around, complete with opportunities to troubleshoot problems, upgrade software on the network, and perform fundamentals of networking such as adding new users. If she does a third co-op, she might be doing substantial computer room work, handling tricky interface issues between Novell NetWare and TCP/IP, maybe even setting up the hubs and routers that form the "guts" of the network. She graduates with a rich and deep understanding of one part of MIS.

Confirming Career Plans at LaGuardia Community College
by Marie Sacino

An internship can provide an opportunity to discover your passion, to make a solid contribution to your employer, and to grow. Zoe Cornielle, a liberal arts student in our social science and humanities curriculum, explored her interest in the field of social work during her first internship at the Hospital for Special Surgery. Zoe was assigned to work in the Department of Patient Care and Quality Management. Under the supervision of a program coordinator and a managed care associate, Zoe worked as part of a health care team to provide education, advocacy, and assistance to outpatients in both rheumatology and orthopedic clinics.

With training, support, and supervision from social work professionals, Zoe began to provide outreach services to patients in various patient waiting areas. Zoe listened to patients' concerns and questions, provided information on education and support groups, made referrals to community-based agencies, and kept records of patient activity.

On my visit to HSS, I got a first-hand opportunity to see Zoe at work. I was so impressed by her professionalism, her ability to engage patients, her understanding and sensitivity of the impact of barriers to health care as well as her dedication to the patients with whom she worked. HSS was also quite impressed: Zoe was invited back for her second full-time internship this past summer. She discovered her passion—helping people—and confirmed her career plans: social work. Zoe expanded her role greatly as she took on the new role of "first" lead volunteer. She had an opportunity to participate in developing training materials and in leading group discussions. Zoe also provided support and supervision to new interns and trainees as they began to work with patients. She now plans to transfer to Hunter College to pursue a degree in social work.

Marie Sacino is Professor of Cooperative Education at LaGuardia Community College.

Meanwhile, Student B doesn't really know what he wants to do with MIS—he just knows that he likes doing stuff with computers. Maybe he starts out with that same Help Desk job but finds it frustrating to deal with impatient end users and to juggle competing priorities and requests amidst numerous interruptions. Next time around, he tries a database development position and likes it more but finds it too much on the opposite extreme—too much time sitting at his computer, not enough variety. Finally, he gets a Systems Analyst job on his third co-op and acts as a go-between for programmers and financial planners who need software. This student graduates with greater *breadth* of experience. He may not command as much money in his first full-time job, but he may have more options available to him now and more doors open to him later. So there are positives either way.

Additionally, any professional experience that you obtain as an undergrad will do much more than improve your technical skills in a given field—the experience will provide you with great opportunities to professionalize yourself. If you're like most students, you may underrate the importance of this. While most students come into internships and co-ops focusing on what technical skills they may be able to acquire, many come away from their first job rather surprised at how much they learn about working that has *nothing to do with learning technical skills and responsibilities.* Every workplace has its own written and unwritten rules about performance and behavior. Organizational politics can have a dramatic impact on your ability to function effectively in a position. Supervisors can vary dramatically in terms of their managerial skills, expectations, and pet peeves. Developing the adaptability to handle different work environments and to obtain great evaluations in situations that require radically different behavior can be a big challenge. Learning the changing rules of the game and making sure that you succeed regardless of varying expectations is a characteristic of the best future professionals.

Most students—especially those working full-time hours in their work experience—find that they feel more confident about their professionalism after each job experience. The discipline required to get to work on time every day and to get your work done well and on time seems to develop good habits that become more automatic over time in most cases. It's often exciting for a co-op or internship coordinator to see a student after one job experience: I was often amazed to see big changes in professional etiquette when these students returned to my office and interacted with me. Frequently, going to work in a professional setting helps you develop a greater sense of purpose both in the classroom and in your professional relationships.

Building a Great Resume and Getting Valuable References

If you're building your experience, then you obviously are also building an impressive resume detailing all of that experience. Just as importantly, if you perform well, you can end up with a long list of respected professionals who will recommend you to future employers. Developing a network of people who are able and willing to assist your future job searches can make a big difference—many jobs are filled through personal connections rather than simply pulling in a bunch of anonymous candidates through an online job site.

Enjoying a Trial Period with Potential Full-Time Employers

Many organizations who hire students for co-op jobs, internships, and other forms of experiential learning are looking for more than a person to do a job for six months—they are using the co-op period to "test out" someone they may wish to employ upon graduation.

As one large co-op employer once told me: "If we hire ten co-op students, we figure that at least nine of them will work out well and get productive work done in a cost-effective manner. If three of those nine are such stars that we want to hire them after graduation, then that's really the ultimate goal for us. After all, at our company, we can't just fire someone—we have to coach them to death!"

Indeed, this organization doesn't allow managers to fire employees who are clearly poor performers. Instead, the manager must hold regular "coaching meetings" and document them heavily. In the end, the employee still ends up being terminated. As you might imagine, this employer really doesn't want to hire the wrong people—that's a mistake that costs thousands of dollars in addition to causing numerous headaches! Hiring co-ops and interns helps them know what they're getting and makes it less likely that they will have to go down that costly and time-consuming path with a wayward employee.

Integrating Classroom Learning with Workplace Learning

Certainly one of the greatest payoffs for students who immerse themselves in a relevant real-world setting is the opportunity to make meaningful connections between theory and practice. Better still, it's a two-way street: Concepts that are hard to really understand in the classroom can come alive for you when you see how they apply to real-world situations.

At other times, you will learn how to do something while on co-op but perhaps not really understand the underlying concepts until you learn about them in a class after completing your work experience.

Better still, co-op, clinicals, and internships can bring home the importance of classroom concepts, sometimes in dramatic and unexpected ways. Students who don't get meaningful, career-related job experiences during their undergraduate years sometimes have a harder time believing that some required courses are all that important. Even if you have a gifted professor, it may be hard for a student to believe that coursework in finance or accounting has any relevance to them if they "know" that their future is in marketing or human resources.

Getting that professional experience as an undergrad can reveal that this way of thinking is an illusion. Years ago, one of my students who completed an MIS position in senior management support at The Gillette Company had to provide computer and audiovisual assistance to some of the most powerful people in the organization. His coursework in accounting took on a newfound urgency for him as he ended up assisting during several heavy number-crunching meetings, in which the executives spoke with great passion about balance sheets, income statements, and other concepts that the student had found only mildly interesting before the job began.

Another student felt rather lukewarm about taking his Organizational Behavior requirement, mainly because the offering was an eight-credit course meeting twice a week for over three hours at a time. Before long, he found that his class was "almost like therapy." It helped him process and understand many elements of motivation, leadership, and group dynamics that had absolutely baffled and confounded him on his previous co-op job.

Coursework outside of your major also can have a dramatic impact on your career, and vice-versa. One of the biggest mistakes students make when picking electives is to just pick something that sounds relatively painless without considering the possible benefits of liberal arts electives. A marketing student might be well-advised to take a communications course that helps build public speaking skills; a civil engineering student with lofty aspirations might be wise to take classes in corporate finance. I knew a student who felt that her self-confidence and interpersonal skills improved dramatically by taking a class in acting. Likewise, there can be good synergy for computer science students and modern language majors who take some electives in each other's disciplines.

One of the funniest stories along these lines came from one of my students who absolutely had to add a social science course to meet a liberal arts requirement for business students. He signed up for Introduction to Psychological Counseling, basically because the class hadn't filled up yet and it fit the requirement. When his next co-op ended up being a PC support job, he couldn't believe his dumb luck: He was shocked to find himself using techniques he had learned in class—such as active listening—when trying to calm down and help computer users who were frequently angry, embittered, and impatient due to their PC problems.

Earning Money (including Part-Time Work)

While co-op and internship earnings will not pay all the costs of education for most students, they can make a nice dent in your expenses. Many internships offer stipends or at least modest hourly pay. Many students also have the opportunity to stay with their employer to work part-time hours after returning to classes. How much money you make will depend mainly on your field and your experience. For example, even an outstanding co-op student in early childhood education will make much less than the average student in accounting, engineering, or computer science. Also, it makes sense that a finance concentrator with no job experience and no coursework in the field will have much less earning power than an upperclassman with classroom knowledge and co-op experience. As for part-time internships, you can understand that someone doing a computer-related job is more likely to get a paid position than someone who wants to work in sports management or at a TV station or record company.

Your earnings as a co-op or intern also can be affected heavily by your flexibility. Having a car obviously will open up numerous opportunities for you versus the student who is stuck on public transportation. While this is true in all fields, it can be especially dramatic for some majors depending on where they are seeking a job. For marketing students at Northeastern, for example, many of the good quality jobs are not incredibly far away with a car—but they are completely inaccessible by public transportation. Additionally, being open to the possibility of relocating to work out of state and/or being willing to work in a variety of areas also will increase your earning—and learning—potential. When you're competing against dozens of students who cannot or will not consider using a car or working out of state, you may find numerous terrific jobs and surprisingly little competition beyond the immediate reach of your university.

Other factors affecting earnings may include grades, the time of year that you choose to work, your effort in the job search (including effort in teaching yourself relevant skills), and soft skills such as communication skills, interpersonal skills, and attitude.

Return on your Investment in Education

Above all, real-world experience gives you a chance to get a nice return on the investment of time, money, and energy that you put into your collegiate career. Studies have shown that full-time co-op students get a nice head start in terms of post-graduate earnings and quality of job opportunities. The more you strive to accomplish, the bigger the payoff at the end.

Learning to Fish

There's a Chinese Proverb: "Give a man a fish and you feed him for a day. Teach a man to fish and you feed him for a lifetime."

As you start to think about getting ready for your first job search, this proverb should tell you what your mentality should be. In my experience, universities and colleges vary dramatically in how much support they give to student job seekers. Some are fantastic, some are mediocre, and some do almost nothing. But it doesn't really matter; sooner or later you're going to be out in the world on your own, and the quicker you learn to fend for yourself as an expert job seeker, the sooner you increase your competitive advantage—and that is something you will be able to enjoy for the rest of your career.

My hope is that when you finish this book you'll feel like you know three times as much about the job search process as your *parents* do right now. So as we think about becoming a job search expert, perhaps the most surprising news—and maybe the most encouraging news—is that from my years working in higher education, as a recruiter, and in the private sector, I've learned that the bar is astonishingly low in terms of what people believe to be good job search skills. As an example, my long-time colleague Susan Bacher and I conducted several job searches a few years ago, working as independent recruiting consultants to small companies. We would typically find that of 100 resumes and cover letters perhaps about 5 percent were ones that you would say were extremely well done. Beyond that 5 percent, there might have been another 15 or 20 percent that were pretty good: They were adequate—often generic, but they covered the basics. The rest of them were usually poorly done, at best, or just truly awful. That's actually good news for you! Employers have learned to develop low expectations. By covering the basics—and by going the extra mile with your resume and cover letter—your application can stand out in that pile of resumes and bring you one step closer to an interview.

If you're like most students, you're probably at least a little anxious about the competition and about the fact that you have so little experience. That's certainly a disadvantage to some degree, but you can make up for some of that lack of experience and level the playing field by outworking the competition. Perhaps surprisingly, it's not that hard to do! So always remember that if you can out-research, out-prepare, out-think, and outwork the competition, you're going to be way ahead of 95% of job seekers for the rest of your life. How does that sound?

GETTING READY FOR A FUTURE REAL-WORLD EXPERIENCE

Maybe your first professional job experience is still a long way off. For some people reading this book, their first co-op, clinical, or internship may be more than a year away. That's a long time, and there's no point in beginning a job search when your availability is in the distant future. Still, there are plenty of things that you can do *right now* to improve your chances of getting a better job when the time comes. But first, it's important to understand a critical question: What do employers *want* when they are looking to hire an intern, co-op candidate, or even a full-time hire coming right of college?

Common Fears

As stated earlier, about 90 percent of Northeastern students that I ever met cited co-op as their number-one reason for picking the program. However, many of them still experienced a good degree of fear and anxiety about beginning their co-op careers. This is natural: Most students recognize the value and importance of practical job experience but begin the program with limited knowledge about the job market and the co-op process as well as significant concerns about their lack of professional jobs in the past. In fact, I would guess that at least two-thirds of college students begin the program without anything more than unskilled-labor positions on their resumes.

Very frequently, students meeting with their co-op or internship coordinator for the first time express concerns about what their first job search may hold: In addition to inexperience, students also worry about the negative impact of poor grades, lack of a car, a sagging economy, and competition from other (presumably better) candidates.

The first thing to remember is to limit your fears and concerns to the things that you *can* control. You can worry about the economy, the job market, and how good other job candidates are—but in the end, worrying about these things won't change them at all.

Fortunately, there are quite a few things that you *can* control. You also may have more going for you than you realize, as you'll soon see.

What are Employers Seeking when Hiring Co-ops and Interns?

When I first took over the MIS program at Northeastern University in March 1995, my colleagues Bill Sloane and Charlie Bognanni suggested that I get out on the road to meet as many employers as possible in order to understand the needs of my program. It was great advice, and it yielded surprising information. I thought I already knew what MIS employers were seeking when they hired co-op students: computer skills, naturally! At that time in the history of information technology, I expected employers to list applications: "Well, we want someone who can use Novell NetWare and who knows Visual Basic or another programming language...."

I did hear some employers say those kinds of things—but only about one-third of the time. Two times out of three, the manager would say something like this: "Computer skills are great—the more the better. But more than anything, we want someone who wants to be here every day, someone who thinks it's fun to learn new things, a hard worker who communicates well and gets along with people.... Someone who can work independently and show initiative but also work in a team... Someone who doesn't complain and moan and whine when something has to be done that's a little *less* fun. We'd much rather have a student who is weak on technical skills and strong in terms of these other qualities than to have it the other way around."

Hiring Co-ops and Interns – An Employer's Perspective
by Steve Sim

From a Microsoft perspective, it's difficult to specify anything in particular, but we look for the core competencies we wish all MS employees to possess:

+ Passion for Technology
+ Big Bold Goal Mentality
+ Honest and Self-Critical
+ Accountability
+ Intelligence
+ Team & Individual Achievement

Steve Sim was a Technical Recruiter at the Microsoft Corporation and is now Co-Founder & Principal Search Consultant at Envisage Recruiting LLC.

After hearing this several times, I asked a few managers to explain why they felt this way. "In six months, I can teach someone a lot about UNIX or Windows NT, assuming that they're smart and motivated," a manager said. "But I can't teach a person to want to come in to work every day."

Another manager flipped it around the other way. "If you haven't learned how to take pride in what you do, how to respect other people, and have a positive attitude in the first 18 years of your life," she mused, "then *how am I going to change all of that in just six months!*"

Even Microsoft—an employer that obviously features an extremely technical environment—basically follows this rule. Look at the sidebar box on the next page, and consider the emphasis.

For most students, this is extremely encouraging news: Students who want to be in an experiential learning program requiring work generally have a strong work ethic. Most students I've met have at least some of those desirable soft skills. I found—just as those managers had told me—that it is indeed very hard to change who a person is as opposed to changing their skill set. This attitude is not unique to MIS employers. Consider what this marketing employer has to say in the following sidebar box:

Hiring Co-op Students – An Employer's Perspective
by Mike Naclerio

Energy and passion: You can teach a student or an employee the skills that are necessary for a position, but you cannot teach someone dedication and enthusiasm. If you build an organization based on quality people, you will get quality results.

Mike Naclerio is the President of Enquiron.

This is not just true in business environments. Consider what one of Northeastern's physical therapy co-op faculty told me when I asked her what her employers want in first-time professional hires:

What Employers Want – A Co-op Professional's Perspective
by Rose Dimarco

They're looking for someone who wants to learn, who's dependable, reliable, and who has some experience in a team environment—whether an athletic team or a debate team. Those are the things that they really are buying when you start school. When you graduate, they'll look more at technical skills, but they'll always be hiring professional behaviors. Always. That consists of how you perform in a "professional" environment.

Rose Dimarco is a cooperative education faculty coordinator in
Physical Therapy at Northeastern University.

Even for students in highly technical disciplines, this holds true. Employers do want to see basic technical skills, but they are not the primary concern when hiring:

What Employers Want – A Co-op Professional's Perspective
by Bob Tillman

Does it look like you have the skills and abilities? Does it look like you have your head on straight, and does it look like you'll show up at work on time every day? Because we're going to teach you everything else. So the question is: Does it look like you'll fit in? Does it look like you have the entry-level skills so you know how to turn a computer on, you know how to plot in AutoCAD already, you know how to bring drawings up? We'll teach you everything else, but you need to look like you can learn. So you need to talk about being able to learn, being responsible, showing up, and doing the job.

Bob Tillman is an Associate Professor and cooperative education faculty coordinator in Civil and Environmental Engineering at Northeastern University.

Of course, there are a few catches here. If possible, most typical managers would prefer to hire someone who has the soft skills AND some relevant technical skills—especially in a tough economy in which jobs are less plentiful. An inexperienced student who is a great person will not get a position if they're competing with great people who also have experience. Additionally, can't any snake oil salesman walk into an interview and *claim* to have a great attitude, excellent ability to work independently, and a terrific work ethic?? Absolutely. But there are steps you can take to change your skill set NOW and to help *prove* that you really have those soft skills, so let's consider those next.

Improving Your Marketability – A Co-op Professional's Perspective
by Rose Dimarco

I'll tell you what you can do: Get the best possible understanding of yourself. When you're president of your class, or when you go and work in a camp job or as a waitress, start looking at what energizes you in that job and what doesn't. Once you know that, you can better assess what a better job is for you at co-op time. It's getting beyond "I only want to work with children," "I only want to work with chronically ill people." It has to do with understanding the role you play at that site: Does that site value what you bring to that role naturally? You're not going to have all the academically critical skills to do the job; everyone knows that. You're bringing *you*, and you have to be able to articulate who you are and what you can offer that environment. There's no such thing as a lousy job; there are just jobs that are incompatible with who you know you are.

Try to be around people who need health-care assistance. That can be an elderly grandmom; that could be a neighbor who has a child with some form of disability. That could be volunteering in a nursing home part-time, even working in a hospital gift shop: You're seeing families going through your gift shop on their way to see someone who is ill. Seeing how all that fits will take time, but there is a connection between the healing process that's underway on that floor and that conversation in the gift shop when that mom and dad were heading up to see their child, and what they did to try and make things better. I would say that any experience involving some sort of service can go on your resume, and employers will value students who have volunteered and have exposure to different areas.

Rose Dimarco is a cooperative education faculty coordinator in Physical Therapy at Northeastern University.

Ways to Improve Your Marketability before you Start Your Job Search

This has to be one of the most underutilized steps that you can take, and there's nothing to keep you from starting to do this right away—even if your next job search is not on the immediate horizon. Here's the key: start devoting some time toward improving your knowledge of your field. A criminal justice student could go out and do informational interviews with professionals in law enforcement and security. A veterinary science student would gain valuable experience and demonstrate a great deal about her interest in her field by volunteering at an animal shelter. For a finance student, this could mean reading *The Wall Street Journal* or *Smart Money* or any number of other periodicals or books that will help you understand stocks and bonds, mutual funds, investment philosophy, and concepts such as risk versus reward and the present value versus the future value of money. Just about any information technology student (whether majoring in computer science, engineering, or business) would benefit by picking up computer skills on their own—whether through using online tutorials, reading books such as *HTML for Dummies*, or attending on-campus workshops on specific computer skills. I once worked with a student who had earned about five computer certifications on her own. This absolutely raised the eyebrows of potential employers. Likewise, taking meaningful courses in other majors such as Computer Science or English Composition instead of some bunny course to get an easy grade also can boost your technical and soft skills.

You're the Product – A Co-op Professional's Perspective
by Erin Doyon

When preparing for the job search and all that comes with it, think of yourself as a PRODUCT. If you are a product that you're trying to get an employer to purchase, everything you do to prepare becomes part of your brand and marketing. When writing your resume, picture it as a billboard. If you were creating a billboard, you would want to use all the space, make sure it was neat, easy to read and interesting. After all, this is your advertisement.

Think of your appearance as your packaging. If you were purchasing a product, you would look for a clean, sharp-looking package. If employers are thinking of hiring you—purchasing your product, basically—they too will be looking for clean, sharp-looking packaging.

Lastly think of your interview as your commercial. This is your opportunity to sell your product, yourself!

Erin Doyon is an Assistant Director of Cooperative Education in Engineering at University of Massachusetts Lowell.

Making Connections with Professional Associations

Joining a professional association in your field is another way to make yourself more marketable... but that's not the only reason to do so. If you attend professional association meetings and events, you'll have an opportunity to rub shoulders with professionals in your field. This is a great way to do some networking that eventually could lead to an interview, a co-op job, an internship, or even a full-time job after graduation. Also, your conversation with these professionals can be informal informational interviews: What do professionals in your field actually do? What do they like most and least about their jobs? This may help you figure out if you're in the right field or not. These informational interviews sometimes even lead to regular job interviews. For more on how to conduct informational interviews, read the appendix on the topic in the back of this book.

Another great thing to know is that while some professional associations can be expensive to join, they may offer substantially discounted student membership rates. For example, as of summer 2013, the Council of Supply Chain Management Professionals (SCSMP) charged professionals $295 for an annual membership, but students only had to pay $35 to join and have the opportunity to receive career-related newsletters, attend conferences at reduced rates, and many other benefits. Ask your co-op, internship, or career services coordinator— or an academic faculty member—for information about professional associations in your field and whether they would be worthwhile for you.

Making the Most of All On-Campus Resources

Most universities have tons of resources that you pay for with your tuition, whether or not you take advantage of them. Most universities and colleges have Departments of Career Services—featuring numerous resources that you may find valuable. You can research jobs in different fields, take tests that help you build self-awareness about how you might match up with different careers, and perhaps even have a practice interview videotaped and critiqued. In particular, you may want to look into whether a campus professional can administer the Myers-Briggs Type Indicator, Myers-Briggs Career Report, the Campbell Interest and Skill Survey, or the Strong Interest Inventory. The Myers-Briggs tests are often useful in understanding your personality, which can translate into a better sense of what elements you should seek in a job. The various interest inventories are great for seeing how your preferences and dislikes match up with professionals who are happy and successful in a great variety of fields.

Your university library is a good source for periodicals relating to different fields, careers, and organizations. Most universities also have counseling centers—good places to go if personal problems are causing you difficulties, whether job-related or otherwise. Another little-known fact is that some counseling centers also can help with issues such as time management and test-taking anxiety.

Taking Advantage of Online Resources

Even if you aren't able or willing to get assistance from professionals on campus, there are some online options that may prove helpful. If you Google terms such as "Myers-Briggs" or "Campbell Interest Inventory," you'll get links to sites that offer online testing for a fee. Some sites offer free testing as well—try Googling "Free Myers-Briggs test," for example—but you may be surprised to fill out a 70-item test and then be told very little... unless you THEN shell out some amount of money.

Taking Career-Related Courses

Increasingly, many universities are offering and even requiring career-related courses. Some—such as the excellent Gateway To The Workplace course at LaGuardia Community College in New York—are mandatory prerequisites to obtaining an internship or co-op job through the program. Given that these courses are often one-credit, pass-fail courses, some students might be tempted to go through the motions in these courses, doing just enough to get by. However, that would be a missed opportunity. For example, the University of Massachusetts Lowell is building a strong cooperative education program, and their course offers all sorts of tools and techniques that are invaluable to young professionals. These classes give you a chance to get questions answered, undergo some career counseling, learn

---

Utilizing On-Campus Resources – A Co-op Professional's Perspective
by Ronnie Porter

We now encourage students to obtain part-time positions or internships over the summer to prepare for getting their first co-op job. It would really depend on the field they're interested in. We might direct them to Career Services. There might be other resources on campus: we might direct them to the departments to check with faculty. We encourage them to really take advantage of their work-study positions, maybe working with a faculty member on research or some capacity like that to further develop their skills. We would really ask them to think about making the best use of any opportunities like that to develop their transferable skills.

Ronnie Porter is a cooperative education faculty coordinator in Biology at Northeastern University.

---

the fundamentals of resume writing and interviewing, and start to understand the logistics of how the co-op process works for you. It also can help you develop a good relationship with a co-op coordinator who can be a resource for you during all of your undergraduate years.

Start Owning the Responsibility for Your Success

One characteristic of interns and co-op students who are highly successful is that they own the responsibility for their success. In other words, a great co-op student is one who doesn't wait for things to happen but instead makes things happen for themselves. Take, for example, the student who came to see me ONE FULL MONTH *after* the official start date for his first co-op. Why did he blow off working with the co-op department? Well, a couple of friends had told him that the job market was tough and that he probably wouldn't be able to get a professional job. In talking to him, I quickly learned that he had good communication skills and a car. I had to tell him that basically 100 percent of our students with cars had been able to find related jobs in their majors—even in a bad economy. What a shame that he listened to people who knew little about the situation: Based on gossip and speculation from uninformed classmates, he went out on his own and got a job as a cashier in a restaurant. He looked absolutely sick when I told him that people with less going for them than him were making as much as $16/hour doing work directly related to their major!

Show some initiative as you plan ahead for your future co-op. When you interview for a psychology job and are asked about some aspect of the field, you don't want to say "I don't know anything about that because we haven't covered it in class yet." Maybe you can talk about reading Irvin Yalom's excellent book *Love's Executioner*, which features remarkable tales of psychotherapy. Likewise, journalism students should be able to cite *The New York Times* articles that they thought to be excellent; political science students should be able to speak—very diplomatically, of course—about political issues in their city, state, or in the nation. Hiring managers look for results-oriented self-starters who don't sit back and wait for someone to force them to learn a new skill set or about relevant developments in the field.

A great deal will depend on your outlook. If you have negative expectations about your co-op or internship, you are more likely to focus on the negatives in your job. If you take the attitude that hard work, good performance, and a cheerful tone can overcome the negatives in most jobs, you probably will find that to be true. The key is to start taking small steps toward success.

Co-op Success Factors – A Student's Perspective
by Mark Moccia

A student should be active as soon as the college career begins. The key to landing the job you want is not throwing pennies into a fountain, hoping for the Gods of Co-op to "bestow the perfect job upon thee." A student must work hard to improve grades, add skills, participate in clubs, and take on other activities to show they are hard working and potential leaders.

Equally as important, students must first decide their priorities before looking for a job. Some students might be looking to make good money, gain valuable experience, work for a large company, small company, etc. Once this is decided, the student then can begin to search for particular jobs.

Mark Moccia was an Accounting/MIS student at Northeastern University, Class of 2002.

GROWING AND MANAGING YOUR DIGITAL FOOTPRINT

Here's a concept that may be new to you, as a first-time professional job seeker. It is important to start thinking about growing and managing your digital footprint. What do I mean by that? Well, it's not my own concept, but I will explain.

Just as you leave behind a physical footprint when you go for a walk on the beach, you have a digital footprint. However, on the beach your footprints wash away in an afternoon, while your digital footprint lasts indefinitely. As an aspiring professional, you want to have a digital footprint which is fairly large and attractive—which is not always one and the same.

How does a person manage to create a large and attractive digital footprint? Much of your digital footprint is based on what people would find when they Google you online. Of course, people are able to do more extensive research if they have the know-how or the right software, but in most cases "garden variety" searches are done using Google.

The fascinating but horrifying thing to realize is that *anything* that you put online or even anything that *somebody else* posts or writes about you online—including in social media or blogs—is part of your digital footprint. The worst case is if your digital footprint includes an arrest record or other unsavory information. This might include all sorts of online activity: making a stupid comment on someone's blog or website, creating a review on TripAdvisor where you describe what is effectively underage drinking, you name it.

Digital Footprint Horror Stories

I have seen some horrifying examples. Several years ago, *The Boston Globe* wrote an article about a young woman who was not hired following an interview. She blogged about how the interviewer was an idiot and that the process was ridiculous. The interviewer found out about it, and an online war of words began. Now if you were to Google this woman—or this interviewer—you would see the whole story. It doesn't reflect well on either of them.

A few years ago when I was doing some recruiting, I was asked to hire a young professional right out of college. One candidate who I spoke to seemed to be a potential fit for the job, but I happened to do a Google search on him and discovered his blog. This blog covered pretty much everything about his life. Some of it was benign—what movie he had seen and things like that—but he had also written about other things. He wrote about his frustrating job search with a great deal of sarcasm and bitterness. This included a reference to me calling him for a phone screen and how he was hopeful about this but also fearful that it would be yet another failure. I dug even deeper and found that he revealed some incredibly personal information. He shared his insecurities about his romantic and sex life. This was obviously very awkward for me to read as a recruiter. After some debate, I decided to send him an e-mail to let him know that his blog was readily findable through an online search. Given its personal nature, I suggested that he may want to reconsider posting it with his name attached to it, or reconsider posting it at all. I didn't hear back from him after that point, but I'm sure he was mortified. The blog was taken down.

Anything you put on the internet is a lot more findable than you may think. I've had students put things up on a social media site under a pseudonym thinking that would be a clever way to make their online persona anonymous. But then one of their friends would write in the comments, "Hey there nice to see you on this site, Jamie Mastodon!" I've been able to find students this way and not always in the most flattering of situations. They hadn't put their name in there, but somebody else did.

The Power of Social Media

According to a blog called Digital Marketing Ramblings, Facebook had 1.1 billion users as of June 2013. About 350 million photos were uploaded to Facebook each day at this time. Google+ has been growing quickly, with 343 million users as of June 2013. Meanwhile, there were about a half *billion* tweets sent via Twitter every single day as of late 2012.... And Twitter has over a half billion users as well. Instagram was up to 130 million users as of this writing.

These numbers testify to the wild popularity of these sites and apps. Be thoughtful, though, about your exposure on these sites. They can be places where you could end up inadvertently sharing aspects of your life that would not be appealing to an employer who is looking for the best candidate to fill a professional position. There are any number of ways you can get tripped up on any of these sites as well as ones like Reddit, Tumblr, and YouTube.

In fact, getting too comfortable on these sites is one of the great dangers. Twitter, for example, is very searchable; I can't tell you how often I've read posts there that would reflect poorly if an employer ran across them. Remember: The Internet is in no way a private communication vehicle. If you are sending tweets, you always want to look at them from the point of view of an employer. What would an interviewer or a recruiter think if they came across it? Would they say "Wow, this person's impressive!"? Or would they say "Wow, this person doesn't show very good judgment."?

The same is true with Facebook. Obviously it's a good idea to have privacy controls on Facebook, but it is no guarantee that people won't see your posts. In fact, I know of cases where a student was asked to sign onto Facebook during an interview to show the interviewer his or her profile. Now, will this happen to you? Usually it won't, but it could. You might say it's unfair or unethical, and I would understand why you would feel that way.

Do Employers Really Look at Social Media Use?

But I also have a question for you: Why put inappropriate stuff on Facebook? Is it really necessary? Will you miss out by not doing that? Why show photos of yourself engaged in underage drinking or something that is otherwise going to be a red flag to an employer? These digital displays can have an effect on your professional life. A few years back, there was a viral story online about an intern who called in sick, so he could go to a Halloween Party hundreds of miles away. He then posted a picture of himself in costume, holding a beer, and noting the location. The employer saw it, and the student was out of a job shortly thereafter. If you Google "Fired Over Facebook" or "Not hired because of Facebook," you'll see all sorts of similar examples.

A 2011 *Forbes* infographic showed that 69 percent of employers have rejected a candidate because of what they saw on a social networking site. It also revealed that only five percent of employers don't use these sites to screen employees. So what would be a red flag for an employer checking out your profiles, posts, and tweets?

- Badmouthing a current or former employer

- Alluding to your use of drugs and alcohol

- Lying about your experience and qualifications

- Making discriminatory comments about others based on race, age, ethnicity, gender, sexual orientation, etc.

- Posting inappropriate comments or photos

- Demonstrating poor communication skills

Your Online Reputation – A Former Co-op Student's Pespective
by Rebecca Harkess

Before sending out resumes, you should ensure your online reputation is portraying you in a manner that you would like potential employers to see. Check all of your social media accounts to make sure your privacy settings are at the right levels, and Google yourself to see what comes up. Also make sure your LinkedIn profile is up-to-date and professional.

Rebecca Harkess was a Business Administration/Supply Chain major at Northeastern University, Class of 2009. She is now a Supply Planner at Keurig.

It's easy to be careless with social media and you don't want to learn the hard way. What you can do now is to build your online reputation and start being mindful of the power and level of exposure of these online networking and communication sites. Start thinking about your social media activities in the context of your digital footprint.

Creating a LinkedIn Profile

When I wrote the first edition of this book in the late 1990s, LinkedIn didn't even exist. Created in 2003, LinkedIn first struck many professionals as a curiosity—not something to take too seriously. Ten years later, LinkedIn had amassed over 200 million profiles worldwide. It's now the premier social networking website for professional purposes.

As a result, you really need to create a LinkedIn profile if you haven't already. While it's important to avoid making mistakes on other social media sites, LinkedIn is an opportunity for you to make a real positive impact on your digital footprint—if you do it right.

If you go to www.LinkedIn.com, you'll find that the site makes it easy to create a profile. Therefore, I won't describe that here. However, I would like to share the must-do steps when creating a new LinkedIn profile:

1. *Don't put it off!* Most college students probably know that LinkedIn exists, but many of them believe that there's no point in creating a profile until you've graduated college. That's a mistake. While your job experience may be unimpressive for now, your LinkedIn profile is still an opportunity for you to show a potential employer that you are giving thought to how to set yourself up for a professional career. It's also never too early to start making connections with people on LinkedIn... but more about that shortly.

2. *Think of it as an online resume.* In addition to your resume and possibly a cover letter, your LinkedIn profile may be the first example that an employer sees of your work. As a result, it's crucial that your profile advertises you effectively. Every spelling error, typo, or poorly worded summary or job description may be held against you. Take your time to get your profile right. At the very least, it can show people that you have some sense of how to present yourself professionally.

3. *Wear professional attire for your headshot.* One way your profile differs from your resume is that it can and should have a photo of you. On Facebook, you may well have a profile photo that's very informal. On LinkedIn, you want a formal headshot— usually showing either just your head or perhaps from the chest or shoulders up— and you should be wearing something that you would wear in a business formal work environment. Even if your experience is light, you want your appearance to say, "I can adapt to working in a business environment."

4. *Consider writing a summary that highlights your professional brand.* What are some words or phrases that might describe who you really are as a worker? Do you have stories to prove that those words or phrases are accurate and not just wishful thinking? If so, you can think of those qualities as your "professional brand." Maybe you're a "resulted-oriented people person," a "quick learner," or perhaps you're "adept at learning new software applications." Maybe you're a "social media expert" or an "effective writer." Regardless, you might want to write a few sentences as a summary that previews what you have to offer a potential employer. You also could list specialties or specific interests within your field.

There's an example on the next page.

SUMMARY

Results-oriented journalism major with significant experience in writing blogs, feature stories, and hard news. I have earned a reputation for thriving on deadlines while writing clear, concise, cliché-free text for online and print publications.

Specialties: Current events, local news, sports, human interest, business, trends, technology, lifestyle.

5. *Make sure that your job descriptions are accurate and consistent with your resume.* In the next chapter, I'll describe how to write a job description. Refer to that if necessary. The most important thing is that your dates and duties match up, and that you are not overstating your experience and qualifications. A 2011 Forbes survey mentioned lying about qualifications as the biggest reason why they have not offered a candidate a job when it came to use of social media.

6. *Make connections with people you know on LinkedIn.* I get requests all of the time from people who want to connect on LinkedIn. I always say yes to someone I know—unless it's someone I really don't want to know! But I do think it's foolish to try to connect with people you don't know... or to accept invitations from people you don't know. What's the point? If you sent an invitation to the CEO of some company, would they accept? Perhaps, but would it do anything for you if you didn't know that individual personally? I highly doubt it.

So focus on people you *do* know and not so much your friends at this early stage in your career. Connect with professors and teachers who think highly of you as well as managers and experienced employees with whom you've worked. Connect with family friends and acquaintances—especially those who work for companies that interest you or are in your field or industry.

Over time, you can and should build up a LinkedIn network of hundreds of connections, a little at a time. Some day—perhaps not for years—you will apply for a job at some organization where you don't know anyone... but maybe someone in your LinkedIn network works there or knows someone else who does. Then you can reach out to that connection and see if you can get some inside information—or maybe even an introduction to someone who's hiring.

In short, it's a good idea to take steps now that will help you get yourself a job later—even if it's not until you're 21, 25, 35, or 50!

7. *Add "Skills & Expertise" appropriately so you can be endorsed.* In the last couple of years, it's become possible for people to endorse their LinkedIn connections for various skills. LinkedIn has some sort of algorithm that will look at your profile and take its best guess as to what skills make sense for you. Some of these will make sense, but you also should add others as you see fit.

Once you have some connections, by all means endorse them IF you truly believe that they have a given skill or area of expertise. When you endorse others, they'll often

18

endorse you.

8. *Recommend your connections... and request recommendations if necessary.* It can be very powerful to have several people recommend you on your LinkedIn profile. It just means asking them to write a paragraph or two about what makes you special and what you have to offer. Often, you don't even need to ask for a recommendation: If you write one for someone you know and respect, they frequently will respond in kind.

Having a solid LinkedIn profile will pay off for you eventually. Over time, you can often see who views your profile on LinkedIn. And when you apply for a job on LinkedIn someday, it will be an easy click for people to view your profile. You absolutely cannot build a great LinkedIn profile—complete with connections, endorsements, and recommendations—in a day or even in a few months. Start working on it now!

LinkedIn – A Co-op Student's Pespective
by Mary Beth Moriarty

LinkedIn has been a huge help for jobs. It isn't as personal as Facebook, but it allows me to get in touch with people I have met on the job and at conferences. Sometimes I don't remember people's names, so I can quickly look up someone on my phone before going up to them, so it seems like I didn't forget important details. If I am looking for an 'in' to a company, it allows me to search connections and find out if I can connect to anyone there.

Mary Beth Moriarty is a PhD Candidate in Plastics Engineering at the University of Massachusetts Lowell.

Blogs, Websites, and Your Digital Footprint

These days, anybody can be a publisher. By that I mean that it's pretty simple these days to create your own website or blog. Using WordPress or Tumblr, you can create a basic site that you can use as your own online pedestal for voicing whatever opinions you might have.

But should you create your own blog or website? That depends. A blog or website can be a positive, a negative, or a neutral non-factor to a potential employer. It's a negative if your site has offensive content, or—as in my earlier blog example—if it simply shows questionable judgment. It's also a negative if it makes a poor impression from the standpoint of style— either visually or in showing that you can't string together a few sentences intelligently.

Your site will be a neutral non-factor for you if it's well done but has no relevance to your field or career. If you have a nice looking blog about your favorite sports team, band, or hobby, then that usually would do you no harm—unless the band or hobby is offensive or you write in a way that might raise eyebrows.

A blog or website can definitely work in your favor if you're writing intelligently about your field—or if you're showcasing skills that definitely matter to a prospective employer. For a graphic design or architecture major, a website is a must these days. Journalism or photography majors also benefit from being able to point people to their work. For a student in a computer-related field, a site could be an opportunity to showcase your coding ability. For many other majors, a blog is a good way to share your knowledge or insights on your field: A finance major could share links to recent investment news, commenting on them in the process. An engineering major could use a website to show people an academic project: What problem were you trying to solve? How did you solve it?

Blogs or sites like these definitely give you a bit of a competitive advantage if done well. They tell people that you are *really* interested in your field and that you're already taking strides toward becoming a member of a professional community of practice.

JOB SEARCHES IN THE DIGITAL AGE

The whole process of applying for a job has changed dramatically since the late 1990s. That means that your parents might not know how to help you deal with job searches in the Digital Age. With that in mind, let's talk about how you can ready yourself for a job search in an era where employers and candidates alike can be overwhelmed by a hiring process that requires real savvy with job sites, document management, and e-communication.

Here is the most important message: The Digital Age will reward those who apply selectively and carefully over those who indiscriminately barrage employers with their resumes. If you think about it, it's ironic. Once upon a time, applying for a job was hard work. Not to sound like your grandfather, but in those days we couldn't copy and paste—we had to type up each cover letter from scratch. We had to print out cover letters and resumes before sending them out via snail mail.

As for looking at job listings, there were only a few ways to do it two decades ago. You either used personal connections, or you picked up the Sunday newspaper and read a chunky Help Wanted section.

Everything has changed. You can find thousands of jobs listings on dozens of websites from around the world, and you can apply for a job in a couple of minutes if you choose. And because it's so easy to apply for a job online, why not take an extra 20 or 30 minutes to really do it right? You can always copy and paste an old cover letter and rework it to some degree.

However, *that almost never happens*. People can't be bothered. When I've read applications as a recruiter, you get the feeling that most people don't even read the whole job description. They just click "reply" and attach a resume—maybe without even an accompanying note, let alone a cover letter.

This is pathetic... but, as noted earlier, it's also an opportunity for you to stand out by making a little more effort. If you're applying for engineering internships, you could start off with the same basic cover letter, but then you can customize without writing it from scratch every time. You adjust the letter to refer to requirements of the position and needs of the employer.

If you're applying for three different types of jobs, you can prepare three different kinds of cover letters. Early in my career, I did this quite often. I had a resume that highlighted my ability to create intellectual property as a consultant, but I had a second one that showcased my managerial experience and a third that focused on my work as an educator. All of the jobs were the same, of course, but what I highlighted on the job descriptions varied based on who would be reading that particular resume.

We'll be talking more about how to customize your background later in the book, as we review Interviewing in Chapter Three as well as the appendices on cover letters and a technique that I call bridging.

How to Use Online Job Sites

There are other factors to consider as you think about your job search in the digital age. One of them is how you can use job sites most effectively to help you to find a job. As noted above, there are an unbelievable number of online job resources. However, most of them are useless to you and a waste of time.

You really don't need to go to Monster or Career Builder or your local newspaper website. You can save a lot of time by focusing your search on a few good websites rather than searching 15 different sites. There are only three or four places you need to focus on for the online aspect of a job search in the Digital Age:

1. *Your on-campus database for jobs through your career office.* In my experience, universities vary a LOT when it comes to the usefulness of their job listings. A good co-op or internship program has better listings than you'll find anywhere else. After all, these are often employers who want to hire a co-op or intern rather than a full-time employee. That won't be true of most job sites. Check out those on-campus listings first.

2. *An aggregating job database site.* Sure, you could find jobs on about a hundred different websites. But don't bother. You only need to go to a few sites that aggregate—pull together—job listings from dozens of other job sites. The best ones I know are www. Indeed.com and www.Simplyhired.com. The really cool thing about those websites is that they are set up to pull in jobs posted almost anywhere; including jobs posted on Monster, Career Builder, through hundreds of company websites, and so forth. All you have to do is plug in a few keywords and a zip code, and you'll get a bunch of listings.

    If you just follow one of those websites you are probably going to come across most of the jobs that are out there online, including LinkedIn jobs. That said, I recommend LinkedIn because the site is easily searchable and it has a great database. And personally, I would apply for a job through LinkedIn's website even if I found it on www. Indeed.com or another site since I find it to be the most effective and user-friendly.

3. *Craigslist (yes, Craigslist!).* One job search site that I've found to be underutilized is Craigslist. Most people think of Craigslist as a place you go if you want to buy or sell an old couch or a bicycle, but many employers have turned to Craigslist as a great alternative for promoting their jobs. Why is that? Because it is reasonable: It only costs $25 to post a job to Craigslist while it costs several hundred dollars to post on many of the major job websites. Both employers and applicants tell me they have sometimes had faster turnaround and more success by going through Craigslist. And, for whatever reason, Craigslist jobs are not picked up by those aggregating websites like www.Indeed. com. Better still, you can click a box on checklist that says "internship" or "part-time."

This will save you a great deal of time, as most employers listing jobs are only looking for full-time, permanent employees.

4. *Company websites.* If there is a company that you're attracted to that hires fairly often, you can sign up for e-mail alerts from that company's website. Then you may get word of openings a little sooner—sometimes the company will even search their own resume database before posting a job.

    Let's say, for example, you're interested in a public relations job and you really want to work at a particular big company in your region. You can go to their website, put in your profile, and check the option that asks them to notify you if there are openings related to your particular area of interest. With this example, you might check off public relations, marketing, communications, or writing. Sometimes you can designate your level of experience, company locations that work for you, and so on. After you've set up your profile, you hopefully will get an e-mail alert every once in a while informing you of a relevant opening and you can jump on that quickly. That's handy!

UNDERSTANDING THE JOB MARKET

As stated earlier in this chapter, you cannot control the nature of the economy, the job market, or cyclical factors that affect the quantity and quality of jobs available in your field. Yet although it does little good to fret about what you can't control, you still need to be aware of these elements and the impact they may have on your job search.

The Economy

The United States economy is large, complex, hard to understand, and certainly impossible to change. Yet you should realize how this can affect you as an individual.

After the housing bubble burst in mid-2007, the United States entered a severe recession. Almost nine million jobs evaporated between 2008 and 2010. As a result the unemployment rate rose to over 10%. Since the official end of the "Great Recession" in June 2009, job growth has been uneven and erratic, shaking the confidence of consumers and employers alike.

Job growth has made steady gains since 2010; however, the population has also risen significantly. The US economy still needs to create many more jobs to make up for those lost in the recession. With these fluctuating dynamics in the job market, many employers have had to lay off employees, restructure their business, and sometimes send jobs overseas, where cheaper labor is available.

How might all of this affect you? Even as the economy continues to grow, we have seen more competition for fewer positions and of course this affects not only the public in general, but co-op students as well. Many students have struggled to get jobs during these years especially if they a) started their job search late, b) were inflexible about what type of job they were able and/or willing to do and where, geographically, they would or could work, or c) were inconsistent in their job-search efforts. Doing everything on time and to the best of your ability is no guarantee of getting a job in a challenging economy, but expending energy on the controllable part of your job search will help you fare better when grappling with something as uncontrollable as the US economy. The amount of effort expended on the job search is the single biggest factor in determining whether or not an individual student is meaningfully employed or not—a much bigger factor than skills and job experience! Most co-op and internship programs are NOT placement agencies—they don't simply assign you to a job; you have to earn it.

Even in a tough economy, it's also important to remember that there can be opportunities if you know where to look. According to Paul Harrington, a Drexel University economics professor who once worked at the Center for Labor Market Studies at Northeastern University, full-time job seekers coming out of school in May 2005 may have fared best if they were willing to look at Portland, Oregon, Washington, DC, and the Rocky Mountain region—especially given that New England had been losing quite a few jobs. In 2013, according to www.Kiplinger.com, the five states with the largest job growth will be Utah, Nevada, Hawaii, South Carolina, and Colorado. Next year, the hot place for new hires after graduation may be the southwest, northwest—who knows? Again, the more you lock yourself into thinking that you MUST work in your local region, the more you are going to limit your options.

The Job Market in Your Field

Your chosen field will have a big impact on the quality and quantity of job options available to you. If you're fortunate enough to be in some fields, you might well wonder what all of the fuss is about with the bad economy. Although the economy also affects job markets—for example, computer science students had incredible options in the mid-nineties but struggled when the technology sector cooled off in 2001 and 2002—you will always be affected by the simple laws of supply and demand. Health science majors sometimes have had great options in an otherwise bad economy, but I also have seen years in which the supply of nurses outweighed the demand, as one example.

If the demand in the job market for professionals in your field is greater than the supply of workers available, you may have some amazing options, even as an entry-level co-op student. But if you're in a field that is popular with college students who are competing for a limited number of jobs, then it's a very different story.

In the previous section, I mentioned Paul Harrington. Along with Neeta Fogg and Thomas Harrington, Paul Harrington wrote a book called *College Majors Handbook with Real Career Paths and Payoffs, 3rd Ed.* This 2013 publication is a great resource for understanding how your choice of major affects your future earnings potential. According to the 2012 edition, recent college grads who were pre-med majors came out on top with an average salary of $100,000, followed by computer systems engineering grads at $85,000, and pharmacy majors at $84,000. Engineering and other math/science majors filled out much of the top 15 majors on the list.

In the co-op realm, though, let's consider a few specific examples. Recently, it became more difficult for students to complete all of the requirements necessary to become Certified Public Accountants (CPAs). As a result, a significant number of students have drifted away from this concentration. Yet companies still need people to do accounting work, and accounting firms are still hiring at a healthy rate. The result is that accounting students now enjoy one of the best job markets amongst business students, as the supply of jobs is greater than the number of co-op students who are able and willing to fill them.

On the other side of the coin, there are always students who want to get into what I often call "sexy" jobs. A "sexy" job involves working in a field that individuals between the ages of 18 and 25 find to be glamorous. Imagine how many people in your age range want to work in the music industry, fashion, television, professional sports management, publishing, and advertising. Likewise, how many co-op students would want to work for organizations such as Reebok or the FBI or in the White House?

Given that so many students want to work in these fields or with these organizations, the result is that these employers often opt for students who will work for free as interns instead of hiring paid co-ops. If you really want to work in a "sexy" field, be prepared to work for little or nothing…. Or be creative about how you break into the field.

When I worked with Northeastern's entrepreneurship students who wanted to get into sports management and who fantasized about working with the Boston Red Sox, I would tell them about my friend Tom Ford. Tom got his MBA and wanted to get into professional baseball, so he got the best job he could get to gain experience: He became a jack-of-all-trades for the Idaho Falls Braves—a low-level minor league baseball team. Tom did everything from groundskeeping to taking tickets to picking out goofy sound effects to play over the loudspeaker when a foul ball went into the press box. He often worked 12+ hours a day for pitifully low wages. But within a few years he landed a dream position: general manager for a team in the high minor leagues in Tom's home state of Tennessee.

So you can break into glamorous fields if you're willing to pay the price in terms of time and money. The other way to do it is to acquire hot skills and use those skills as a way to differentiate yourself from other candidates. A few years ago I did a presentation on interviewing at a national co-op conference. Afterwards, two gentlemen from the CIA introduced themselves. Without any prompting from me, they said "Tell your students that if they want to work for the FBI and CIA, the way to do it is to major in computer science, MIS, or computer engineering. You have no idea how many criminal justice students contact us, and we're not interested in them!"

You always have to think about whom you're competing with for jobs and how you're going to be able to say, "I'm different!" We'll talk about that more in the Interviewing chapter.

Time of Year

Your ability to get the job of your choice also can be influenced by the time of year during which you hope to land that job. For students at Northeastern, the two most common choices are to work for six months starting in early January or to work six months starting in mid-June. At other schools, the timing may be different. Regardless, first-time students trying to pick one of the options often ask, "Which is a better choice?"

Basically, if your program lets you choose what time of year you do your co-op or internship, there are tradeoffs either way. There are more job opportunities available in early January because fewer students are available to work during that time of year—yet this also means that there is more competition from other students in the same program, and you also may need to be in school during the summer—which some students think is great but others don't like.

If you start work during the late spring or early summer, you're competing with everyone else in the collegiate world who is seeking a summer job. Thus, there are fewer jobs available, but there also might be fewer students from your program seeking a job at that time. If your program allows you to work more than the three months that a typical summer-only worker can promise, this also gives you an edge over students from conventional programs.

As we saw when considering "sexy" jobs, what you want to avoid is doing what everyone else does. Again, how can you differentiate yourself from other candidates? For example, the worst thing you can do as a Northeastern student is look for a summer-only job: Then you're competing with every other college student PLUS all of your classmates who can work for six months. Not recommended.

Your chosen field also may have a different supply of jobs at different times of the year. About two-thirds of our accounting students choose to be on co-op for the first six months of the year due to tax season. This is a win-win situation because organizations can get help for their busy season and not have to pay for year-round people who won't be necessary during the summer and fall. Meanwhile, students get to work in action-packed jobs, which are always preferable to slow-paced work environments.

Having Realistic Expectations

This is especially true for first-time co-op students. A co-op or clinical coordinator sometimes meets with nursing students who think that their first job as a nursing co-op will entail providing direct care for patients—even though their background is limited to prerequisite courses in anatomy and physiology. Then there is the entrepreneurship student who wants to own a restaurant some day and thus gets a job in a restaurant, believing that she will be making decisions about the menu. Or the computer science student who believes he will be a key member of a software development team, taking the lead in designing a new software application for the company. Wrong, wrong, and wrong!

No company in their right mind is going to hand major decision-making power to a business intern or co-op student who has not even taken a single course in finance or marketing! Legally, health care providers have to be very careful about what they allow co-ops, interns, and clinical students to do. For American Sign Language students, most job opportunities require fully trained professionals with degrees. As a result, the best that an ASL co-op or intern may be able to hope for is a position that provides them with informal opportunities to practice their ASL skills with deaf people, rather than a role in which he or she is an "official translator."

More than anything, your first co-op is a great opportunity to gain initial exposure to the professional world in the field of your choice—just "being around" in that kind of environment can be a good learning experience, even if your job duties entail monotonous Quality Assurance software testing to find and document programming bugs or chopping vegetables up at a restaurant or being a "sitter" in a hospital: basically sitting by a patient in an Intensive Care Unit for hours to make sure that they don't pull any of their tubes out (all possible duties for the students mentioned in the previous paragraphs).

Co-op students need to work their way up the ladder by proving themselves in whatever role they are given. Repeatedly in this book, you will hear about how co-op success—versus mere survival or outright failure—is all about *momentum*. Co-ops and interns are often given low-level tasks when starting a new position. Why? Employers want to see what you can do, and they often want to give you tasks that you can handle to build confidence and start off successfully.

If you take on these low-level tasks cheerfully and efficiently, you may find that you are suddenly being asked to take on more and better projects. Fail to do them with the right attitude or without success, and you are less likely to get more advanced work to do. Having realistic expectations about your first job will enable you to approach the job with a good attitude—an understanding that you may need to work your way up in the organizational world.

JOB SEARCH OPTIONS

At a large institution, it is very unlikely that a co-op, internship, or career services coordinator will hold your hand throughout the job search process. Cooperative education programs will usually do a great deal for some of their students—generally the ones who are planning ahead, putting considerable energy into their co-op careers, and actively seeking their advisor's guidance and direction. However, given the size of student loads, coordinators just don't have enough hours in the day to call you up regularly during placement season to ask why you haven't come in with your resume. It's really up to you to be on top of what you need to get done and when you have to do it in terms of the placement process.

Working with a Co-op or Internship Coordinator and/or Career Services Department

If your university has a co-op/internship coordinator or career services department, by all means take advantage of these resources. At schools with established programs, these career professionals are the liaison to hundreds, even thousands, of jobs. The co-op/internship or career services coordinator should have a good understanding of the specifics of the job market in your field and region. Plus, he or she talks to hundreds of employers about their employment needs. If you don't work with a coordinator, you won't have access to all kinds of information!

The best advice I can give you regarding working successfully with your co-op or career services coordinator is to treat this individual in the same way that you would treat your supervisor in the workplace. Use your interactions with co-op coordinators as opportunities to hone your professionalism.

What does this mean in practical terms?

- When meeting a coordinator for the first time, introduce yourself, shake hands, and clearly state your reasons for the office visit.

- Be on time to appointments with these professionals. If you absolutely cannot make an appointment, call in advance to cancel instead of just being a no-show.

- Be sensitive to the coordinator's need to juggle multiple priorities on a tight time schedule.

- When faced with uncertainty, assume the best: For example, if your coordinator asks you to change your resume, assume that it's with your best interests in mind, not to inconvenience you!

- If you need to state concerns or air conflicts, try to do so in an upbeat, solution-oriented way rather than simply blowing off steam or complaining.

- When in doubt about what you should do in *any* situation—before, during, or after you obtain your job—ask your coordinator.

It's definitely in your best interest to develop a good working relationship with your coordinator. Inevitably, when great new jobs come in, coordinators think first about the students whom they know well and who are in touch with them regularly. With large student loads, students can easily fall off their radar screens. Stay in touch regularly to make sure that doesn't happen, and you likely will be the beneficiary of a wealth of good advice and assistance in the job search process. "I just haven't had time" or "You're not available at times that are convenient to me" just don't cut it as excuses—it only takes a minute or two to write an e-mail or leave a voice mail with an update. More often than not, your coordinator also can make accommodations to meet with you if the posted appointment times or walk-in hours don't correspond well with your availability.

Finding a Job on Your Own

Some students may find it useful or even absolutely necessary to find a job without much help from their college or university. Some schools don't have formal co-op or internship coordinators or programs. Even if you go to a big co-op school, you may want to look for your own job for various reasons. A Northeastern student seeking a job in his home state may need to find her own job—especially if the desired job is outside of New England, southern New York, or New Jersey. You also may need to or want to find your own job if you are seeking work in a field that your co-op department typically doesn't work with. Examples might be some of those "sexy" fields that were mentioned earlier in this chapter: music industry, fashion, sports management, and advertising come to mind.

Although your job search falls outside of the conventional paths available through your school, you still have options. However, there are a few things to bear in mind before striking out on your own:

1. *Always check with your co-op or internship coordinator before approaching any companies.* If you have a connection with IBM, for example—even one through a classmate, friend, or family member—it would be a mistake to approach the company without getting clearance from your co-op coordinator first. The reason is that your school may have already established a co-op relationship with them, and both IBM and

the co-op department may perceive you as trying to "beat the system" or doing an "end run" instead of legitimately following the process as other students do. In some cases, you may need to discuss your job lead with the appropriate co-op coordinator before making contact to avoid any misunderstandings.

2. *You must get your co-op coordinator's approval before accepting any job found on your own, and you must get that approval BEFORE the beginning of the work experience.* Not all jobs qualify as co-op positions. For many students at Northeastern, the jobs must be full-time positions (minimum 35 hours/week) and they must be appropriate to your career; other programs may be more flexible and less strict about what qualifies as a co-op, but you need to be sure. Also, your coordinator is responsible for knowing your whereabouts on co-op and for submitting data on your salary to the university administration. In most programs, coordinators simply will not give a student credit for a work experience if they fail to discuss the position with her or him beforehand—even if the student obtained a fantastic position on his own.

3. *Even though you are pursuing your own job, don't forget that your co-op coordinator can be very helpful to you in your job search.* Sometimes coordinators can give students job leads depending on their circumstances, and most coordinators can help with resumes, cover letters, networking tips, and advice on how to sell the idea of co-op to an organization. Take advantage of this resource. Also note that Appendix C in the back of this book has information on how to write a cover letter. You would be amazed at how many long-time professionals really have no idea how to write cover letters effectively. Learn now!

4. *Be sure to complete the appropriate paperwork with your co-op coordinator.* Have a copy of an agreement form (or any other paperwork required by your school) ready to fill out and give it to your coordinator upon locating a suitable position.

Coming Up with Job Options on Your Own

For most students, one of the most challenging parts of finding their own co-op job is managing to get in the door for an interview. Although some employers do advertise internships on sites like Craigslist or other sites, many employers don't usually put co-op or internship job listings on any job site. The trick is becoming more creative about how you come up with options. Here are some suggestions:

1. *Network through family and friends.* As stated earlier, don't use family and friends to get to employers that already work with your school's co-op or internship program—discuss this step with your co-op coordinator first. After clearing that hurdle, you'll find that networking is the single most effective way of finding your own job.

Can't Find the Perfect Job? Hire Yourself! – A Co-op Professional's Perspective
by Deborah Hunt

Sometimes students have a dream of running their own business someday. Believe it or not, it might be possible to make that happen much sooner than you think. I have worked with many students who have tried doing something entrepreneurial for an internship or co-op job. While this has its downsides, it can be a great learning experience for students who are open to exploring the possibility of creating a business as an alternative to the traditional co-op job.

any colleges now offer entrepreneurship courses and have on-site innovation/entrepreneurship center that give students opportunities to get involved. Research shows that employers look for this type of experience when hiring for entry-level positions. They aren't concerned if the business/ project succeeded or failed, but that the student had that experience and learned from it.

Students who are entrepreneurs often develop better soft skills such as communication and teamwork that employers are seeking. Employers also find that students with an entrepreneurial mindset have more accountability for their actions, are more aggressive, and know how to execute. Therefore, some employers would prefer to hire these students over students with more traditional internship/co-op experience.

Starting your own business can be the ultimate reality check for a young entrepreneur. Many students have "cool ideas" for a company, but not every cool idea turns out to be a viable business opportunity. Here are a few questions to consider before deciding whether this is a smart option for you:

• What would it cost to launch and run your business? Ideally, a student-run business won't cost much to get going. You probably would need to register a business name with your town or city, and you might want to have business cards and a simple website. But unless you're independently wealthy, you'll want a business that requires very little expense in the way of equipment, advertising, and raw materials. Don't risk any money that you can't afford to lose!

• How easy is it for you to connect with potential customers? A big success factor is how simple it is to reach people who might want to buy your product or service... and to convince them to hire you. You have to do some homework to learn if there is a real market for your business.

• Can you afford to not make money from your co-op job or internship? While it's nice to fantasize about making big money as a student entrepreneur, that often doesn't happen. Some students really need to do work that is guaranteed to bring in some money to help with rent or school expenses. If you're in that category, starting your own business might be a bad idea.

• Can you keep the business going without compromising your academic success? The best student businesses are ones that don't result in having you work 80 hours a week on top of taking classes. A business where you can work more or less hours in a given week depending on what else is going on in your life is ideal.

Things to note if you plan to do this as your co-op:

• Start the process early! You'll need to plan a cycle in advance just as you would if you were doing a traditional co-op or internship. Maybe even sooner if you need to line up resources to make it happen.

• If you hope to get credit for the experience, you'll need to get approval of your project/business and may need lead time to find a sponsor or mentor to work with during the co-op period. It would be very unusual for a school to give you credit for your own business after the fact: Get approval before you start!

> - Many of the college innovation centers provide workshops or boot camps that help you prepare.
>
> - Be sure you sign up and know the dates and timelines for this.
>
> - Most important – keep your co-op advisor informed of your plan and work with your advisor according to what the structure is at your college for this type of co-op. Your advisor can help you avoid potential problems and make sure you get as much as possible out of this learning experience.
>
> - I've seen student entrepreneurs run all sorts of businesses—Web design, a laundry/dry cleaning delivery service, freelance computer consultant, e-commerce entrepreneur, you name it. There are plenty of ways to make money out there, and, more importantly, learn a great deal about who you are and what makes a business tick.
>
> *Deborah Hunt is an Employer Relations Specialist for Wentworth Institute of Technology and Founder of Career-Creations.*

An entrepreneurship/small business management student of mine several years ago came to see me and announced that she wanted to find a job in Denver. She had a cousin who lived there but otherwise knew no one in Colorado. Together, we worked hard on how to network. Armed with that knowledge, she began grilling her cousin: Whom do you know who works in a small business? Where do they work? What's their phone number? When she found people who worked in small businesses, she tried to get them thinking about her situation: Could your company use someone to work on marketing projects? Someone to help with computers? An individual who could crunch numbers, work as a good team player, and serve as a Jill-of-all-trades?

Even though she experienced a lot of rejection, the student stayed positive, upbeat, and persistent—to the point where people really *wanted* to help her find a job. Plus she tried to avoid any dead ends: Anyone she talked to was an opportunity to get more names and phone numbers. Finally, she got a fantastic job, working for a small business that helped other businesses put together IPOs and go public. How many people did she have to go through to make this happen? The job was obtained through her cousin's boyfriend's father's friend's friend!!! It just shows what you can do if you are willing to expend some energy in an intelligent, directed search for your own job.

2. *Check out job boards and newspaper listings.* Many Northeastern undergraduates could benefit by using HuskyCareerLink, which you can access by going to www.northeastern. experience.com on the Web. Hundreds of employers list jobs through HuskyCareerLink. Find out if your school has a similar site that is worth checking. Some employers are purely interested in hiring full-time employees who have completed their degrees (or who will do so very soon), while others can be approached about co-ops or internships and are interested in forging bonds with the university. Some even list temporary or hourly positions that are appropriate for a student seeking a co-op job.

Beyond that, there are numerous job boards out there. Earlier in this chapter, I mentioned specifics about how to use sites such as www.Indeed.com and Craigslist. Additionally, there are a few national sites that might be appropriate for students interested in specific types of jobs. One intriguing site is idealist.org, which claims to list jobs from roughly 100,000 nonprofit and community organizations. They list paid internships and volunteer opportunities spanning the globe for those interested in civic-minded ways to gain experience and broaden your exposure to the world. Similarly, www.thenonprofittimes.com lists nonprofit jobs by state and offers tips and articles on the latest trends in the NPO sector. Journalism students can go to www.asne. org (American Society of Newspaper Editors) to see dozens of paid internships with newspapers. There are many other possibilities broken out by region or field—ask your co-op, internship, or career services professional for other ideas.

3. *Making Cold Calls.* Telephoning, e-mailing, or stopping in at an employer is a last resort because you will put in a lot of energy without much return in many cases. You can improve your chances by targeting larger employers, checking whether there is information about co-op jobs on their website, and then getting in touch to express your interest.

Selling a Company on the Value of a Co-op Employee

One of the best things about finding your own job is that it is a great way to test your ability to be entrepreneurial. You have to not only sell yourself in the interview as you ordinarily would: Often you will need to be able to articulate how cooperative education works and why it benefits potential employers. Here are some key points to hit:

1. *Co-op employees and interns represent cost-effective labor.* In many cases—especially with corporate jobs—these employees are a less expensive resource than the alternatives, such as contractors or temps.

2. *Co-ops/interns do not need to receive benefits.* Health care benefits and paid vacation time are expensive to employers; many companies are under pressure to keep their "headcount" (full-time employees who are eligible for benefits) at a minimum. Co-ops and interns are one way to help achieve this goal. Note that co-ops are NOT contractors: state and federal taxes DO need to be withdrawn from your pay.

3. *Co-ops/interns can provide long-term help but are not a permanent commitment.* If you can make yourself available for at least six months, that's a long time—long enough for you to provide a return on the investment the company may need to make in training you. However, the company need not make any commitment beyond the six months to you or other co-op students or interns. This may be important to start-up companies, which may need help now but are unsure about what their future needs may be. Likewise, even large employers may be reluctant to commit to a permanent hire during times of economic uncertainty. Hiring a co-op or intern for three to six months is far preferable to hiring a full-time employee without knowing if they will need to lay off the person in the next year. Better still, when the economy turns around, these programs mean that the organization has been able to maintain a recruiting pipeline.

4. *Interns and co-op students have much at stake and are therefore more motivated than other temporary workers usually are.* People who work as temps usually do so simply to make money. Co-op student workers usually focus on learning as much as they can and securing a good reference for future employment. As a result, co-ops often show

more interest and effort in their jobs.

Your coordinator may be able to provide you with an introductory brochure about co-ops and interns for potential employers and other materials that may be useful to you in marketing yourself as a temporary student/employee.

Now that you have a good understanding of how to plan ahead for your first professional job, you are ready to tackle the nuts and bolts of the preparation stage: writing a resume, learning how to interview, and generally ramping up for your job search.

EMPLOYER ROUNDTABLE

What would be some smart things for a co-op or intern to do BEFORE going out on their first co-op or internship—maybe even months before—to be that much more ready for a successful job search and productive time as an employee? Let's see what several employers have to say:

First, decide what your ideal internship, as well as life after school, will look like. Once you answer that question, then you can gear your preparation to that goal. In broad strokes, internships will be broken down into two types of companies—large ones and small ones. If you want to hone your skills in your area of expertise, and you want to ensure that resources will be available for you to do that, then aim toward the large company. If, on the other hand, you have the soul of an entrepreneur, and you want to experience several areas of a business, then a small company is for you.

This choice will influence the classes you select. If you are aiming for a large company, then you want to sharpen your axe in the area in which you hope to be gainfully employed. Your course selection should reflect this more concentrated approach. If you are aiming for a small company, then you will want to learn material that encompasses more than just your area of study. In my field, this includes a broad scientific and engineering foundation. For instance, if you are a mechanical engineer, it will behoove you to learn the basics of chemistry and electrical engineering. It might even behoove you to take a course in accounting.

If you want to be more than just a worker squirreled away in a lab or stuck in some other narrow technical role, learn how to communicate. That means honing your writing and presentation skills. Communication skills—more than technical ones—will determine how high you climb the corporate ladder.

- Mark Spencer, President, Water Analytics

Research the company in which you will be doing your assignment. You should have a good understanding of the types of products or services that the company provides.

- Ryan P. Derber, SPHR, Segment Human Resources Manager,
PolyOne Corporation

Gain familiarity with any of the "desirables" that you do not have. For example, if the co-op position desires "familiarity with mechanical testing equipment," and you don't have this skill base—but got the job anyway—you should try to fill the gap.

- Dennis Burke, Senior R&D Engineer, Depuy Synthes, Johnson & Johnson

Most students trying to land a co-op or internship will be applying for their first job related to their field of study. That means that you are most likely competing with others who have little or no experience related to the job at hand. This is probably the only time in your career that this set of circumstances will exist for you. With that said, you do have an opportunity to separate yourself from the others who are being considered for the position. The best way to do that is to study the job description for some clues as to what the employer is looking for, and then make sure you are prepared to talk about how you match up with those attributes. Be ready to describe examples of how you are a fit. If the company is looking for someone who can work with minimal supervision, be prepared to talk about something you did where you had to figure out how to succeed on your own. If the job description talks about working well with a team, be prepared to discuss your role as a team member and an example of how you provided an unselfish benefit to the team. Think in terms of how to create a benefit to the employer and examples of how you are the right choice.

-Dennis Tully, President, MTD Micro Molding

Talk to the hiring manager regarding what projects you will be working on and get prepared a little bit for that.

- Wentao Wang, ETP Engineering Manager, Pfizer Global Supply

STUDENT ROUNDTABLE

What would be some smart things for a co-op to do BEFORE going out on his or her first co-op—maybe even months before—to be that much more ready for a successful job search and productive time as an employee? Here's what several students and alumni think:

Before I went out on my co-ops, I researched potential companies to apply to. I would tailor my resume to the different companies. For example: if it was a manufacturing company, I would emphasize my manufacturing experience and projects; if it was a research position, I would highlight more of my relevant experience for R&D. I would also go get a haircut and buy some clothing for the job interview. Looking like you want the job can speak volumes to potential employers.

After getting the job, I would make sure to pack up any course notes or reference material that might be helpful on the job. You may only use it once while on the job, but you don't want to be that student kicking themselves for not bringing a helpful resource. I would also pay close attention to what people are wearing and how formal the atmosphere is.

You don't want to wear a suit if the dress is casual. When in doubt ask HR, or your new boss, what the dress is generally like.

- Mary Beth Moriarty, PhD Candidate, Plastics Engineering,
University of Massachusetts Lowell

If you're like me, you didn't receive and accept a job offer until almost a week prior to the start date of your co-op. My first co-op, unlike the majority of my peers, was out of state, requiring me to relocate for an extended period of time. The best thing I did was immediately contact the people I knew in the area. Within that week I was able to secure an apartment solely because of my network."

The second action item I took was to visit both the area I was going to be living in, and the company I was going to be working for, prior to my start date. Going in anywhere blind is both stressful and time consuming. I took a day trip, drove up to Burlington, Vermont, met up with my contacts and future employer, and familiarized myself with the area. This made my transition from Massachusetts to Vermont and school to work almost seamless.

- Jared Peraner, Market Development Specialist,
Consumer & Electronics, Nypro Inc.;
BS, Plastics Engineering, 2012, University of Massachusetts Lowell

---

The very first co-op opportunity that a student has can be exciting and nerve-wracking leading up to the first day of work. I know that my first experience caused a bit of anxiety weeks in advance as I labored over the question of whether or not I was prepared. Looking back, the one thing that helped me and prevented more elevated levels of anxiety and stress was having previous work experience and having a good idea of what to expect from my employer. It doesn't really matter what the job is or who your boss is, as long as you're in a position where you're working regularly, working under supervision, and hopefully working hard. In my case, I worked on my grandfather's farm mowing fields on a tractor and picking up brush. Those duties weren't quite the most relevant tasks to mechanical engineering, but they taught me how to work hard for an employer, follow instructions, and work every day.

- William Teter, Mechanical Engineering student,
University of Massachusetts Lowell

CHAPTER ONE REVIEW QUESTIONS

1. Name at least four of the benefits of working as a co-op or intern.

2. List three things that you could do now to make yourself more marketable for a future position in your field.

3. Why do many hiring managers consider soft skills more important than technical skills when hiring co-ops, interns, or graduating seniors?

4. How could you improve your digital footprint this year?

5. When seeking a job in the Digital Age, what does the author describe as the best websites to review to save time while seeing as many relevant jobs as possible? Name at least three specific sites.

6. What does the text describe as the single biggest factor in determining whether or not an individual student is meaningfully employed or not?

   A. The economy
   B. The job market in your field
   C. Skills and experience
   D. Amount of effort expended in the job search
   E. Flexibility, including willingness to relocate

7. Name at least three ways in which co-ops and internships are beneficial to employers.

CHAPTER TWO
Writing An Effective Resume

INTRODUCTION

Your resume is a vital component of an effective job search. It is a personal statement and advertisement of who you are. You may have more talent, knowledge, and skills than any other applicant for a particular job. However, if you don't get an opportunity to communicate those qualities to an employer, you may never get the chance to demonstrate your abilities. A good resume will provide you with that opportunity. It WILL NOT get you a job but it CAN get you an interview.

As you will see in this chapter, there are different schools of thought on how resumes should be written. This creates some degree of confusion, as you may come across contradictory advice when you talk to employers, look at resume tips online, or consult your professors. Some co-op and internship coordinators or career services professionals believe that resume writers should go beyond describing simply what they did to weave in soft skills demonstrated in previous work experience. Alternatively, your co-op coordinator may encourage you to put some "spin" on your job descriptions—encouraging you to describe *how* you did a given job or *what* made you a good or great employee in a given position. That will help a potential employer *infer* what soft skills you have. However, other co-op coordinators believe that it's best to emphasize what you did and not force the potential employer to wade through a long-winded job description—especially given that a prospective employer may only look at your resume for 60 to 90 seconds! From this perspective, the idea is to use the interview to convey your soft skills and anything more qualitative that the interviewer may want to know about your previous positions. Some employers believe that resumes are somewhat overrated (see box on next page).

Conversely, some employers believe resumes are *critically* important. This type of employer may not call a student in because of a careless typo or a poorly organized resume. There is definitely no one "right" way to prepare resumes. For example, some people believe that an

37

Interests section is completely meaningless. Yet I also have had more than one employer tell me that they can't imagine why anyone would be foolish enough to exclude this element from his or her resume.

Resume Writing – An Employer's Perspective
by Mike Naclerio

Not much impresses me on resumes. I don't spend much time reviewing them and view them as a mere formality. The personal interview is what counts, and where you can truly determine whether an individual will fit into your unique working environment.

Mike Naclerio is the President of Enquiron.

Your best bet is to find out what your co-op or career services professional believes would work best for you, given your work history as well as your field. After all, this individual has direct communication with the employers who will receive your resume, so they generally have the best idea of what will resonate with interviewers. You also need to think about what feels right and comfortable for YOU. Maybe your brother's girlfriend thinks you should do your resume a different way—the approach that *she* used in getting some fantastic job—or your mom is an HR manager who sees hundreds of resumes per year and believes she knows what is best for you. In the end, though, your co-op coordinator is the one who has dozens of co-op jobs available, whereas your brother's girlfriend probably doesn't have any! Make sure your coordinator understands your goals and values: Are you comfortable, for example, with a resume that really sells your skills? Once your coordinator knows you, trusting that person's judgment is usually the best move. Of course, you also need to feel comfortable that your resume truly reflects the real you. Even if you are urged to have a resume that features a "hard sell" of your skills, you shouldn't do so unless you're comfortable with that.

Just about any professional would agree on many factors that differentiate a strong resume from a poor one. An effective, competitive resume is one that highlights your best achievements, accomplishments, and contributions at work, at school, and in the community. It also can reflect your hobbies, interests, and background, making you into a three-dimensional person instead of a name on a page. A strong resume also must be *flawless* in terms of typos or errors—after all, if you can't get things right on your resume, why would anyone expect you to have excellent attention to detail as an employee?

In contrast, a mediocre resume will provide minimal work and academic history plus extremely basic job descriptions. Also, a poor resume is unattractive to look at—maybe it's hard to read due to small type or poor alignment, perhaps it is just very inconsistent in terms of formatting. A weak resume also will have poor grammar or outright errors on it: failure to abbreviate properly, misspelled or misused words, or significant omissions. Employers often go through dozens of resumes in search of a handful of interview candidates. If you want your resume to stand out positively from the rest of the pile, you need to invest considerable time and thought. Therefore, to learn how to write a winning, professional resume, read on!

WRITING YOUR RESUME

The first step in writing your resume is easy. It has to do with the way your resume will look when it is finished. Remember, appearance does create a strong first impression. Just as you would not go to an interview dressed in a t-shirt and shorts, your resume also needs to look professional. The following five tips will help you to have a "good-looking" resume.

Resume Writing – A Student's Perspective
by Keith Laughman

One of the greatest attributes of this book is its coverage on resume building. The first time someone writes a resume he or she might be too humble to beef themselves up. A resume is a marketable representation of who you are; it's the first and sometimes only impression that employers see of you. You want to create a sharp image in their eye and leave an imprint on their mind when they are done looking at your resume. This is what sets you apart from everybody else and this is why Northeastern is number one with its co-op program.

Throughout your lifetime, you will be revising your resume constantly. It's important to put a lot of energy into developing it for the future. Students should understand that a good resume takes time and thought. The process of building a resume is also a great opportunity for the student to learn more about themselves and how they have dealt with certain people and situations in the past, thus preparing them for the next big step, the interview.

Creating a resume was actually a fun experience for me. It helped me realize that I did much more at work than I thought and that although I had few skills relevant to my major, I had many interpersonal skills. These skills are just as effective as technical skills. Technical skills can be learned; you may have interpersonal skills, but they need to be developed! Four years later and I am still using the co-op guidebook as a resource to improve and refine my skills.

Keith Laughman was an MIS/Marketing student at Northeastern University, Class of 2002.

FIVE RESUME TIPS

- As a co-op student, your resume generally should be only ONE page in length on 8 1/2 X 11 inch bond paper.

- Use neutral colors when selecting bond paper (white, ivory, off-white, gray).

- It is recommended that you type your own resume on a word processor and save it on disk or flash drive. This will enable you to make changes and corrections at any time. Also, most students will need to upload their resume onto the school's computer system and/or give an electronic copy of their resume to their coordinator.

- Almost everyone uses Microsoft Word when writing their resume, and 90 percent of resumes seem to use one of Word's default fonts—Calibri or Times New Roman—as a result. Dare to be different! Experiment with other fonts. Arial is one reliable alternative... and there are many others such as Garamond and Helvetica. Just don't go too wild—especially as unusual fonts may cause you problems when submitting a resume online or converting it to a PDF format.

- Your resume should reflect you as a professional and as an individual—do not directly copy from the sample resumes in this chapter. Employers have commented on how too many resumes look exactly alike. Write your own!

Writing a Resume – A Student's Perspective
By Amber Zapatka

A good resume is one that is true to who you are. Don't try to spice up your resume with fancy words, and don't put down skills that you are not truly proficient with them. If you are okay with a skill or program, write "exposure to," so your potential employer knows you have at least used the program or are familiar with a skill.

Bad grammar and misspellings are my biggest pet peeve. If you are trying to look professional, really give your resume a good look-over and make sure everything is correct. Lastly, don't try and make it look fancy. This is you on a piece of paper. It doesn't need a cute border, elaborate lines or font, or thesaurus words. And if you cannot back up your resume in person, then you have some edits to make.

Amber Zapatka was a Plastics Engineering major at University of Massachusetts Lowell, Class of 2011.
She is now a Project Engineer at Nypro.

SECTIONS

Your resume will be broken down into a number of separate sections, which will be used to describe aspects of your life and qualifications. Every co-op resume should include sections on:

- Education

- Experience

- Skills

Depending on your background, you also might include several other possible sections, such as Interests, Military Experience, Volunteer Experience, Memberships, Major Accomplishments, and Professional Certificates or Licenses.

HOW TO START

Every resume should start with an introduction. When you meet someone for the first time, you always tell them your name. Your resume is the same. Your name should be at the top, either centered, left, or right—whichever you think fits best. Address, telephone number(s), and e-mail address are critical. Employers need to reach you should they want to interview you or make you an offer! Therefore, include a permanent (family) and temporary (local) address if they are different. Remember, your resume may stay on file for over a year with an employer while you move in the meantime. Your permanent address and telephone number will ensure that you can always be reached for a job offer. Likewise, you always want to include a reliable e-mail address that you check regularly. If you're always having trouble with your Gmail or Yahoo account because you exceed the storage limit for messages, you need to do something to make sure that that won't make it difficult for a potential employer to reach you.

It's advisable to make sure that the number and address you want employers to call first is on the left-hand side, as they are most likely to use that one.

For example:

JANE SMITH
Janesmith89@gmail.com

CURRENT ADDRESS	**PERMANENT ADDRESS**
7 Speare Hall, Box 10	**89 Fifth Avenue**
Boston, MA 02115	**Natick, MA 01760**
(617) 377-0000	**(508) 555-0001**

International students who use an Americanized nickname can include that on their resume. It could look like this:

WAI MAN "Andy" LAM

What if you have an extremely difficult to pronounce name and are afraid that an employer may be reluctant to call you as a result? Recently, we heard of one enterprising student who included the pronunciation of his name right below it. You could do that like so:

OLUMIDE NGUNDIRI
(first name pronounced "oh-LOO-mee-day")
olumide@yahoo.com

EDUCATION

While you are still a college student, the education section is usually listed first. Upon graduation, this section often moves below the EXPERIENCE section. When writing the education section, you should use the following guidelines:

- Format: reverse chronological order (current university listed first, other universities and colleges second, high school last)

- Include anticipated degree (i.e., Bachelor of Science Degree in Business Administration; Bachelor of Arts Degree in English) and expected month and year of graduation (e.g., May 2018)

- Include concentrations and dual concentrations or minors, if applicable

- Honors: include GPA if 3.0 or above and any scholarships received (Compute your GPA to no more than two decimal places: 3.45 is fine; 3.4495 does not indicate greater honesty or make any significant difference to an employer)

- Include activities related to the University, especially leadership roles

- Include the above information for transfer schools

- If you are financing a significant portion of your education yourself, you could opt to include that fact. For example:

Financing 80% of college tuition and expenses through cooperative education and part-time job earnings.

Here's how the section might look:

<u>EDUCATION</u>

UNIVERSITY OF MASSACHUSETTS LOWELL	Lowell, MA
Bachelor of Science Degree in Business Administration	May 2017

Dual Concentration: Marketing and Finance
Minor: Communications
Grade Point Average: 3.2
Activities and Honors: University Honors Program, Joe Smith Memorial
Scholarship, Intramural Basketball, Residential Life Representative, Outing Club
Financing 75% of tuition and living expenses through cooperative education earnings and part-time job income.

Many students who have not yet had significant work experience will find it helpful to include their high school education in this section. Since your resume is written in reverse chronological order, the recording of your high school experience would come AFTER your university or college notation.

EXPERIENCE

This is the most vital section of your resume. This is the time not only to list where you worked and what you did, but to list your accomplishments and achievements! Take time to think about what you want to say—it's worth doing right! Here are some key points:

- *Include company name (the official name), location, job title, and dates of employment.* Employers want to see this information in order to determine exactly what you have done and how long you spent doing it. They might use this information to contact your present or previous employer in order to find out more about the relevance of your experience and the accuracy of your statements. Note that you probably shouldn't bother listing a job if you only did it for a month or two: Fairly or unfairly, it may raise questions about your ability and willingness to keep a job.

- *Jobs should be listed chronologically from present position, then backwards.* List your present or most recent position first, then your second most recent and so on. As you go through your university years, you probably will be getting more and more advanced jobs. If you have already had two internships jobs related to your major, for example, you certainly wouldn't want it to look like your retail job in high school was your most important experience to date. One exception to this rule: If your most recent job experience was not related to your major—for example, a part-time restaurant job that you did while attending classes—you might want to have a section called "Relevant Job Experience" or "Internship Experience" *first*, followed by another section called "Other Job Experience" or "Part-time Job Experience," etc.

Don't Sell Yourself Short – A Co-op Professional's Perspective
By Erin Doyon

Most students I meet with have never held a professional job. In fact, some have never held a job! You are a student, and employers know that. Employers are not looking for you to know how to do the job, but that you know how to learn! Make sure your resume demonstrates the skills you have been acquiring over your years as a student, including your high school years. The missed opportunity for many students on their resume is projects they worked on—maybe even as early as their freshman year of college. These projects are often in a team setting, and they will help you demonstrate your ability to learn among many other skillsets. If you have these projects on your resume, it will tee you up to tell stories about them in your interview, demonstrating your ability to learn!

Erin Doyon is an Assistant Director of Cooperative Education in Engineering at University of Massachusetts Lowell.

- *Sentences should always begin with an action verb.* Avoid starting sentences with weak linking verbs such as had, got, did, etc. Use verbs that convey confidence, such as handled, improved, managed, designed, etc. There is a long list of great action verbs toward the end of this chapter. An alternative is to start with a compelling adverb: "Effectively handled," "Successfully managed," etc. There is a helpful list of action verbs on page 61.

- *Do not underestimate the power of word choice: Use power words, not passive words.* For example, don't say "Got information on orders for people who asked for it." Instead, say "Responded effectively to customer and colleague requests by tracking order status on computer and over the telephone."

- *Do not use personal pronouns such as "I," "me," "we," or "them."* On a resume, this amounts to stating the obvious. If your name is on the top of the resume, the reader knows that the statements refer to you unless you state otherwise.

- *If possible, include accomplishments as opposed to just listing responsibilities.* Never begin a sentence with "Responsibilities included..." or "Duties include...". This type of beginning may capture *what* you did, but you need to go further than that. Starting with action verbs helps you capture what you did and *how* you did it. Were you good at your job? If so, tell us why. If not, well, then stick with your responsibilities, simply stated.

- *Quantify and qualify whenever possible.* For example: "Increased sales by 15%," or "Increased sales significantly by using suggestive-selling techniques." Either of these statements tells the reader much more about precisely how well you did or how you went about accomplishing this task. This is far preferable to simply writing "Sold products." Notice how much more powerful the following descriptions are when the large, bold-type descriptive part of the sentence is added:

  - Owned and operated snowplowing business **grossing $3,500 a winter**

  - Hired and supervised **five** employees

- ○ **Using Harvard Graphics**, created a **750-page color** presentation for the annual sales meeting

- *Highlight transferable skills.* As stated earlier, professionals disagree as to whether so-called "soft skills" or transferable skills—such as interpersonal skills or attention to detail—should be included in a resume. However, most professionals agree that job seekers who have NO experience in their chosen field should consider including at least one or two specific soft skills in each job description. Think of it this way: Let's say you're a human resource management concentrator who has never worked in a corporate environment. Perhaps the only jobs on your resume are working as a waiter and as a house painter. In all probability, you will not want to wait on tables or paint houses as a co-op employee. Therefore, most co-op coordinators—but not all—believe that it's helpful for inexperienced candidates to include some transferable skills on your resume.

How can you identify what your transferable skills are? Ask yourself two questions: Were you good at the job you did? If so, why? Was it because you managed to figure out how to do the job well in a short time (**ability to learn quickly**)? Your ability to keep customers happy (**customer-service skills** or maybe **interpersonal skills**)? Was it that you never missed work or showed up late (**dependability** or **strong work ethic** or **positive attitude**)?

The transferable skills that you choose to highlight will depend heavily on your concentration and the type of co-op job that is being sought. As co-op coordinator Rose Dimarco points out in the following sidebar box, it also depends very much on what purpose the resume needs to serve. If you're in a co-op or internship program in which the coordinator arranges the interview schedule for the employer, this calls for a very different resume compared to a situation in which the resume alone must get you in the door! She also emphasizes that sometimes it's enough to imply that you have a specific transferable skills. For example, why bother saying "demonstrated ability to multitask" when you could have a bullet as follows: "Simultaneously handled telephone calls, in-person customer service, data entry, and invoice processing." I think that the reader will figure out that you are a bona fide multitasker!

Look at the list at the end of this chapter for a more complete list of transferable skills for various majors and concentrations.

Certain verbs are very helpful to know when capturing transferable skills. Some good examples are displayed, demonstrated, utilized, exhibited, showed, and used. Often you can start out a job description sentence using one of these verbs and an appropriate adjective in front of a transferable skill. For example:

- ○ Demonstrated excellent interpersonal skills when....

- ○ Utilized solid communication skills when....

- ○ Displayed outstanding ability to learn quickly while....

Tailoring Your Resume – A Co-op Professional's Perspective
by Rose Dimarco

A resume initially gives you a script. When you think about what you're willing to put on paper about yourself, it typically reflects how you're going to explain yourself. So are we talking about a resume that's going to *introduce* you, or is it going to be a *leave-behind* that is going to help an employer remember you and differentiate you from someone else? It might introduce you and that may be the only decision-maker that they have to determine whether they call you for an interview, and that might adjust your resume somewhat. I'm just concerned that you're not boastful; that it's factual, but you also give yourself credit for what you've done.

If transferable skills are things that you feel are of value, that's what I would help you put on a resume in such a way that the interviewer reading it would conclude those things that you know about yourself: That you're a hard worker; that you're flexible—you don't necessarily want to use those terms on a resume, but you want them to conclude that from reading it. That's the art of resume writing in general, but in health care those are the things that we want to bring to the surface.

Rose Dimarco is a cooperative education faculty coordinator in
Physical Therapy at Northeastern University.

A "transferable skill cheat sheet" toward the end of this chapter has lists of these verbs and a summary of this transferable skill formula.

Note that you need to be a little careful about throwing transferable skills around. The worst thing you can do is to just mention these skills and leave out anything about what you actually did on the job. Employers need to know what you actually did—even if it was simply mopping floors or washing dishes! Also, be careful not to overuse the transferable skills—working one or two them into each job description may be adequate. Above all, NEVER claim that you have a certain transferable skill unless you are confident that you really have that skill—and that your former employer would agree. At worst, overemphasizing the transferable skills may come off as "BS" to some employers—especially if they believe that you're using them as a smokescreen to hide the low level of what you really did. Calling a garbage collector a "sanitation engineer" doesn't change the nature of that smelly job. Likewise, it can come off as insincere overkill if you say "Demonstrated outstanding ability to learn quickly when maintaining lawns." How hard is it, really, to learn how to mow a lawn? In that case, it might be better to keep it simple: "Efficiently mowed lawns for neighborhood customers."

- *Take time to think about how your job/contribution fits into the "big picture."* When capturing your job experience on a resume, don't just think about what tasks you did each day. Instead, consider the importance of these tasks with relation to what helped the organization accomplish its goals. For example: Don't just say, "Created window displays." Instead, show how your work made a small but important difference for your employer: "Generated customer interest by creating innovative window displays."

- *Either the bullet/outline format or the paragraph format is acceptable.* When writing up your job description, use which works best for you. If your job experience is complex and relatively hard to explain, the paragraph format may work best. If you had

45

numerous and highly varied job responsibilities, you might find the bulleted format easier to use. It's up to you.

Resumes – An Employer's Perspective
by Myretta Robens

In a co-op resume, we mostly just look to see that it is neat and grammatically correct. Experience is not essential. In fact, one of my favorite resumes included the line, "Demonstrated a positive attitude while cleaning out horse stalls." I figured that if Sara could do that, she could handle anything our users threw at her. And that turned out to be the case.

Myretta Robens was the Director of Technology Operations at Harvard Business School Publishing. She is now the published author of two romance novels.

- *Volunteer experience can be included under EXPERIENCE or in a separate section.* Although you can be flexible about where to include volunteer experience, just make sure that you don't fail to include it somewhere on your resume. Working as a volunteer can show concern for others as well as a desire to learn through unpaid experience.

- *In most cases, write out numbers below 11.* Unless you're writing about percentages (e.g., 5%), you generally should write out numbers from one through ten (e.g., "Utilized two database programs"); higher numbers are written numerically (e.g., "Generated 75 leads for potential sales").

Remember, the Experience section usually is what a potential employer studies to make a preliminary decision about whether you can do the job. An ordinary description means you are an ordinary person. Now is the time to show an employer that you are extraordinary. The following are some helpful hints on how to do that.

A STEP-BY-STEP APPROACH TO WRITING UP YOUR JOB EXPERIENCE

Writing job descriptions takes time, effort, and practice. But once you learn how to do this effectively, you will have mastered a skill that will help you for the rest of your career. Let's look at a step-by-step formula to writing effective job descriptions. Note that the changes in each step are indicated by having the text underlined: You would not underline any job description text on a real resume.

In the interest of giving equal time to two different perspectives, the first example will incorporate transferable skill phrases; the second will show how to write a job description without touting your soft skills.

Step 1
Write down the organization's name and location, then the job title and dates of employment on the second line:

SANTA'S TREE FARM   Kent, CT
Laborer   November 2012 - Present

Step 2

Write down in simple terms the various duties you have or had in a given job:

SANTA'S TREE FARM Kent, CT
Laborer November 2012 - Present
- ♦ Plant trees and help them grow.
- ♦ Mow property.
- ♦ Cut down trees for customers, accept payment, and tie trees to customers' cars.

Step 3

Unless you worked for an organization that almost everyone knows (such as Pizza Hut), consider adding details about the nature of the employer and the purpose of the job:

SANTA'S TREE FARM Kent, CT
Laborer November 2012 - Present
- ♦ <u>Working as only hired employee for small family-owned business</u>, plant trees and help them grow <u>to ensure that adequate supply of Christmas trees is available each winter.</u>
- ♦ Mow property <u>regularly to make sure that trees have adequate exposure to sunlight and room to grow.</u>
- ♦ Cut down trees for customers, accept payment, and tie trees to their cars.

Step 4

Add quantitative details and professional terms when possible to bring the experience to life:

SANTA'S TREE FARM Kent, CT
Laborer November 2012 - Present
- ♦ Working as only hired employee for small family-owned business, plant <u>over 300 trees annually</u> and help them grow to ensure that adequate supply of Christmas trees is available each winter.
- ♦ Mow property regularly to make sure that <u>all four varieties of evergreen</u> trees have adequate exposure to sunlight and room to grow.
- ♦ Cut down <u>approximately 200 trees per year</u> for customers, accept payment, and tie trees to their cars.

Step 5 (Optional)

Add a phrase or two containing transferable skills in order to capture how well you did the job and what you might be able to provide to a co-op employer in a more professional setting:

SANTA'S TREE FARM Kent, CT
Laborer November 2012 - Present
- ♦ Working as only hired employee for small family-owned business, <u>exhibited an outstanding work ethic</u> when planting over 300 trees annually and helping them grow to ensure that adequate supply of Christmas trees is available each winter.
- ♦ <u>Demonstrated strong attention to detail</u> when mowing property regularly to make sure that all four varieties of evergreen trees have adequate exposure to sunlight

and room to grow.
- ◆ Cut down approximately 200 trees per year for customers, accepting payment, and tying trees to their cars.

By crafting this type of job description, a student shows a potential employer that they have many qualities that might be desirable in an employee. Again, note that the inclusion of transferable skills is generally considered to be a good idea if you lack experience in your field of choice. As you advance in your career and obtain jobs that are directly related to your field, the explicit use of transferable skills becomes less important. But if you fail to include them when you do not have highly relevant job experience, you are asking an employer to make a mental leap in terms of figuring out whether you have any qualities that might be useful to her or him.

ANOTHER EXAMPLE OF THIS STEP-BY-STEP APPROACH

One of the great advantages of using this step-by-step approach is that it will make your interview easier. If you take the time to nail down an excellent description of your job and employer, then that becomes one less thing that you will need to worry about accomplishing during the interview itself... when you won't have much time to think about what to say! Instead of having to explain the basics of your previous experience, you can build on the resume by diving into specific examples of the points made on your resume.

Let's consider another step-by-step example, leaving out the transferable skill formula this time around:

Step 1

Write down the organization's name and location, then the job title and dates of employment on the second line:

FENWAY PROJECT ADMINISTRATIVE OFFICE   Boston, MA
Office Assistant   April 2013-Present

Step 2

Write down in simple terms the various duties you had in a given job, like this:

FENWAY PROJECT ADMINISTRATIVE OFFICE   Boston, MA
Office Assistant   April 2013-Present
- ◆ Schedule and organize events.
- ◆ Perform research and administrative tasks.
- ◆ Recruit and train student interns.

Step 3

Add details describing the nature of the employer in question and the purpose of the job:

FENWAY PROJECT ADMINISTRATIVE OFFICE   Boston, MA
Office Assistant   April 2013-Present
- ◆ Schedule and organize events and <u>community services for needy socioeconomic</u>

groups in inner-city Boston.
- ♦ Perform research on <u>corporate and nonprofit organizations to identify strategic methods for getting donations of resources</u>.
- ♦ Recruit and <u>motivate college students to participate as volunteers</u>.

Step 4

Add quantitative details and professional terms when possible to bring the experience to life:

FENWAY PROJECT ADMINISTRATIVE OFFICE Boston, MA
Office Assistant April 2013-Present

- ♦ <u>In a timely manner</u>, schedule and organize events and community services <u>for over 50 inner-city Boston teenagers</u> in needy socioeconomic groups.
- ♦ Research <u>roughly 250</u> corporate and nonprofit organizations to identify strategic methods for <u>soliciting</u> donations of resources.
- ♦ Successfully recruited and motivated ten college students to participate as volunteers.

From this job description, we get a much better sense of who this student really is. We get a sense of her research experience, altruistic motives, and ability to juggle tasks—without directly mentioning these soft skills. A hiring employer could infer that the student was responsible and motivated. As you will see when you read the chapter on interviewing, these qualities are probably the most important that any potential supervisor wants to see in a new hire.

PASSIVE VERSUS ACTIVE VERBS

If, after all this, your resume is still lacking something, try to review your use of verbs. Remember: never use passive verbs where you can use active verbs instead. The following is a list of POWER words for inclusion in your resume.

PASSIVE VERBS	ACTIVE/POWER VERBS
Maintained	Enhanced
Assisted	Contributed (to)
Answered	Directed
Spoke to...	Resolved problems
Sold	Increased sales by...
Taught	Instructed
Processed	Expedited
Received	Earned
Coordinated	Negotiated

As mentioned earlier, a more comprehensive list of action verbs in various categories is available toward the end of this chapter.

Capturing Other Types of Experience

Probably some of you are saying, "What if I don't have any job experience?" For cultural reasons, many international students may not work at all while in high school. And some

US-born students may have minimal experience or almost none at all. Still others might believe—quite rightly—that they would be better off using the valuable real estate of their resume to emphasize academic projects that are directly relevant to an employer's needs, minimizing less relevant jobs in the process.

Obviously, you should check with your career professional if you think that this applies to you. But certainly you can write up an academic project under your experience section if it's relevant to a potential employer.

What would a section along these lines look like? Here's an example from a plastics engineering major at University of Massachusetts Lowell:

RELEVANT ACADEMIC PROJECTS
Electrical Connector Moldflow Evaluation   December 2012
♦ Conducted multiple assessments of an existing part and analyzed test results using Moldflow software
♦ Provided multiple design and process improvements

This section might go above or below your job experience (if you have any) depending on its priority from the employer's perspective. Just as with any job description, you would want the description of an academic project to include active verbs and convey your accomplishments.

COMPUTER SKILLS (OR SPECIAL SKILLS)

This is a very important section and should be included on your resume. Every college student will have at least some basic computer skills. This is the place to state what they are. Do not overstate your abilities, but don't be modest either. You need to state your abilities clearly. Are you proficient with, familiar with, or do you just have exposure to a particular software program? Can you work with PCs, Macs, or both? In this technological age, stating your computer skills can be the edge you need to get an interview—even when pursuing jobs in supposedly non-technical fields such as the humanities and social sciences!

With this in mind, let's take a closer look at how to capture your computer skills on this section of a resume. Sometimes people either will forget about what PC skills they have or—incredibly—feel that they can't put a given skill down because they learned it on their own, outside of the classroom or workplace. Did you know that some employers are actually *more* impressed with candidates who taught themselves how to use software applications? For example, if you taught yourself "just for fun," that says a great deal about your ability and enthusiasm to learn on the computer. With this in mind, here's a quick checklist you can use to determine whether you have included *all* of your relevant computer experience.

Do you have experience with:

• **Word Processing** (Microsoft Word, WordPerfect, etc.)

• **Spreadsheets** (Microsoft Excel)

- **Databases** (Microsoft Access, Oracle, SAP, Lotus Notes, etc.)

- **Customer Relationship Management/E-mail Marketing (Salesforce, Constant Contact, etc.)**

- **Content Management (SharePoint, Box, WordPress, Drupal, Joomla, etc.)**

- **Operating Systems** (Windows 8/NT 4.0/XP/Vista, UNIX, MacOS, etc.)

- **Programming languages** (Objective C, SQL, Python, Ruby, C++, Visual Basic, Android (Java) etc.)

- **Network Administration** (Active Directory, Windows 2008/NT, TCP/IP, etc.)

- **Web Design** (HTML, CSS, JavaScript, PHP, etc.)

- **Presentation Graphics** (PowerPoint, Prezi, Keynote, etc.)

- **Desktop Publishing/Graphic Design/Data Visualization** (Visio, Adobe Photoshop, Tableau, etc.)

- **Hardware** (Hubs, routers, switches, etc.)

Many students are unsure about whether their skills with a given application are good enough to put on their resumes. Obviously, you want to be honest, but you also want to give yourself credit for what you do know. One suggestion for dealing with this dilemma is to break down your knowledge of applications under the categories of "Proficient with," "Familiar with," and "Exposure to." If you have tons of experience with Excel, say that you are proficient with it. If you know how to do formulas, alter columns and rows, and create charts and graphs but not much more, you might say that you are familiar with it. While if you have only used it a few times or your experience is in the distant past, play it safe and say that you just have exposure to Excel. This way you can be honest without selling yourself short.

You also should take care to ensure that you correctly spell the names of any computer applications that you list under the heading of "Computer Skills" or "Special Skills." Use the list on the next page as a quick reference when proofreading your resume. Although this is particularly important if you are applying for an MIS job, everyone should try to make their resume as perfectly accurate as possible... never an easy task when it comes to the bizarre spellings of many software applications.

Note that it's also acceptable to include what version of a program you have worked with (i.e., Novell NetWare 3.x, etc.). This is especially true with operating systems such as Windows, as there is a big difference between, say, Windows 2008 NT and Windows 2008Vista.

Also note that Microsoft Office is a family of Microsoft applications (Word, Excel, Access, PowerPoint, and Outlook) that some employers may buy as one complete package. If you have experience with Microsoft Office, though, we still suggest writing out all of the applications, as some employers may not be familiar with the term. Also, there are different versions of Office, so it may not be clear from that term if you know Access, for example, as that is not included in all versions of Office.

Correct spellings of typical MIS terms
(and acceptable alternatives)

WordPerfect	Microsoft Word (MS-Word, Word)
Microsoft Excel (MS-Excel, Excel)	Microsoft Access (MS-Access, Access)
Microsoft PowerPoint (PowerPoint)	MS-DOS (DOS)
MacOS	FoxPro
TCP/IP	HTML
Lotus Notes	Dreamweaver
Windows 2008 XP	Windows 2008
Windows 2008	UNIX
C++	Novell NetWare
PageMaker	AutoCAD
WordPress	SharePoint
Salesforce	SQL

Now that you know how to capture your computer skills, let's consider other skills that you want to make sure to mention. You should include skills you have in the following areas:

- Language Skills: Fluent in..., Conversational ability in..., etc.)

- Laboratory Skills (see sidebar box)

- Licenses, Certificates and Training (Real Estate, CPR, First Aid)

Here's an example of what your skills section might look like:

SKILLS
Proficient with Microsoft Word, Excel, and PowerPoint
Familiar with Windows 2008 XP/Vista, Prezi, and Access
Exposure to Salesforce, HTML, and JavaScript
Conversational in Spanish

If you have a very strong background in computers—meaning that your knowledge goes well beyond applications such as Microsoft Office—the recent industry standard is to break out your computer skills by category. This is fairly standard for students in MIS, Computer Science, Computer Engineering, and similar majors. Here's an example:

COMPUTER SKILLS

Operating Systems:	Windows 98/2000/2008, MacOS
Languages:	Objective C, SQL
Networking:	Windows 2008 NT, Novell NetWare 6.5, Active Directory
Applications:	Microsoft Word 6.0, Excel, Access, PowerPoint, Adobe Photoshop, AutoCAD
Exposure to:	Python, PHP

Capturing Skills On Your Resume – A Co-op Professional's Perspective
by Ronnie Porter

I really started noticing a few years back that students who did not have much experience and who were not explicit about their skills were not getting jobs. There may be technical skills that they've not really thought about it because they haven't practiced them on a job, but they've learned them in a laboratory setting. So I created a skills list with a set of things that they might have learned in lab that they could replicate in a work setting. I had them start communicating that to employers, and it made a huge difference. On their resume, they would have a section called Laboratory Skills. I found that that made a big difference in being successful. Employers weren't making the leap from Bio I and Bio II to the skill sets, so students had to break it out for them. The interviewer might be an HR person who might not be able to communicate effectively to the supervisor what the candidate is capable of doing.

Ronnie Porter is a cooperative education faculty coordinator in Biology at Northeastern University.

INTERESTS

How you spend your free time reveals another dimension of your personality, as well as important skills such as communication skills, leadership, motivation and initiative, time management, resourcefulness, organization, and energy. It is a chance to include activities, hobbies, and interests—to show you're well-rounded. Interests humanize you—and anything that makes you seem more like a real person than just a name on a page will make an employer more inclined to give you an interview.

Resumes – An Employer's Perspective
by Mike Naclerio

An "Interests" section is a good icebreaker for interviews. It gives the resume a personal/unique touch and is an area I always seek out to open conversations with students in an interview.

Mike Naclerio is the President of Enquiron.

As before, try to be specific. Listing "dancing, reading, sports, and movies" is much less interesting than, say, "ballet, contemporary short fiction, ice hockey, and foreign films." A specific and unique list is much more likely to catch the eye of a potential employer. It also shows that you are serious about your interests and have some depth of character. This makes you come off as a three-dimensional person, and it also can make an employer want to get to know you a little better in the interview. As an ice-breaker question, interviewers may ask you about one of your interests...which is a MUCH easier first question than, say, "Why should we hire you for this job?" Better still, a potential employer may share one of your interests and believe (rightly or wrongly) that the two of you share a connection as a result. That can't hurt!

If you include political or religious organizations or affiliations, be aware that this could work for you or against you. Choosing not to hire you for these reasons would be illegal, of course, but you still run a risk in including certain kinds of information. Imagine writing about your volunteer work for the Republican Party on your resume, then going into your interviewer's office and seeing an autographed photo of former President Clinton! In other words, try to be sensitive to the fact that others may not share your enthusiasms and may even be turned off by them.

Adding Interests to Your Resume – A Student's Perspective
By Daniel Brooks

You definitely should put experiences and qualifications on your resume which you can speak about enthusiastically and intelligibly. Employees will like to see that you were, are, and will be excited and competent when it comes to your work projects.

But also add some personal interests and hobbies on the resume. This will allow a good interviewer to break the ice more effectively and help you relax by talking to you about non-work related activities you find interesting. This will help the employer see your true colors—especially if you can use your interests to showcase some qualities that are also attractive in an employee.

Daniel Brooks was a Plastics Engineering major at University of Massachusetts Lowell, Class of 2012. He is now in the Commercialization Leadership Program at SABIC Corporation.

Avoid anything that might be controversial or that may raise a potential concern. This includes such common college student interests as nightclubs, partying, girls, hanging out with friends, or shopping. You want to show interests that require some intelligence or at least energy.

As a part of your resume, some consider the Interests section to be optional or irrelevant. However, make every effort to include it. It can't hurt you, and it might help you. If you don't think you have the space, take a close look at the rest of the resume and ask yourself why you can't *make* room for this section. If I have students who are skeptical about including this section, I always ask them: "What would you prefer as the first question of your interview: "Why should we hire YOU for this job?" or "I noticed that you're interested in contemporary fiction. Who are your favorite authors?"

Here is a sample Interests section:

INTERESTS
Russian literature, skiing, chess, current events, triathlons, and camping

REFERENCES

And, lastly, don't forget your references and reference page. On your resume, simply write either "References Furnished Upon Request" or "References Available Upon Request" on the bottom. But don't stop there. Create a reference page on the same bond paper that you use for your resume. Be sure to contact your references first to ask their permission to be used as a reference. This will help your reference person to be more prepared and thus able to give you a better reference when called upon by an employer.

You should have at least three references and ideally around five. Try to include two or three professional/work references, one or two academic references, and one or two character references. A character reference is a coach, a religious leader, or a family friend who has known you since you were more or less in diapers, while a work reference is usually a direct supervisor. Include name, title, company, company address, telephone number, and, if you know it, an e-mail address. As long as you include these items, the format isn't critical: some people center their references on the page, while others have them flush left. *Just make sure that whatever format you use is consistent with your resume.*

You should always bring a few copies of your reference page to an interview, so you can give them to the interviewer immediately, if asked. If you're asked to supply references, you don't want to reply "Um, uh.... Can I get it to you in a few days?" A sample of a basic but good reference page is included at the end of this chapter following the sample resumes.

SAMPLE RESUMES

At the end of this chapter, we have included a few sample resumes that you can review to see how other students have captured themselves. These resumes reflect varying degrees of education and job experience as well as many different majors, but they all are unique and effective.

Check out Hannah Snow's resume on page 65. This is the resume of a young woman with no real professional experience, yet it's packed with plenty of attractive attributes. With a variety of extracurricular activities complementing thorough documentation of various jobs and her high school background, Hannah comes across as a substantial individual despite her inexperience. Consistent with what we've covered in this chapter, note the use of powerful active verbs, strong qualitative details, and a determination to include *accomplishments* as opposed to simply listing *responsibilities.* Also note that Hannah has shunned the use of transferable skills in this resume in favor of a more concise approach. As I've indicated, this is a judgment call: Hannah shows here why they are not an absolute necessity if the resume finds a way to convey the individual's strengths.

Look at Lana Schillman's resume on page 66. This is an example of the bulleted list form of resume, as opposed to the paragraphing format. One nice thing about this resume is that she has used the font Arial. As mentioned earlier, employers see many resumes in Times New Roman, which looks fine but doesn't stand out. Elsewhere, this resume has consistent and strong verbs throughout the job descriptions, and it is easy to read.

Of course, this is the resume of a senior: someone looking for one last co-op job. But what if you're looking for your *first* co-op job? Consider the next resume at the end of this chapter. Gabrielle Bueno has an effective approach. She uses the bullet format, which works nicely. Bullets tend to work well in jobs involving a variety of duties and/or jobs that are relatively uncomplicated. This student does use transferable skills effectively but sparingly. Regardless, she is able to imply that she possesses those soft skills. Her job descriptions are thorough but concise. They reflect accomplishments but don't overhype her unskilled jobs. Another point here is the power of extracurricular activities. Although Gabrielle obviously hasn't had a real professional job yet, her school activities are definitely eyebrow-raising.

The fourth sample resume is a great example for students who might be best off by emphasizing things other than their work experience. In this case, Martin Parkhurst is showcasing his technical skills as well as his impressive work with academic projects.

As noted earlier in the chapter, you absolutely can describe an academic project on your resume. For some students, these projects may be more important in the eyes of an employer than any job experience. As a plastics engineering major, Martin wants to emphasize his impressive technical skills first. Then he goes into the projects before briefly describing his jobs. You also have to make a judgment call as to what will matter most to the employer. In this case, Martin clearly believes that his academic experience will get attention.

Next we have a promising student from LaGuardia Community College. Like the first individual we sampled, here is a student whose job experience is longer and stronger than that of many college students. As a result, Pui Sze Ng opts against using the transferable skills within the job description: Her experience doesn't need as much selling as someone who has never had a professional job. Appropriately, she chooses to push her computer skills higher up on the resume, just after the education section. This is her top selling point, and she wants it to be noticed right away. The skills section breaks out her computer skills in a way that will be useful to her prospective employers: It's easy to follow both aesthetically and conceptually. Lastly, the resume is in a font called Verdana—always a good idea for an aspiring computer professional to show that she can get beyond the default font in Word!

As for the fifth and last sample, the first thing that catches your eye with Meghan Brooke's resume is that it is neat and eye-pleasing, with nice use of boldface and italics. This resume also shows how to display both a local and permanent address if you feel inclined to include both. As her job experience lacks work related to her concentration, she has chosen to use transferable skills throughout all of her job descriptions in order to highlight skills that an MIS employer might want to see. Meghan chose the paragraphing format, too, probably because it saves a little space, but she could have used bullets just as easily. This resume attracted multiple interviews and a great entry-level co-op job for her.

As you can see, each of these three resumes differs significantly in terms of how to use font, boldface type, italics, centering, headings, and underlining. Some of the resume writers' choices may appeal to you more than others. There really is a great deal of flexibility in how you make your resume look, as long as you capture each of the required sections on a one-page resume, and as long as your resume is completely free of spelling mistakes or typographical errors.

Is it easy to write an effective resume? Not necessarily. As you hopefully know by now, you may have to be creative to show how some of your past job experience relates to the jobs you plan to pursue. But with considerable effort and a little assistance from your co-op coordinator and/or Career Services, you can write a resume that will help get you in the door for an interview.

MULTIPLE RESUMES

What if you are applying for jobs in more than one concentration? Perhaps you plan to apply for both finance jobs and MIS jobs, for example. One option for those who are more ambitious is to create TWO resumes: one emphasizing your desire to get a finance job, and another focusing on your strong interest and aptitude in MIS. In fact, software applications at some universities actually allow students to upload multiple resumes and then designate which employer should receive which resume.

Is it "okay" to do this? Of course it is! In fact, trying to capture both of these interests in one resume is extremely difficult; you run the risk of coming across as someone who lacks focus or who is "jack of all trades, master of none." This should give you some incentive to consider writing more than one resume. One cautionary note, however: *It is crucial that YOU keep track of which resume has been faxed or e-mailed to each employer. If the same employer receives one of your resumes from your coordinator and another when you arrive for an interview, this is likely to work against you! This is especially true given that many coordinators now use a computerized system for e-mailing resumes—make sure to discuss using multiple resumes with your coordinator before trying to do this.*

Much of the information on each of your resumes will be identical: Obviously, this won't affect your Education section much, and you still list your places of employment. But how you describe your job experience could vary quite a bit. On a finance resume, you would emphasize work experience that relates to financial experience: budgeting, calculating, analyzing, assessing, etc. On an MIS resume, though, you might describe the same job in terms of what computer skills were required to perform these financial duties. Or, if some of your previous job related to computers but some of it didn't, then move your computer-related duties to the *top* of the job description for the MIS resume. On the finance resume, put the computer-related duties lower and don't emphasize them as strongly in your description. In your skills section, the MIS resume should be more all-inclusive, featuring the version number of each software application if possible. Even your interests might be reflected differently on each resume: You might take "investments" off of your MIS resume and add interests pertaining to learning new computer applications, Web design, foreign languages, and the Internet: all of which may be perceived more favorably by an MIS employer. Keep in mind that we're not suggesting that you *lie* about your interests and your job experiences, but rather to emphasize those things which will be relevant to an employer in that field.

THINGS TO AVOID: OBJECTIVES AND TEMPLATES

Now that you are almost through with this chapter, you may be wondering why you have not read about starting off your resume with an objective—especially when many word-processing resume templates prompt you to include one.

First off, *don't use a word-processing template!* They may appeal to those who are lazy and/ or fear that they don't know enough about word processing to make the format look good. Believe me, templates are not the answer. Templates make it extremely difficult for you to revise and update a resume, and they may force you into including or emphasizing items that are not appropriate for an aspiring co-op, intern, or senior seeking his or her first full-time job. A few times a year, someone shows me a resume that was thrown together in a few minutes using the resume template in Microsoft Word. The typical Word resume template is not that attractive—the student's address is small and hard to read, and the experience section's format is rather odd in its emphasis. We have plenty of options here that will work better for you.

As for objectives, they occasionally can be useful but usually are problematic or unhelpful. The problem is that they either tend to say too much or to not say anything at all. Think about it: if you write that your objective is "To find a cost-accounting position with a growing financial services firm," then what happens if you want to or need to apply for something even slightly different? In other words, you end up pigeonholing yourself. The flip side is the objective that really doesn't say anything that we don't already know: "To find a cooperative education position that will help me grow as an aspiring health care professional." Well, I hope so!

The only exception to this rule might be if your true objective is to find something that is very different from what one might infer from your previous experience. Someone who has worked in the psychology field but now wants to pursue a career in marketing could make this crystal-clear with a good objective. Generally, though, you should avoid bothering with an objective on your resume.

After you have written your resume, use the following checklist to make sure your resume meets the successful resume standard.

RESUME CHECKLIST

☐ The resume is one page in length.

☐ The resume has been carefully checked for spelling and punctuation errors as well as double-checked to make sure that all addresses and phone numbers are current.

☐ Job descriptions are grammatically correct.

☐ There are no personal pronouns (I/me).

☐ Job descriptions do not begin with: "Responsibilities included" or "Duties consisted of" or anything similar to those constructions.

☐ Abbreviations of states are correct (i.e., MA not MA. or Mass.)

☐ The format is neat and attractive to the eye.

☐ The format is easily readable.

☐ All major components of a resume are included.

☐ Job titles are listed for each job description.

☐ Dates and place of employment are included for each work experience, and they are written in the same format each time.

☐ Confirm that all contact information is correct. This includes your mailing address, e-mail address, and telephone number(s). Be especially sure that telephone number(s) is(are) correct if you have a land line. (A common error because students tend to move frequently.)

☐ Resume will be copied on 8 1/2 X 11 inch bond paper in white or some other neutral color. Note that plain white paper should be used on resumes given to your coordinator: Nice paper sometimes looks awful when run through a fax machine!

YOUR RESUME IS A REFLECTION AND PERSONAL STATEMENT OF YOU!

Please note that these are suggestions, not requirements. Your resume is a reflection of you, and as such, you should feel comfortable and proud of its contents. While writing your resume, you will be presenting your experience and achievements in the best way possible. However, there is no room for deceit or lies on a resume. Lying on a resume is akin to plagiarism and is not acceptable at any university or in any professional workplace. Grade point averages, dates, computer skills, and achievements must be accurate and honest. You are building a professional reputation and should strive for a reputation known for its integrity.

Resumes – An Employer's Perspective
by Steve Sim

What impresses me on a resume? First of all, honesty impresses me. If you haven't done a whole lot of HTML development work, and you put that down as a skill set, be sure you can answer specific questions about HTML.

Second, clarity impresses me. If you are clear enough on a resume where someone who doesn't know anything about you (or potentially even positions you're interested in) can read your resume and say you're qualified, then it's going to get to my desk.

Third, effective use of space impresses me. Fonts and margins can change to fit your info. One should feel comfortable using them freely.

Steve Sim was a Technical Recruiter at the Microsoft Corporation and is now Co-Founder & Principal Search Consultant at Envisage Recruiting LLC.

While writing your resume, feel free to consult with friends, advisors, teachers, employers, and others whose opinions you respect. However, bear in mind that this guidebook and your co-op/internship or career services coordinator should be your number one resources. Again, be wary of your cousin's boyfriend who claims to be good at writing resumes—a person outside of your co-op program generally has no experience working with co-op students and employers and therefore may be not be a credible source of assistance. That said, *do* have several people proofread for grammatical and spelling errors. "I have employers that will teach you many things that you don't know," says Bob Tillman, associate professor and co-op faculty coordinator for the civil engineering program at Northeastern University. "So on your resume, I have other concerns: let's get rid of all of the dumb mistakes." Many employers will discard your resume as soon as a typo is discovered, the theory being that if you cannot take the time to submit an error-free resume (which should reflect your best effort), then the quality of your work may reflect the same low standards. To put it more simply, an employer might think "If this is the best, I'd hate to see the rest!"

So invest your time wisely and do a superb job! There is no exact formula for a perfect resume, but these suggestions are based on experience, employer recommendations, and research. Learn to do your resume well now, and you will find that this skill will be helpful to you throughout your career.

GOOD LUCK!

ACTION VERB LIST

COMMUNICATIONS

acted as liaison	demonstrated	lectured	publicized
advised	displayed	marketed	published
advocated	edited	mediated	recommended
authored	guided	moderated	referred
commented	informed	negotiated	sold
consulted	instructed	notified	trained
corresponded	interpreted	presented	translated

ADMINISTRATION

administered	distributed	managed	recruited
appointed	eliminated	motivated	referred
arranged	executed	obtained	represented
completed	governed	opened	reviewed
controlled	implemented	organized	selected
coordinated	instituted	overhauled	supervised
delegated	issued	presided	supplied
directed	launched	provided	terminated

PLANNING & DEVELOPMENT

broadened	devised	improved	prepared
created	discovered	invented	produced
designed	drafted	modified	proposed
developed	estimated	planned	

ANALYSIS

amplified	detected	forecasted	researched
analyzed	diagnosed	formulated	solved
calculated	disapproved	identified	studied
compiled	evaluated	investigated	systematized
computed	examined	programmed	tested

ENGINEERING

assembled	installed	operated	replaced
constructed	maintained	planned	rewired
forecasted	modified	remodeled	set up
guided	monitored	repaired	standardized

FINANCIAL/RECORDS MANAGEMENT

allocated	collected	logged	purchased
audited	documented	maximized	recorded
balanced	expedited	minimized	scheduled
catalogued	invested	monitored	traced
classified	inventoried	processed	updated

GENERAL TERMS

accomplished	delivered	originated	serviced
achieved	expanded	performed	strengthened
assisted	handled	provided	transformed
completed	increased	served	utilized

TRANSFERABLE SKILLS IN BUSINESS CONCENTRATIONS

MIS/Computer Science

Ability to learn quickly

Positive attitude/Strong work ethic

Interpersonal skills

Computer skills (be specific)

Communication skills

Dependability/Reliability

Customer-service skills

Willingness to do whatever asked

Patience

Organizational skills

Good judgment

Attention to detail

Ability to juggle multiple duties

Accounting/Finance

Positive attitude/Strong work ethic

Quantitative skills

Responsibility

Computer skills (be specific)

Dependability/Reliability

Organizational skills

Communication skills

Ability to learn quickly

Interpersonal skills

Ability to juggle multiple duties

Willingness to do whatever asked

Attention to detail

Ability to work in teams

Marketing

Verbal communication skills

Writing skills

Positive attitude/Strong work ethic

Ability to do research

Persistence/Drive

Results-oriented personality

Customer-service skills

Selling skills/Persuasiveness

Interpersonal skills

Computer skills (be specific)

Organizational skills

Outgoing personality

Ability to juggle responsibilities

Willingness to do whatever asked

Attention to detail

Ability to work in teams

Entrepreneurship

Initiative/Self-starter

Creativity

Ability to work independently

Willingness to take risks

Ability to identify opportunities

Openness to new ideas

Willingness to play any role

Ambitiousness

Eagerness to learn

Ability to do research

Flexibility

Enthusiasm

Commitment

Willingness to work long hours

Persistence/Drive

Ability to juggle multiple duties

TRANSFERABLE SKILLS IN OTHER MAJORS

Health Sciences/Social Sciences

Interpersonal skills

Positive attitude/Strong work ethic

Sensitivity/Caring

Communication skills

Judgment/Responsibility

Organizational skills

Attention to detail

Willingness to do whatever asked

Ability to juggle responsibilities

Reliability/Dependability

Discretion and integrity

Ability to work in teams

Eagerness to learn

Engineering/Natural Sciences

Analytical skills

Ability to lay out and solve problems

Communication skills

Computer skills (be specific)

Positive attitude/Strong work ethic

Attention to detail

Ability to work independently

Ability to work in teams

Ability to prioritize

Interpersonal skills

Reliability/Dependability

Laboratory skills

Willingness to do whatever asked

Humanities

Communication skills

Ability to research

Presentation skills

Analytical skills

Positive attitude/Strong work ethic

Reliability/Dependability

Organizational skills

Interpersonal skills

Ability to work independently

Ability to work in teams

Willingness to do whatever asked

Criminal Justice/Law

Integrity

Judgment/Responsibility

Analytical skills

Attention to detail

Communication skills

Positive attitude/Strong work ethic

Interpersonal skills

Reliability/Dependability

Ability to work independently

Ability to work in teams

TRANSFERABLE SKILL PHRASE CHEAT SHEET

If you would like to try building transferable skill phrases into your resume, try using this formula: Pick an accurate word from each column below in order to figure out how to graft a transferable skill phrase onto a bullet point or sentence in your Experience section.

VERB	ADJECTIVE	TRANSFERABLE SKILL	LINKING WORD
Demonstrated	effective	ability to learn quickly	when
Displayed	excellent	communication skills	while
Showed	outstanding	interpersonal skills	
Exhibited	strong	attention to detail	
Proved to have	solid	dependability	
Utilized	very good	attitude	
Exercised	consistent	organizational skills	
Used	exceptional	patience	
Possessed	positive	customer-service orientation	
		willingness to do whatever asked	
		ability to work in a team	
		ability to work independently	
		initiative	

Step 1: *Capture what you did in a simple, straightforward way:*

♦ Cleaned out stalls at a horse farm.

Step 2: *Add quantifiable and quantitative details to make the job come alive:*

♦ Working in a busy, family-oriented horse farm, cleaned out 23 horse stalls daily.

Step 3: *If you were GOOD at the job, identify the transferable skills you used in the job and use them to create a phrase using the above formula:*

♦ Working in a busy, family-oriented horse farm, demonstrated positive attitude and willingness to do whatever asked while cleaning out 23 horse stalls daily.

You don't need a transferable skill phrase with every single sentence or bullet, but students without any directly relevant job experience probably should make sure to use at least two per job…. assuming you were GOOD at that job! One way or another, find ways to make your resume do more than list WHAT you did. Capture HOW you did it and WHY you did it well.

Hannah Snow
1234 Singha Street, #42 Morgan Hill, CA 02115

(617) 555-6543   E-Mail: hannah103194@hotmail.com

EDUCATION

San Jose State University   San Jose, CA

Candidate for Bachelor of Science Degree in Business Administration   May 2017

Concentration: Marketing   G.P.A. 3.6

Awards and Activities: Dean's List, University Honors Program, Vice President Membership for the San Jose State University Marketing Club, Chamber Singers

Live Oak High School   Morgan Hill, CA

High School Diploma   June 2013

Awards and Activities: National Honor Society, Student Government Association, Varsity Soccer Captain

EXPERIENCE

Mari Calendars Restaurant   Morgan Hill, CA

Waitress   January 2012-Present

- Advise customers on menu selections based upon their likes and dislikes.
- Resolve all issues in designated section including opening and closings, table setup, and assured food storage at appropriate temperatures.
- Utilize suggestive selling for specialty food promotions.
- Process cash and credit transactions, calculating customer receipts to analyze percent allocation to restaurant wait staff and hostesses.

Gap Incorporated   San Jose, CA

Sales Associate   May 2010-August 2011

- Worked on selling floor as a part of sales team to meet daily sales goal.
- Consistently increased customer sales through add-ons.
- Directed customer complaints to appropriate department for satisfactory resolution.

Super Seafood   Monterey, CA

Chef's Assistant/Cashier   June 2009-September 2009

- Steamed all lobster and shellfish dishes in a popular seasonal take-out restaurant and fish market.
- Stocked fish case, wrapped fish, and operated cash register.
- Precooked 100-200 lobsters every night for the next day.

VOLUNTEER EXPERIENCE

Junior Achievement Academy   Gilroy, CA

Volunteer Mentor   January 2014-Present

- Teach high school students business and leadership skills.
- Recognized at Financial Executives International annual banquet for participating with the program.

SKILLS/INTERESTS

Computer Skills: Knowledgeable in Windows 95/98/2008 ME, MS Word, MS PowerPoint

Languages: Conversational French, beginning Spanish

Certifications: American Red Cross CPR, First Aid

Interests: Traveling, baseball, piano, photography

Lana Schillman
99 Tovar Road, Apt. #6, Chestnut Hill, MA 02167
(617) 490-9999   e-mail: lanas@aol.com

EDUCATION

PASON UNIVERSTY   Boston, MA
Candidate for Bachelor of Science Degree in Business Administration   May 2017
Concentration: Management Information Systems   **GPA**: 3.73
Honors: Dean's List

Activities: Lacrosse Club, Robotics Club

EXPERIENCE

ROCOCO INVESTMENTS   Boston, MA
Architecture Assistant   June 2013 – Present
- As a member of the system architecture group, take part in the design and development of a database application system. Repository will be internally used as a decision support component required for impact analyses.
- Understand the systems, their interfaces, the databases, and the overall architecture of the information system.
- Understand the logical model and model representation of the repository.
- Formulate the application's business requirements.
- Design and develop the application user interface utilizing PowerBuilder 5.0.

INTEGRITY FINANCIAL SERVICES   Boston, MA
Systems Specialist   June 2011 – April 2013
- As a Member of LAN restructuring task force, effectively worked toward simplifying file naming conventions on network, and combining drives.
- Created queries and reports for management evaluation, utilizing Crystal Reports.
- Created and updated Excel spreadsheets for Actuarial purposes.

HYANNISPORT CRANBERRIES INC.   Lakeville, MA
Human Resources Intern   Jan. 2011 – May 2011
- Modified organization charts by utilizing Lotus Freelance Graphics software application.
- Performed queries to determine if there were suitable internal or external candidates for specific job requisitions.
- Used Resumix database to ensure that resumes were on the computer system.

SKILLS AND INTERESTS

Computer Skills: Knowledgeable in MS Access 2.0, MS Excel 5.0, MS Word 6.0, PowerBuilder 5.0, Lotus Freelance Graphics 2.0, Crystal Reports 5.0, Windows 2008, Windows 95, 2000, 2008, Windows NT 4.0, UNIX, Mac. Familiar with C++, SQL, and Visual Basic.
Languages: Conversational in Hebrew; Exposure to Spanish.
Interests: Aerobics, cross-country skiing, contemporary fiction, and Web page design.

References furnished upon request

GABRIELLE BUENO

750 Parker Street, Palo Alto, CA 94563 ● 510.499.0000 ● bueno.ga@neu.edu

EDUCATION

Golden Gate University
San Francisco, CA

Candidate for Bachelor of Science in Business Administration
June 2015

Concentration: Supply Chain Management and Marketing

Honors: GPA: 3.9; Dean's List; Sigma Alpha Lambda (Honors Fraternity)

Activities: Vice President of Programming and Community Service, Golden Gate University Marketing Association (GGUMA) (present); Committee Chair, College of Business 2013, Class Council (2012-present); Vice President of Finance, GGUMA (2013); Treasurer, Longoria Hall Dormitory (2011-2013)

Balamonte High School
Portola Valley, CA

College Preparatory Curriculum
June 2011

Activities: Editor-in-Chief, Balamonte Yearbook (2010-2011); President, YMCA Youth and Government local chapter (2008-2009); Founder and President, CARE Community Service Club (2009-2011)

WORK EXPERIENCE

Golden Gate University Department of Residential Life
San Francisco, CA

Office Assistant
Sept. 2012 – Present

- Provide administrative support to Resident Director including: answering phones, filing, data entry, auditing residents, assisting with move in/out procedures
- Effectively resolve problems for students and staff
- Market dorm events to 526 residents
- Handle confidential student files and work with a high degree of autonomy

GAP Inc.
Walnut Creek, CA

Sales Associate
May – August 2011

- Consistently provided customer service and greeted every customer
- Used suggestive-selling techniques to market GAP credit card and promotional add-on items
- Worked efficiently in a team environment when processing shipments containing thousands of units for inventory and display
- Assisted with implementation of corporate marketing programs by assembling visual merchandising campaign materials in store

Ablove-Sloane Yearbooks
Walnut Creek, CA

Event Planner, Administrative Assistant
March – August 2010

- Efficently organized computer and graphic art workshops, client parties, and a week-long camp for 300 students
- Handled a wide range of office duties, creating PowerPoint presentations and organizing travel for company employees servicing over 80 schools
- Utilized strong attention to detail when processing payments and creating invoices

VOLUNTEER EXPERIENCE

Horizons for Homeless Children
Sept. 2012 – Present

Spend two hours a week working with underprivileged infants to aid early childhood development

SKILLS AND INTERESTS

Proficient in Microsoft Word, Microsoft PowerPoint; Familiar with Microsoft Excel; Exposure to FileMaker Pro, Adobe InDesign

Interests include: event planning, community service, scrapbooking, working with children, exercising

References provided upon request

Martin Parkhurst

Phone: (555) 555-5555

99 Maple Lane, Lowell, MA 01854

E-mail: MartinParkers97@gmail.com

EDUCATION

University of Massachusetts Lowell

Lowell, MA

Bachelor of Science, Plastics Engineering, May 2018

GPA: 3.2

TECHNICAL SKILLS

- *Processing* – Injection Molding (Roboshot, Argurg), Blow Molding (Rocheleau), Single Screw Extrusion (Davis Standard, Welex, and Berlyn), Rotational Molding (Wensley), Thermoform Molding (Maac), Vertical Rubber Molding (Freudenberg), Twin Screw Compounding, Blown Film Extrusion (Battenfeld Gloucester)
- *Testing* – Tensile Properties (Instron), Flexural Strength, Izod Impact, Shore Durometer Hardness, Rockwell Hardness, Melt Flow Rate, Coefficient of Friction, Charpy and Izod Impact, TMA, TGA, DSC, FTIR, Capillary Rheometer, Heat Press, Vacuum Press, Glass Adhesion
- *Software* – SolidWorks, Moldflow, MS Word, Excel, PowerPoint

RELEVANT ACADEMIC PROJECTS

Electrical Connector Moldflow Evaluation   December 2012
- Conducted multiple assessments of an existing part and analyzed test results using Moldflow software
- Provided multiple design and process improvements

Preparation of Environmentally Responsive Hydrogel   Fall 2012
- Prepared dye-filled hydrogels that change color and absorb acidic waste excreted by living cells in a given medium to extend cell life

Screen Window Frame Profile Extrusion Die Design   Fall 2012
- Applied knowledge of materials, the extrusion process, and SolidWorks to design and prototype an extruder profile die

ENGINEERING EXPERIENCE

Plastics Engineering Department, UMass Lowell

Lowell, MA

Polymer Science Lab Teaching Assistant

Fall 2012

- Successfully aided undergraduate students in various polymer experiments
- Effectively managed lab areas to ensure all supplies were available

ANTEC

Orlando, FL

Student Poster Presenter, 2nd Place Qualifier

May 2013

- Conducted research on the preparation of environmentally responsive hydrogels
- Presented findings alongside peers to the Plastics Industry Council

Innovative Plastics

Southborough, MA

Assistant Project Engineer Co-op

Jan. – May 2013

- Effectively solved design complications and material processing problems
- Served as primary liaison between engineering and technician teams

Design House

Clinton, MA

Assistant Process Engineer Intern

June – August 2012

- Assisted process engineers in optimizing new mold designs
- Aided project engineers in formulating layouts

Pui Sze Ng

57 Durutti Avenue, Staten Island, NY 10201
Phone: 718-222-0000, Fax: 718-222-9990, E-mail: puisze@yahoo.com

Education

LaGuardia Community College/CUNY, Long Island City, NY
Associate of Applied Science Degree – January 2016
Programming and Systems Major, Business Minor
Honors: Dean's List

Skills

Software	Programming Languages	Operating Systems
• Word 00/13	• Visual Basic 6.0	• Windows 2008/NT/00
• Excel 00/13	• Visual FoxPro 6.0	• Dos 5.x/6.x
• FrontPage 00/	• C++	• Novell Netware 4.x/5.x
• Adobe Photoshop	• HTML	• Macintosh OS 8.5

- o Customizing computers, constructing PC systems, troubleshooting and implementing software applications
- o Strong analytical skills
- o Detail-oriented and dedicated to problem-solving
- o Excellent interpersonal and organization skills

Work Experience

Manhattan University   New York, NY
Network Technician and End-User Support Specialist   August 2012-Present
- Work with relative independence to meet CIS project deadlines, including the setup of computers and printers for the registration department, faculty, and student labs.
- Install and configure Windows 2008 Workstations, TCP/IP, and applications.
- Run RJ-45 CAT 5 wires and terminate into Keystone jack preparing workstations for LAN services and internetworking.
- Use a variety of equipment, such as wire scopes and port scanners, and applications, such as IP browser, FTP, and IRC software to complete projects.

Robins USA   Long Island City, NY
Accounting Office Assistant   June 2011-July 2012
- Used Excel to create accounting spreadsheets.
- Posted financial entries to journal and ledger utilizing customized software.
- Organized, sorted, and maintained financial records and profiles.

Interests

Technological trends via hands-on experience, online technology resources, computer technology magazines, gourmet cooking, jazz, outdoor activities.

References

Business and personal references available upon request.

MEGHAN C. BROOKE
e-mail: brooke.mc@neu.edu

<u>Local Address</u>
145 Gallatin Street
Bozeman, MT 02115
(907) 465-8822

<u>Home Address</u>
6856 Camera Circle
Ocala, FL 22454
(255) 788-8642

EDUCATION

BIG SKY UNIVERSITY   Bozeman, MT
Bachelor of Science Degree in Nursing   May 2014
Cumulative GPA: 3.6 (4.0 scale)
Honors: University Honors Program, Dean's List
Activities: Health Sciences Club (Treasurer), Big Sky Student Ambassadors, Ultimate Frisbee Club
Planning to finance 60% of tuition and living expenses through cooperative education earnings

MANATEE HIGH SCHOOL   Ocala, FL
College Preparatory Curriculum   June 2010
Honors: Who's Who Among American High School Students, National Honor Roll, National Honor Society
Activities: Varsity Tennis, Ocala Packers Hiking Club, Students Against Driving Drunk

EXPERIENCE

KOHL'S DEPARTMENT STORE   Ocala, FL
Point of Sale Representative   June 2009-August 2010
Increased customer participation in Kohl's credit program by persuading customers to enroll. Exhibited close attention to detail while performing cash and credit transactions and calculating customer receipts. Demonstrated ability to learn quickly while using the credit computer and cash register. Greeted customers.

GOLDEN YEARS SENIOR CENTER   Ocala, FL
Volunteer   June 2008-Sept. 2008
Demonstrated warmth and caring when working with over 75 geriatric residents. Consistently exhibited patience while dealing with demanding population on a daily basis. Effectively juggled multiple duties by answering phones, delivering food and mail, and engaging in personal conversations with residents. Taught interested residents how to use Internet. Stocked supplies.

COMPUTER SKILLS
Knowledgeable in Microsoft Word, Microsoft Excel, Windows XP/Vista.
Familiar with Microsoft Access, Microsoft PowerPoint, and HTML.

INTERESTS
Skiing, ice hockey, camping, Scandanavian literature, drawing, and theater.

References will be furnished upon request

MEGHAN C. BROOKE
e-mail: brooke.mc@neu.edu

Local Address
145 Gallatin Street
Bozeman, MT 02115
(907) 465-8822

Home Address
6856 Camera Circle
Ocala, FL 22454
(255) 788-8642

REFERENCES

Mr. John Shumbata, Store Manager
Kohl's Department Store
777 South Garfield Drive
Ocala, FL 22454
(255) 555-3388
e-mail: j.shumbata@kohls.com

Mr. Anthony Zamboni, Facility Manager
Golden Years Senior Center
5544 Manatee Highway
Ocala, FL 22455
(255) 555-3000
e-mail: azamboni@goldenyears.com

Ms. Susan Bacher, Family Friend
43 Locklear Cove
Kissimmee, FL 22103
(313) 555-1111
e-mail: susan_bacher@hotmail.com

Dr. Joseph Pepitone, Professor
Timothy Paul School of Nursing
Big Sky University
24 Lone Mountain Avenue
Bozeman, MT 90601
(906) 373-0001
e-mail: j.pepitone@bigsky.edu

Dr. Singha Piqaboue, Associate Professor
Timothy Paul School of Nursing
Big Sky University
24 Lone Mountain Avenue
Bozeman, MT 90601
(906) 373-0003
e-mail: s.piqaboue@bigsky.edu

EMPLOYER ROUNDTABLE

What advice do you have about writing resumes? What makes for a good resume? What bugs you on resumes that you see?

First impressions really will make or break you as a candidate, and your resume is your first impression. Your resume needs to be concise, well organized and professionally laid out. In the age of spellchecking, typos and grammatical errors are inexcusable and will doom yours to the round file.

You're a student, and no employer expects to see a history of impressive job titles in your background. What he or she will look for is a demonstrated history of self-initiative. Did you get up at 5 AM every day to deliver papers, or did you flip burgers? Don't try to overstate your credentials. I recently read a resume in which the student worked at a restaurant and stated that he was "skilled with a toaster." Being well rounded is important, but don't make the mistake of filling your resume with nothing but minor achievements, such as "member of the ultimate Frisbee team." Choose a handful of activities in which you expended a maximum effort, such as "violinist with school chamber music group."

If you really want to go where few interns have gone before, customize your resume for every employer you target. For instance, if you will be interviewing with a company that makes medical devices state in the objectives section that you are especially motivated to gain experience in life sciences. (Just don't lie if it's not true.) If you are able to glean information about the company's needs, then stress your skill in that area.

- Mark Spencer, President, Water Analytics

Be yourself. Write your resume in vocabulary that you understand and that you would normally use. Interviewers will use your resume to ask you questions about your experience, so you also need to be able to back up everything you put on a resume. There is nothing worse than asking a person a question about something they listed on their resume and being told that the interviewee does not know what it means or that it was typed incorrectly.

- Ryan P. Derber, SPHR, Segment Human Resources Manager,
PolyOne Corporation

Spelling. Many will toss a resume for bad spelling.

- Dennis Burke, Senior R&D Engineer, Depuy Synthes, Johnson & Johnson

Keep it neat and easy to read, make sure there are no spelling errors, etc. Keep it simple.

- Wentao Wang, ETP Engineering Manager, Pfizer Global Supply

STUDENT ROUNDTABLE

Now that you've had experience with the job search, what advice do you have about writing resumes? What makes for a good resume? What bugs you on resumes that you see?

I think resumes that are to the point are the best. I like it when resumes use different adjectives and verbs instead of the same words over and over again. They need to be easily read and organized. I love it when headers are easily distinguished from the body of the resume. Super small font is one of my pet peeves as well as complex graphics. It is okay to leave something out on the resume and bring it up in an interview.

- Mary Beth Moriarty, PhD Candidate, Plastics Engineering,
University of Massachusetts Lowell

The 'real world' that everyone talks about preparing for is fast paced. Your resume should be tailored to fit that lifestyle. Your resume hits HR's desk, and they will look it over quickly. Your best attributes should be highlighted first; make them short, concise and clear. Attract their attention with strong action words and they'll be inclined to read further into the details and ultimately pass your resume along to your potential employer.

- Jared Peraner, Market Development Specialist,
Consumer & Electronics, Nypro Inc.;
BS, Plastics Engineering, 2012, University of Massachusetts Lowell

CHAPTER TWO REVIEW QUESTIONS

1. Name at least four transferable skills that you have to offer a potential employer, and identify where you developed each skill.

2. Does it always make sense to list job experience in reverse chronological order, starting with the most recent job? Why, or why not?

3. What are the pros and cons of specifically listing your transferable skills on a resume?

4. What is the best way to indicate your varying degrees of knowledge of a computer skill or a language?

5. Name five specific interests that you have, choosing only ones that would add value to your resume. Also, list three interests that should NOT be included on any resume.

CHAPTER THREE
Strategic Interviewing

INTRODUCTION

When students are preparing for an interview, they often ask the following question: "Should I try to make it sound like I would be a great candidate for this job, or should I be honest?"

The answer is, simply, "Yes." Many future co-ops, interns, and full-time job seekers don't realize that this is not an either/or question: There is no reason you can't be honest while effectively selling yourself as an outstanding job candidate. Learning to do so is a two-step process: You need to identify which of your skills, experiences, or personal characteristics might be attractive to a particular employer. Then you need to learn how to articulate these qualities to the interviewer in the process of answering questions... and asking questions!

By the end of this chapter, you should have a better idea of how to strategize for interviews: How to show the employer that there is a strong connection between your unique characteristics as a job candidate and the job itself, as it is described in the job description.

Mastering this art will boost your chances of obtaining the best jobs. Depending on your major, the job market, the interviewer's approach, and your school's way of doing business with employers, your interview could be anything from a brief "sanity check" to a grueling interrogation. Talk to the professional at your school about what to expect, but—when in doubt—always assume that the interview will be a challenging test of your ability to research, prepare, and execute strategically.

INTERVIEWER AGENDA

As mentioned earlier in the book, these days I work for Bates Communications, a consulting firm specializing in leadership communication. Our CEO, Suzanne Bates, has written an excellent book called *Speak Like a CEO: Secrets for Commanding Attention and Getting*

Results. In it, she describes a simple, powerful tool called the Audience Agenda System. At work we sometimes half-kiddingly say that it's the only communication tool that anyone needs. It's just an extremely useful way to get your thinking process going when you're preparing for *any* form of communication: a presentation, a speech, a one-on-one meeting… even an e-mail.

Here's how it works: On the left-hand side of the page, you write what *you* want to convey to your audience. What's on your mind? What do you want them to know? Let's show how this tool could be applied to a student's job interview. In this example, we'll imagine that the student is a plastics engineer. First, let's see what the student is thinking:

STUDENT AGENDA	INTERVIEWER AGENDA
• I'd really like to work close to home. • I want this job: It pays really well! • Will I get to have my own office? • I hope my boss is ready to spend a lot of time mentoring me. • I want to do lots of challenging, interesting work that will help me learn!	

Next we have to use what Suzanne calls "180 Thinking." In other words, we now want to look at the interview from the *other* side of the desk! Envision the person who will manage this plastics engineering co-op or intern. The manager is probably swamped with projects and receiving dozens—maybe hundreds—of e-mails every day. He may have mixed feelings about hiring a co-op or intern. This young professional could be a big help, but there are many ways in which a "rookie" could be a real liability, too. So let's focus on the right-hand side of the page and imagine what the interviewer might be thinking going into this interview:

STUDENT AGENDA	INTERVIEWER AGENDA
• I'd really like to work close to home. • I want this job: It pays really well! • Will I get to have my own office? • I hope my boss is ready to spend a lot of time mentoring me. • I want to do lots of challenging, interesting work that will help me learn!	• Does this guy have any relevant skills or experience to do what I need him to do? • Will he be worth the time it will take me to train him? • Is he going to be one of these entitled college kids who has no experience but expects glamorous work? • Will he free me up or need a lot of hand holding to get stuff done? • Does he seem to have the soft skills that are necessary? I don't have the time or energy to teach those!

What do you notice about the two agendas? They're almost completely different, aren't they? The student is on a very different wavelength. But what should he do about that? Suzanne Bates likes to say that she's a simple person who believes in simple solutions. Then she draws a giant 'X" through the left-hand side of the page!

The lesson is that if you aren't focusing on your audience's agenda, your communication will *fail*. So when you prepare for an interview, you have to do as much as you can to understand the interviewer's point of view. What are the interviewer's concerns? Find out as much as you can, but you also will have to make some reasonable assumptions. If you can focus first on addressing the interviewer's concerns rather than your own selfish interests, you are far more likely to make a great impression. You do need to be honest, but you also have to make sure that all of your answers emphasize how you can make life easier or better for the interviewer—not for yourself.

BASICS OF INTERVIEWING

Before your resume has been transmitted to a potential employer, there are several basics that you should know about interviewing. While many may seem like common sense, sometimes we find that sense is less common than we would like to believe. Accordingly, see how you rate in terms of the following:

Voicemail Messages

Making sure you have an appropriate voice mail message is an important start. Then you need to check it regularly during your job search. The best employers know that they need to act quickly if they hope to hire the best co-op candidates. If employers have trouble contacting you, they may move ahead and hire someone else. At the very least, they may experience frustration in attempting to contact you. Obviously, this is *not* the kind of first impression you want to make. So check your voice mail and e-mail at least twice each day once you start the referrals process.

If you have a land line, it's sometimes reasonable to be cautious about putting your home number on a resume due to unreliable or unpredictable roommates. If you list your cellphone number on your resume, then you run the risk of having an employer call you while you're on a noisy subway or some other awkward situation. With a cellphone, you also have to worry about annoying delays, echoes, and garbled speech depending on the quality of your service.

Most students do use a cellphone. If you do, though, be careful about when and where you pick up the phone while in the thick of a job search. If in doubt, just let it go to your voice mail—and then call back promptly from a quiet place with good reception.

Another point on this topic: Your voice mail message and initial conversation will give the potential employer their first opportunity to hear how you present yourself. As such, you want to leave a highly professional message, one that is clear and concise. For example: *"Hi, you've reached Tom Olafsson at 555-1234. I cannot answer your call right now, but please leave a message, and I will call you back as soon as possible."* There have been many horror stories about students' outgoing messages with loud music and obnoxious roommates saying ridiculous things: "Yo, we're down at the pub with a bunch of pitchers—Later!" We had one student whose *girlfriend* left a provocative message on his machine—not the best introduction to a potential employer! Sometimes it's not even clear whether the caller has dialed the right number. On a more subtle note, many students simply mumble, sound half-asleep, or fail to express themselves in an upbeat, professional manner.

Basically, your outgoing message won't determine whether or not you get a job. At best, it may be completely neutral. At worst, it can create the beginnings of doubt about whether you have the basic professionalism to communicate in a corporate environment. And if life without a humorous outgoing message seems unbearable, you can always change it after you have started your co-op job.

Phone Etiquette

When speaking to a potential employer on the phone, make sure to be professional in your speech. Try to avoid "yeahs" and "uh-huhs." Speak with energy and enthusiasm—even if you're not sure if you want this particular job. You want your first conversation with a potential employer to be positive and effective. If you're called to arrange an interview, make sure that you have your calendar on hand. Try to be flexible about what days and times you can meet. If you have another commitment, say so politely and suggest what days would be best for you. Tell the caller that you're looking forward to the interview and eager to find out whether this job would be a good match for your skills. Make sure to ask for the location of the interview, ask for the individual's phone number in case you must reschedule the interview due to an emergency, and confirm the date and time before you hang up.

Attire

Make sure that your professional wardrobe is in good shape *before* beginning the interview process. Many students have wound up buying a new suit or outfit right before going on an interview: In fact, one student forgot to take the price and size tags off of his new suit and was nicknamed "Tags" for his whole six-month co-op job! You don't want to be shopping before an interview when you could be researching the organization, so plan ahead.

Men should wear dress shoes, a suit, a shirt, and tie. Your shoes should be polished. Your shirt should be a light color, usually white, light blue, pink, light green, etc. Your suit preferably should be some shade of gray, blue, or black... NOT some unusual color like green, flamingo pink, etc. Go light on cologne. As for ties, it is generally best to be conservative: Wear something that doesn't stand out too much. To our knowledge, no one has ever failed to get a job because they wore a boring tie. This rule is especially true of jobs in conservative fields, such as finance and criminal justice. If in doubt, check with your co-op coordinator.

Women should wear dress shoes, nylons, a dress or a skirt and blouse, or a suit. Make-up should not be excessive; wear little or no perfume. If you're applying for finance and accounting jobs, a very conservative suit would be appropriate. Although some women balk at wearing nylons—and these days there are many jobs for which they are not considered necessary—you should always wear them for interviews... even on hot summer days.

Some students object to these guidelines, feeling that their individuality is being compromised. Well, that's true. Basically, if having a pierced tongue or nose ring, a Mohawk haircut, or wearing funky clothes is more important to you than getting a job, go right ahead but be prepared to accept the consequences. Fairly, or unfairly, potential employers *will* judge you based on how you present yourself at an interview. Are you really interested in "fitting in" and "being one of the team," or is it more important to make a statement about your individuality with your appearance? The choice is yours.

Hygiene

You shouldn't have to receive a gift-wrapped bar of soap from a friend, roommate, or co-op coordinator to know that hygiene is an important consideration. In an interview, hygiene is either neutral or a negative; it goes unnoticed or it distracts the interviewer from the task at hand.

You should shower or bathe before any interview. Make sure your hair is neat and clean. Use deodorant, and make a habit of having a breath mint on the way to an interview. It can be a real distraction, and no one wants to work next to someone who has a hygiene problem!

Punctuality

Short of death—your own or that of an immediate family member—or severe illness, there is never really an acceptable reason to be late for an interview or to fail to show up altogether. Even arriving with a few minutes to spare can only increase any anxiety you feel about being interviewed. With this in mind, there are a few things you can do to avoid being late to interviews:

- Set your watch ten minutes ahead.

- Go to the office the day before to make sure that you can find it, and so you know how long it takes to get there. Frequently, the interviewer will meet you in the lobby and ask you if you had trouble finding the office. Imagine what he or she will think of you if you respond by saying, "Oh, no... I drove out here yesterday to make sure that I could find the building, so I had no trouble being on time today." This is far preferable to beginning the interview with some excuse about why you're ten minutes late.

- Assume that the trip will take you 30 minutes longer than you expect it will. If you allow a great deal of extra time, the worst-case scenario is that you will arrive 30 to 60 minutes early. If you do arrive early, use the extra time to review the job description, review your research, and go over questions you would like to ask the interviewer. If you're completely prepared, take a brisk walk around the block to put any excess nervous energy to use. Don't go into the reception area an hour early—that can be awkward for the interviewer, who may feel obliged to see you sooner than the scheduled time. At most, arriving 15 or 20 minutes early is reasonable.

PREPARING FOR A SPECIFIC INTERVIEW

Working with a co-op/internship coordinator or career services professional, you will look at job descriptions and choose several jobs that you wish to target. So what do you do after an employer calls you and arranges an interview? For any employer, be sure to bring extra copies of your resume and the names, addresses, and phone numbers of your references on nice paper. But how do you prepare for an interview for one *specific* employer? Let's consider several steps in the preparation process:

Knowing the Job Description

First, make sure that you have a copy of the job description. Memorize all the specific skills that the employer is looking for in a job candidate. Start thinking about how the employer would view you as a job candidate in terms of the skills needed for the job. What would the employer perceive to be your strengths? Your weaknesses? Try to understand what it was about your resume that attracted your employer as well as what concerns you may need to overcome to get the job.

One of the most underrated aspects of interview preparation is to research the job description. Many job candidates think of "interview research" as purely looking up facts and figures about the company. As mentioned below, this is important... but it also can be misguided. Think about this example: Let's say a job description mentions that you will be using a Crystal Reports database to do research on market segmentation for an athletic shoe company. Would it really be the best use of your time to memorize the company's total revenues, stock price, international offices, and so forth? Not really: If you aren't familiar with Crystal Reports or Symantec Ghost and/or with the concept of marketing segmentation, get on the Internet and use word searches until you come up with something. Anybody can say that they are a quick learner when they are being interviewed, but few people *demonstrate* their ability to learn quickly by doing appropriate research for an interview. Obviously, you can't learn a software application overnight, but with a little effort you can learn enough to have an intelligent conversation with the interviewer. That will help your cause much more than annual report data.

Researching the Organization

Doing strong research on potential employers is one thing that separates excellent job seekers from average ones. Start by asking your co-op or career services professional. They may have student job descriptions that they can share with you; they may have visited the site. Best of all, they might be able to give you contact information for someone who has worked in that exact position! Imagine what you could ask that person to prepare yourself. This takes a little initiative, but this step can give you eye-popping information to use in the interview: "I spoke to Ben Birkbeck about his experience as a co-op, and I was excited to hear that there are opportunities to work closely with patients at your site." You may want to ask about the supervisor's style, the nature of the work, the organization's culture, the possibility for employment after graduation or in future co-op periods, etc. You can even ask what the interview will be like!

For general company information, the Internet or your school library can be a valuable resource. Talk to a reference librarian if necessary about how to find company news. For publicly-traded companies, you can find recent information at websites such as www.nasdaq. com or at any number of financial services websites. Once you have assembled several sources, look them up and take notes on what you read. Companies will be impressed if you do this homework before the interview.

Here are some other tips for searching via the Web.

Google it: Obviously, Google is a great place to start for researching a company. You also could go to the News menu on Google in order to find any recent developments with an organization. This can be a great way to come up with some topical questions at the end of your interview.

When you do a search, watch out for companies that have similar names or various branches in different locations: Make sure you're researching the right one.

With Google, a few little tricks will greatly enhance the effectiveness of your search. For example, don't just type in John Hancock, because it will pull up every website that has the name "John" or "Hancock" in it... which is NOT very helpful. Instead, put quotes around the words: "John Hancock". This tells the search engine that you ONLY want URLs with that word combination.

Leave no stone unturned in your research: In my experience, students give up far too easily when doing research for an interview. Here's an example: A small company interviewed six of my students. Five looked in the files, looked in the library, looked on the Internet, and found NOTHING. They gave up. The sixth student did all of the same things and also found nothing. But he kept trying. He looked at the job description again, and saw this phrase: "We provide software solutions for the vending industry." He decided to go back to the library and back onto the Internet, learning as much as he could about the vending industry and how software was utilized in it. He learned a LOT about the industry, the competition, and key issues that probably were facing his potential employer. Then he walked around campus with a notebook, looking at the vending machines: Who made them? Who serviced them? How sophisticated were they in terms of software? Armed with this information, he was able to have a sophisticated conversation with the interviewer about vending. And, of course, he got the job. So remember, you can use the Internet to research the *industry* and the *competition* as well as the company itself.

Using LinkedIn to Research the Interviewers – A Student's Perspective
by an Engineering student at UMass Lowell

The company that ended up offering me a co-op asked me to come in for an afternoon of onsite interviews. To prepare, I looked up each of the interviewers on LinkedIn and came up with a list of my own questions tailored to each individual's area of expertise. When you know so much about another person's background, it becomes critical to walk the fine line between insightful questions and creepy statements revealing that you have memorized the entire past employment history of your interlocutor. The best questions will let them show how smart THEY are while revealing how smart YOU are. I found this interview preparation strategy to be effective.

From an Engineering student at University of Massachusetts Lowell.

In similar ways, you need to think creatively about your research: If the product/service is consumer-oriented, go see it in action or how it is displayed and sold. Talk to people who might use the product or service, and ask them their opinions of it. Get a feel for the job as well as the company.

Any information that you can dig up may prove useful in the interview. Later in this chapter, we will show specific ways that you can impress an interviewer with your research.

STRATEGIZING

Matching Your Skills to the Employer's Needs

The most crucial aspect of a great interview is demonstrating that your skills and personal qualities are a great match for what the employer needs in a co-op worker. You may have excellent grades, terrific skills, and a great attitude, but if you can't explain why YOU are a great MATCH for THIS JOB, you may be out of luck. You need to demonstrate concrete reasons that your skills and qualities are a good match for the position-specific information in the job description. If a co-op candidate fails to strategize in this way, the employer may tell the co-op coordinator something like this: "Mary seemed like a great person with good skills, and I really liked her attitude. But I'm not convinced that she meets our needs."

How can you avoid being "close but not quite" when going after a job? Consider the following example. The Littlefield Rehabilitation Center has a nursing co-op job available for a student with "great empathy and patience, some experience working with the elderly or disabled, a basic understanding of nursing, and a willingness to work long shifts."

Student 1 and Student 2 have identical skills: Both are solid "B+" students who have only limited experience with the elderly. Both have taken only prerequisite coursework in nursing, but they do have volunteer experience working in hospitals during school vacations.

In the interview, both students are asked the following question: "Why should we hire you for this position?"

Student 1 says: "I'm a hard worker, and I've always wanted to work for a rehabilitation center. I think this job would give me a lot of good experience, especially the exposure to the geriatric population. So I look at this as a great opportunity."

Student 2 says: "I know you're looking for someone who is extremely patient and empathic. Here are my references—please call my supervisor at the hospital and ask her specifically about those qualities. As for working with the elderly, my experience is limited—but in preparing for the interview today, I talked to some students who worked at your Center; it sounds like you are doing some amazing things with treatment! Looking on the Internet, I was surprised to find that a third of your beds are utilized by younger patients recovering from head injuries, so I've already started reading up on subarachnoid hemorrhages and their clinical manifestations—I want to be ready to hit the ground running in this job! As you can see on my resume, my real strength is working with people, whether I've worked as a hospital volunteer or as a waitress. So I think I bring a strong background to this position."

Who would you be more inclined to hire? Neither student has excellent skills, but Student 2 did a much better job of showing the employer the connections between her skills and the job description. Student 1 answered the questions more in terms of why she would like to have the job instead of focusing on why the employer would want to hire her. As such, the employer might see this student as a far better match for the job... even though the two students have identical skills!

By tying your answers to the job description, you show the potential employer that:

- you are industrious enough to prepare effectively for an interview.

- you are persuasive, self-confident, and sensitive to the employer's needs.

- you have an awareness of what your skills are and how ready you will be to do the job well—right from the start.

One good tip is to go into any job interview with a solid strategy featuring three or four compelling reasons why the interviewer should hire you to do that specific job. Being focused like this will make a big difference.

We will consider more examples when we look more closely at interview questions.

VERBAL AND NONVERBAL INTERVIEWING SKILLS

Obviously, interviewers are very interested in what you have to say. However—especially in some fields—employers are interested in *how* you say it. Many interviewers may not consciously notice what you're doing right or wrong in this sense, but these behaviors still may have a critical impact on whether or not you get a job offer.

Verbal Skills

Keep in mind the following when interviewing.

Speak at a reasonably loud volume. Make sure the interviewer can hear and understand you. If you're not sure, ask.

Don't speak too fast. If you speak quickly, the interviewer may miss the strong points that you are making, or simply fail to remember. Slow down: especially when making an important selling point about yourself. When asked a question, don't be afraid to pause before answering or between giving each of two or three points about yourself. Brief silences can be a powerful tool; they can be used when you want to emphasize something strongly.

It's easy to overlook just how *hard* it is to be an interviewer: All at once, the interviewer has to listen to your answer while trying to assess your answer and think about the next question to ask. If you never come up for air or give time for your points to be digested, the interviewer won't remember much of what you've said. One interviewer told me that I "use silence effectively" as an interviewee. I thought that was a strange compliment at first—aren't interviews all about what you say? Really, though, she was just saying that I was giving her enough time to juggle all her various thoughts as an interviewer.

Watch out for "verbal tics." We all have verbal tics, y'know? Um.... you should, like, try to not use them during an interview, y'know? Yeah, they like make you seem totally immature and unprofessional, right?

Seriously: Almost everyone has a tendency to fill the empty seconds between phrases and sentences with little bits of meaningless slang. Doing this occasionally will go unnoticed, but doing it repeatedly can become a major distraction. In practice interviews, I have heard students use the word "like" as many as 12 times in one lengthy sentence! Many people don't even believe they use these phrases constantly until they see themselves on videotape. Slowing down your speech will help reduce these annoying, meaningless phrases. If you fail to reduce these phrases, you may come off as inarticulate, immature, or unprepared. It takes practice to get out of these habits, but it's worth it, y'know?

It's also especially easy to lapse or relapse into these habits when being interviewed by someone who is younger. Even if you feel like you connect with an interviewer who is of comparable age, don't slip into unprofessional, informal speech habits.

Speak with a professional tone. Save your slang expressions for conversations with friends and significant others. When describing your job experience, for example, avoid terms like "stuff" and "things." Be precise; use a broader range of vocabulary.

Vary your tone. Avoid speaking in a monotone. Make your voice sound excited when talking about things that interest you. This will keep the listener interested.

If English is not your primary language: Make sure that you know how to answer typical interview questions in English. Speak loudly and slowly, and cheerfully offer to repeat something or rephrase something if the interviewer doesn't seem to understand you. If asked about your understanding and use of English, discuss what you have done and will do in order to improve your communication skills in English. If appropriate, you also might mention previous job experiences in which employers were concerned about your English skills but eventually found that this was not a problem for you or your co-workers.

Nonverbal Skills

People can often say a great deal in an interview without even opening their mouths. Therefore, pay attention to the following guidelines:

Handshakes: Shake hands firmly when meeting the interviewer or anyone he or she introduces you to. Keep your thumb up as you extend your hand to shake. If you tend to get sweaty palms when you're nervous, try to wipe off your hand frequently (and subtly) while waiting for the interviewer to arrive in the lobby.

Eye Contact: As much as possible, make eye contact with the interviewer. Don't stare, but don't let your eyes wander around the room at any time; you may be perceived as having a short attention span or as being uninterested in the job.

Body Language: One of the really interesting things about your gestures and body language is that you often don't even notice what these things are signaling to others. One of my colleagues at Bates Communications was talking to me recently about one of her executive coaching clients who was getting vague feedback about being "unpolished." After studying her client for a while, she realized that the biggest issue that this person had was that she slouched constantly. When she told her client this, the client became defensive: She didn't believe she was doing it...not until my colleague slyly took a few iPhone photos of her during a meeting! Her slouching was making her come across as uninterested and unprofessional, and she hadn't even realized it.

How are you supposed to improve your body language without the benefit of an executive coach? The answer is video. Your school may be able to videotape a practice interview that you can review. If not, an iPad can do the trick. In my job, I use FlipCams to record our clients' presentations all the time, and I can tell you that *no one* likes to see themselves on video! However, it's an invaluable way to see yourself as any audience—or interviewer—will see you.

During your interview be sure to sit up straight, and lean forward a little. In addition to avoiding the deadly slouch, don't lean back, or fold your arms: This comes off as being defensive, laid-back, or unfriendly. When you're not using your hands or arms to help express a point, keep them on your lap. Don't put them in your pockets, as you may distract the interviewer by jangling change. Avoid drumming your fingers, fiddling with your hair, pen, jewelry, or clothes, and never chew gum. Try to *smile*! And whatever you do, be sure to silence your phone... and NEVER pull out your phone for any reason during an interview! Recent research has mentioned that as a real pet peeve of employers.

Using notes/Taking notes: There is no simple answer to this question. In some fields, job interviews are comparable to making a formal sales presentation. In this case, failing to use notes may indicate that you have done little preparation for your interview/presentation. You will give the impression that you are "winging it," which—even if you're good at it—may not send the message you want to send. Conversely, other business employers might feel that relying on notes indicates that you are *not* adequately prepared.

When moderating a co-op employer discussion panel recently, I was intrigued to hear that some employers are very impressed when an interviewee takes notes during the interview. These employers felt that the note takers were showing sincere interest and good attention to detail. They cautioned, however, that you need to be judicious in exactly what you write down. Otherwise, note-taking can be very distracting and also may keep you from making adequate eye contact.

In most cases, using notes or taking notes will not be necessary in business interviews. But if you are afraid of "blanking out" or failing to cover several points, you might try using them... as long as you are not reading directly from them or looking at them constantly. If you are unsure about what is most appropriate for your field, ask your coordinator. We will talk specifically about how to use notes later in this chapter.

TURNING NERVOUS ENERGY INTO AN ALLY

Some people enjoy interviews, but most people experience at least some nervousness about them. Feeling nervous is a completely normal and rational reaction to going on an interview. After all, you want to make a good impression, and you want to make sure you get the best possible job for each co-op period. You care! That's a good thing.

In my last couple of years of being a cooperative education coordinator, I did a practice interview with a student who came off very poorly indeed. He was completely rattled and very visibly nervous, much more so than the typical student usually is. Afterward, we talked about the interview, and I asked him to give a self-critique.

He shook his head. "I couldn't believe how incredibly nervous I was—even when I was just waiting in a chair outside your office before the interview started," he said.

This interested me. "What were you thinking about while you were waiting for me?"

He looked puzzled for a moment and had to think it over for a good while before answering. "I guess I was thinking that I'm really not qualified for this job, and I don't know how to interview. I have no idea if I even would want this job, so I don't know how to approach this."

As it turns out, I had looked at his resume and realized that he was a starting player on one of our Division I sports teams. "Tell me," I said, "What do you do to prepare before a game? Do you sit in the locker room thinking, 'This team is really great, I don't have a chance against these guys?'"

He laughed. "Of course not! I do the opposite; I visualize myself making plays and feeling confident out there. I go through the game plan in my mind and review different scenarios to get myself ready."

I loved it. "You already *know how* to deal with your nervous energy!" I told him. "The same things you do to get ready for a game or performance are the same things you need to do to get ready for an interview," I explained.

That was a turning point for him. Sometimes we just don't know what we know. The same is true for you. While you might not have any experience getting ready for a job interview, you probably have had to deal with focusing your energy for some sort of performance—whether it's for a school play, an oral report, or a big sports game. Tap into your preparation ritual, and it will help.

One big mistake that many individuals make is believing that their goal should be to eliminate any nervousness that they feel. The more you try to order yourself to be relaxed, the harder it becomes to do so.

Here is a more helpful strategy: Remember that nervousness is nothing more than energy. The last thing you want to do is go into an interview without any energy! The trick is to *use* your nervous energy in positive ways. If you begin to feel nervous during an interview, put that excess energy to use by:

• speaking louder and with more enthusiasm

• using your hands to be more expressive instead of keeping your arms folded

• focusing harder on the interviewer, listening closely to what he or she is saying

• pushing yourself to come up with excellent questions and answers

Perhaps most importantly, remember this about nervousness: People can never tell exactly how nervous you are if you don't tell them. In mock interviews, many of my students will openly admit that they're nervous. This is a mistake. The interviewer can rarely tell if a student is nervous, and admitting nervousness sometimes makes the interviewer focus on trying to determine how nervous the person is instead of really listening to his or her answers. In some cases, admitting nervousness may make the interviewer feel awkward or nervous too. Regardless, discussing nervousness only moves you both further away from determining whether you are a good match for the job.

Interviewing – A Student's Perspective
by Mark Moccia

I fit the "sweaty palms" prototype perfectly on my first interview. I previously worked in an office environment, although I did not have a formal interview because my mother hired me! I thought I would not be as nervous because of the ease with which I handled my practice interviews. Despite my glowing confidence from the day before, I was nervous from the moment I woke up that morning. When I arrived at the office, I was sweating as if it were 100 degrees outside; the only problem with this is that it was only 75 degrees and cloudy! I experienced all the nightmares that come with nervous first interviews; I stumbled over words, dropped things on the floor, and apologized 50 times, along with many other little, embarrassing moments.

The most important lesson I learned from this interview is to relax and be yourself. I was trying too hard to impress the interviewer (who was the President of the company, which did not help matters) when I should have been selling myself more. It is important to impress the interviewer but you have to earn this right through hard work. You simply cannot impress the interviewer with your "uncanny multitasking ability" if you have never experienced multitasking.

It is important to figure out your strengths and sell those to the interviewer. It is also important to figure out your weaknesses and what you are doing to improve on them because interviewers will ask that question frequently. Finally, as mentioned earlier, the more research you perform on the company before the interview, the more questions you will have for them at the end of the interview when you hear the dreaded, "Do you have any questions for me?" This was pretty ugly for my first interview; I believe my response was, "Uh, uh, no. I do not believe I can learn anything else from this interview." BIG MISTAKE!

Mark Moccia was an Accounting/MIS student at Northeastern University, Class of 2002.

Here are a few other ideas about how to keep nervous energy from becoming a negative force for you in interviews:

- Try to get in a good workout a few hours before the interview if possible. That will get rid of excess energy and improve your state of mind.

- Avoid caffeine.

- Formulate a specific strategy for each interview: Come up with at least three specific reasons why YOU should be hired for THAT specific job description.

- Prepare yourself thoroughly by considering how you would answer typical questions and by doing extensive research about the company.

- Allow yourself plenty of time to travel to the interview location.

- Practice your interviewing skills by working with your co-op/internship coordinator or with the Career Services Department.

- Practice answering questions aloud with a friend, roommate, or family member. Often you *know* the answer... but it can take practice saying it aloud to make it come out as smoothly and concisely as possible. If I'm sharing a story in an interview or speech to prove a point, I will try to practice it out loud at least ten times before using it with a live audience. It really helps! If you do practice with friends and loved ones, though, remember that these individuals generally aren't experts. Practice with them to get used to saying your answers out loud rather than to seek useful criticism.

It's hard to overemphasize the importance of thorough preparation. In the classroom, when are you most nervous before taking an exam? It's when you really haven't studied and aren't prepared. The same is true for interviews: When you know your stuff, you'll be much more at ease.

People who learn to use their nervous energy effectively come off as energetic, enthusiastic, motivated, and focused in interviews... even though they have butterflies and knots in their stomach the whole time!

ORDINARY QUESTIONS, EXTRAORDINARY ANSWERS

Although it is impossible to anticipate every question that an employer will ask you in an interview, you should be prepared to answer the typical questions that arise in many interviews. Preparation makes an enormous difference in being able to deliver extraordinary answers to ordinary questions.

Individuals with little interviewing experience seldom give "bad" answers to questions. However, many people fail to understand the difference between a pretty good answer and an extraordinary one. In this section, we will dissect the most common interview questions and show you specific examples of mediocre, ordinary, and outstanding answers to these questions.

1. *"Tell me about yourself."*

In one form or another, this is a fairly common opening question. You may be asked about your background, or about what kind of person you are. Many people—particularly those who have failed to prepare—dislike these questions and struggle to answer them. The question seems incredibly broad and general: There are a thousand things you could talk about. However, those who are well prepared look forward to this kind of question. Basically, the interviewer is giving you a very open-ended question: You could choose to talk about almost anything in your response.

Why do interviewers ask this question? For one thing, it's an ice-breaker, a way of easing into the interview before asking tough questions about your skills. Another reason employers ask this is because it's a quick way to test your judgment. What you choose to say about yourself says a great deal about your personality and character.

There are many possible ways to answer this question effectively. Here are some guidelines to bear in mind:

1. *Don't waste time telling interviewers what they already know.* Many students answer this question too literally, telling the interviewer that they go to UMass-Lowell, that they're a finance major, etc. Your resume and the fact that it was faxed by a given co-op coordinator makes this kind of information very obvious.

2. *If you're not given a specific question, focus on why YOU are a good candidate for THIS specific job.* An open-ended question is always a good opportunity to sell yourself. Talk about what the job description requires and why you represent a good match for these requirements.

3. *If you are an unconventional candidate for a job, discuss why you are interested in this job and why you are a strong candidate.* For example, if you're a finance major who is interviewing for an accounting or MIS job, you should explain why you are excited about an opportunity in one of these fields and how this job relates to your career goals. In other words, anticipate an employer's concern and deal with it enthusiastically.

Let's look at some possible answers to *"Tell me about yourself."*

Mediocre answer:	*"I live in Brookfield; I'm an accounting major; I like sports, reading, and rollerblading, and I'm a sophomore."*
Ordinary answer:	*"I'm a hard worker, and I've got solid grades and good co-op experience. I think this job would be really interesting, and I'm eager to learn from this experience. I'm persistent, and I expect a lot of myself."*
Extraordinary answer:	*"Working in public accounting is my objective. I have excellent grades in my accounting classes, and I did a great deal of bookkeeping in my first co-op job. I have a strong combination of classroom and professional skills, and I'm dedicated to proving myself in a public accounting environment."*

Can you see how different these responses are? The first tells the interviewer almost nothing that couldn't be inferred from reading the resume. The second conveys a positive attitude but tells the interviewer nothing about why the person would be good for THIS job as opposed to any other position. The third response shows that the job candidate read the job description carefully and has thought a great deal about why the position is a good match for his or her skills and traits. It also shows initiative by referring to research that the candidate did to prepare for the interview (provided the candidate really DID do that research). With this kind of response, you can go a long way toward showing an employer how your skills connect with a given job opportunity.

But what if the employer really was asking the question to find out more about your interests outside of work? Well, he or she can always ask a more specific follow-up question, which you can answer accordingly.

2. "I see on your resume that you're interested in _____. Tell me more about that."

This is another common ice-breaker question. Some employers may ask about your interest in books or skiing or whatever in order to help you relax and have a less artificial conversation with them.

This type of question also illustrates why you should always list some of your hobbies and interests on your resume. Basically, an employer is hiring an individual: not just a list of skills and qualifications. Talking about your hobbies and interests gives you an opportunity to make yourself a real person in the employer's eyes: hopefully, a person they would enjoy working with for a lengthy period of time. Believe it or not, this type of question can also help you sell yourself for the job, sometimes in subtle ways.

For example, one of the first questions that *I* get asked in most interviews is about my interest in writing fiction. When I get asked about it, I'm delighted: For one thing, it gives me a chance to speak about something with great enthusiasm. More importantly, though, this type of question allows me to convey personal qualities that may be very useful in the job at hand. If a job requires creativity, communication skills, persistence, patience, listening skills, etc., I can mention these qualities as aspects of fiction writing that have proven valuable to me.

Let's look at some examples relating to a fictional student named Pete Moss, a marketing student who lists his interests as follows: Photography, camping, skiing, and volunteer work. Check out some possible options for Pete if he's asked about his interests during a marketing interview:

"I see on your resume that you're interested in camping. Why does that interest you?"

Mediocre answer:	*"Yeah, I like to go up to Vermont once in a while. I guess that just being outdoors is what appeals to me. It's relaxing."*
Ordinary answer:	*"Yes, I try to go as often as I can in the summer. I find that it's a good way to clear my mind on the weekend, so I can return to work on Monday with a good focus."*
Extraordinary answer:	*"Besides being a relaxing way to recharge my batteries, camping is enjoyable to me because it requires a combination of characteristics: resourcefulness, good judgment, planning, stamina, and thinking on your feet. Some trips can be quite challenging, and I like to challenge myself."*

An employer who hears the first answer might wonder whether Pete can handle being indoors for six months! At best, this answer won't hurt you. The "Ordinary Answer" is better: It shows that Pete values a balance between work and other interests, and that he sees his weekend time as a way to be more energized in the workplace. However, the "Extraordinary Answer" reflects a job candidate who really "thinks marketing" and is able to make some subtle but creative connections between his career interests and his personal interests. With this answer, he never says anything directly about being a good candidate for the job, but the employer may start thinking that Pete's individual traits fit nicely with a marketing position.

But what if Pete had been asked about one of his other interests? Let's consider some options:

Photography: *"Photography appeals to my creative side, which is a very strong aspect of my personality. I also enjoy photography because I like the challenge of trying to capture something in a picture. It's like marketing, where you're trying to capture the nature of a product or service with one simple slogan or image. I like that."*

Skiing: *"I haven't skied for very long—only three or four years—but I really enjoy everything about it. I like researching different ski mountains, finding out which appeals to me, and trying to sell my friends on which one I think is the best. On the mountain, I like taking on challenging terrain without sacrificing technique. I've improved very quickly."*

Here we see two different approaches. In the photography example, Pete ties his interest in photography directly to its relevance in the field of marketing. In the skiing example, though, Pete is more subtle. He describes many aspects of skiing that are appealing to him, but the interviewer also can see that he's demonstrating many traits that are useful in a marketing job: researching, salesmanship, reasonable risk-taking, an outgoing personality, and a focus on results. The interviewer may be more likely to think of this student as a job candidate without even realizing why he or she feels that way!

Whatever your interests are, think about how you would talk about them if they come up in an interview. Are there connections you can make between your interests and a co-op position? If you can learn to do this well, an interviewer may be pleasantly surprised at your ability to turn a simple ice-breaker question into another showcase of your abilities.

3.   *"Why should we hire you for this job?"*

If the interviewer has a more aggressive personality, you may hear this exact question in an interview. If not, you may find it in a more polite form (i.e., "What is it that makes you a good candidate for this job?"). In either case, the question an employer is *really* asking can be broken into many possible questions:

•   How much self-confidence do you have?

•   Are you a good match for this job?

•   Do you *know* if you are a good match for this job?

•   We expect you to sell our products or services, so how well can you sell yourself?

•   Can you articulate your strengths clearly, confidently, and realistically?

Answer this question directly, focusing on your experiences, attitude, and aptitude in relationship to the job requirements as explained in the job description. In other words, don't just tell the employer why you're a good person, or a good candidate for *any* co-op job. Focus closely on why you are a good match for *this* co-op job. And if you don't have everything they're looking for in terms of skills, present a strategy for overcoming this obstacle.

Mediocre answer:	*"I've always wanted to work in this field, and I'm kind of intelligent. I think I could probably do a pretty good job."*
Ordinary answer:	*"I'm hard working; I have good grades; I'm eager to learn more, and I learn quickly. I also have good job experience that relates well to this position."*
Extraordinary answer:	*"According to the job description, you want someone who knows AutoCAD, and who has strong communication skills. In my class, I was the AutoCAD expert, and I help most of my friends with that and other software at school. As for communication skills, I encourage you to contact any of my previous employers. They'll tell you that I not only have excellent communication skills: I also was well-respected by my colleagues on a personal and professional level. I also noticed that you prefer someone who has used Oracle. Since reading the job description, I've familiarized myself the basics of this program and am confident I could hit the ground running by the time this work period starts."*

The first answer gives the employer absolutely no incentive to hire the job candidate. Even worse, the candidate comes across as someone who has little or no confidence in himself/ herself. The "Ordinary answer" is more positive, but it's rather generic: If an interviewer talks to ten students, this kind of answer will turn up three or more times. To stand out, you have to push your skills. In the "Extraordinary answer," the job candidate talks with confidence about past job experiences and shows a keen awareness of what the prospective job demands. If the employer didn't see these connections when looking at the resume, he or she will be clear on them now.

4. *"Why did you choose Plastics Engineering (or Communications, etc.) as your major?"*

An employer who asks this kind of question hopes to learn more about how focused, enthusiastic, serious, and mature you are. There are many good ways to answer this question, but there are also several bad ways. Thus, some helpful hints:

- *Show that you have a career plan.* You don't want it to sound like someone imposed the major on you, or that you're only majoring in it because some advisor or relative suggested it. Don't be vague when presenting your reasons. Relate the career plan to the job. If you have notions of going to law school, for example, don't talk about that option when you're dealing with a public accounting firm looking to recruit interns and co-ops after graduation.

- *Show some excitement.* One option is to tell the interviewer a short anecdote about what first excited you about economics, history, etc. You might mention a high-school job experience, a previous internship, a classroom experience, or some extracurricular activity that inspired you to major in your given concentration.

- *Make sure to connect your response to the interviewer's job description.* If you're seeking a job within your concentration, this should not be difficult. However, if you're pursuing a job in a different concentration or major, you are very likely to be asked about this discrepancy. If you're a psychology major, why are you interviewing for a job as a webmaster, for example? There may be plenty of good reasons, but you will need to make the connection. Otherwise, the employer may perceive a mismatch between you and the job.

Here are some sample answers for a student who is asked why he or she chose physical therapy as a major.

Mediocre Answer:	*"I dunno; I think it's kind of interesting. My dad says that the economy stinks for just about everything except the health sciences these days, so I figured it would be the best way to make a lot of money."*
Ordinary Answer:	*"I've always seemed to do well in my science courses, and I've enjoyed working with people in various jobs over the years. I think it's just a nice fit for my abilities."*
Extraordinary Answer:	*"I think I've always been a natural for the physical therapy field: In fact, I had to undergo physical therapy at the age of five, when I broke my arm falling off my bike. I'm great with people; I'm caring, and I really want to be in a healing profession that can help others in the way that I was helped as a child. I can't imagine another major that would fit so nicely with these qualities."*

What if someone is interviewing for a marketing job but actually majors in, say, communication studies? The interviewer may ask: "Given that your major is communications, why are you interested in a marketing position?"

Mediocre answer:	*"Well, no one wanted to hire me for a communications job... ."*
Ordinary answer:	*"I think it would be interesting, and it would give me broader experience in business in general."*
Extraordinary answer:	*"I major in communication studies because there are many skills associated with it that I need to master to become a successful businessperson. I have the same interest in marketing, but I feel that many aspects of it—understanding the mentality of customers, knowing how to pitch to a specific market niche, and having a good mind for numbers and business—come naturally to me through my experiences in a family business. I decided I should use my college classes to improve on my weaknesses... not to build on what are already my strengths."*

5. *"I see on your resume that you worked for Organization X last summer. What was that like?"*

Employers have much to gain by bringing up one or more of your previous job experiences. They want to:

- determine whether your experience at *that* job makes you a better candidate for *this* job.

- see how well you can articulate what another organization does and what your role was for that organization.

- see whether you have a positive attitude about previous work experience.

Keep these things in mind when working on an effective response to this question. Most interviewers will ask you about prior job experience, and you want to be ready for it. Follow these guidelines:

- *Describe what the organization does.* Unless the organization is very large or well-known in its field, you may have to use a sentence or two to explain the nature of the work done by the organization. Show the interviewer you can capture the big picture of what a company does.

- *Describe what you did at the* organization. You probably did numerous things in your job at Organization X. Focus primarily on what you did well, what you enjoyed, and— most importantly—how it relates to the job for which you are currently interviewing.

- *Go beyond what is stated on your resume.* The interviewer can read, so you have to say more than what is written on your resume. This is why it is so important to tie your work experience to the description of the job for which you're applying.

- *ALWAYS focus exclusively on what was positive about the work experience.* Even if you hated your boss and found the job boring or unsatisfying, focus on the positives about the experience. Nobody likes a complainer or whiner, and the interviewer may start wondering if you might have significantly contributed to the problem and therefore would be a "risky hire."

Here are some responses interviewers might hear in response to "Tell me about your job at Organization X."

Mediocre answer:	*"Well, I did some pretty tedious office work: You know, answering phones, sending faxes, things like that. It wasn't much fun, and my boss was a pain, so I definitely want something different this time."*
Ordinary answer:	*"I worked for Organization X in Anytown for my last co-op job. I worked in an office and did a lot of administrative support work: xeroxing, answering phones, basically doing anything to help out the team."*
Extraordinary answer:	*"Organization X makes galvinators, which are electronic parts used in the automotive industry. I was an Administrative Assistant, responsible for handling many clerical jobs in the Finance Department. The job was a good entry-level experience; the best thing about it was just having a chance to work alongside finance people and getting to pick their brains about the company's financial operations. That's why I'm interested in the position at your company: I'll get more exposure to the world of finance and get a chance to use some of the new skills I've picked up in my finance classes over the last six months."*

Obviously, all three responses reflected a job that was not too demanding or exciting. The extraordinary answer, though, shows that you can be honest about this kind of job while still focusing on the positives of the experience.

6. *"What would you say are your strengths?"*

This question makes some interviewees uncomfortable: People often don't like feeling that they are bragging about themselves, fearing that they will come across as egotistical. But remember: if you don't sell yourself in an interview, who will? Interviewers ask this question to assess your self-confidence, maturity, and self-awareness in addition to how well your strengths match up with the requirements of a job.

Here are a few guidelines to bear in mind when answering this question:

Be honest. On the one hand, don't exaggerate about your abilities. If you say you have a given technical skill, many employers will follow up with a question to assess how well your knowledge matches up with your claim. Or—if you do get hired by saying you have a skill when you actually don't—the truth will come out shortly after you start the job. Lying about your credentials is grounds for immediate dismissal with most employers.

On the other hand, be honest about what you *can* do. Many co-op candidates sell themselves short when asked about their strengths. If asked about their experience with computers, for example, some candidates will say they don't have any... overlooking the fact that they have taught themselves many software applications and, sometimes, even programming languages. Yes, self-taught skills count when you are asked about your strengths, skills, or experience in a given area.

Describe your strengths in terms of the employer's needs. One common mistake in answering this question is failing to tailor your reply to the employer's needs. Sure, your strengths may include fluency in speaking Swahili and Swedish, great speed in using a slide rule, and the ability to program in C#, but how are these skills going to help you as a candidate for a marketing position?

Before the interview, decide which of your strengths you should emphasize. If a telemarketing position primarily requires persuasiveness, excellent communication skills, and the ability to do straightforward mathematical calculations, you should strategize accordingly. In addition to citing examples of experience you've had that required persuasiveness, for example, you should plan on presenting yourself in an extremely persuasive manner. You also might cite a strong grade in a business statistics class. In contrast, you might not focus on your PC skills or your marketing research experience. However, you might cite these skills heavily if interviewing for a position requiring these talents.

Let's consider some possible responses to the strengths question. Let's say that the job in question is a finance job requiring good experience with numbers, an ability to work as part of a team, and knowing how to calculate present values.

Mediocre answer:	*"I guess I'm a good worker, and I've done pretty well in most of my classes. I'm really good with computers too, especially spreadsheets and stuff."*
Ordinary answer:	*"I'm a real self-starter; I'm motivated and eager to learn. I got an A- in my finance class last semester, and I have strong writing and presentation skills."*
Extraordinary answer:	*"I consider myself a real team player: I have no problem in doing any task that will help my team achieve our goals. I've always been a natural with numbers, although I do find a calculator is most effective for calculating present values. I learned about present values in my first finance class, and my ability to calculate them probably helped me earn an A- in the course."*

Although the second answer discusses many bona fide strengths which may help the candidate land a job somewhere, it goes into little detail regarding strengths that will prove beneficial to *this* employer. The extraordinary answer covers all of the areas mentioned in our mini-job description. Of course, this answer is only effective if the candidate is prepared to "walk the talk." A shrewd interviewer may follow up this question by giving the candidate a simple problem that requires the calculation of a present value. Be prepared to back up any claims that you make in an interview.

7. *"What are your weaknesses?"*

Less experienced interviewees dislike this question, probably because they're afraid of exposing a legitimate weakness that the interviewer will use against them in making a hiring decision. Or the interviewee may worry about giving an answer that really isn't an honest weakness, which may come off as an insincere response.

The good news is that this is not a difficult question to answer *as long as you are prepared to answer it*. You'll need to think it through beforehand because coming up with a good answer on the spot is quite challenging. Here are some basic guidelines in answering this question:

Start off your answer by acknowledging your strengths. You don't want to dwell on negatives more than necessary when answering this question, and you want to reinforce your strengths to make sure the interviewer understands them. One way to make sure you acknowledge your strengths is by starting your answer with "although" or "despite": "Although I have solid skill and experience in areas X, Y, and Z...."

Avoid cliché responses. Frequently, interviewees will cite "working too hard" or "being too focused on the job to the detriment of having a social life," etc. This kind of answer comes off as a cliché, at best, and insincere and defensive, at worst. In a way, you're telling the interviewer that you feel a need to dodge the question, as if you have something to hide.

Choose a legitimate weakness, but not one that would keep you from getting a job that you want. There are many ways to do this. If you are opposed to a job that would require 12 hours of work each day, you can describe your weakness as "I burn out if I have to work 60 hours a week on a regular basis." You can go on to explain that you get your work done efficiently, that your strength is in prioritizing, and that you have no objection to working long hours when necessary as long as it isn't every week. This kind of answer may keep you from getting a job... but it might be a job that you wouldn't have wanted anyway.

Keeping the job description in mind is also helpful when thinking up good weaknesses. If you're applying for a nursing job that requires good interpersonal skills, strong communication skills, and great attention to detail, your weakness could be the fact that your computer skills are limited to word processing and doing research on the Internet. Sure, you don't know databases, but you may not need to for this particular job. If you're a computer science student looking for a software development position, you probably wouldn't have a weakness such as shyness held against you. If a job description mentions the need for someone who is able to work independently with little supervision, you could discuss your inexperience in working with groups. If a job description mentions a hectic, unstructured work environment with unpredictable demands, you could state your weakness as follows: "I find that I tend to get bored easily if I'm forced to do the same job day in, day out. I don't deal well with a steady routine and a rigid structure, which I find stifling and monotonous. So I think that would be a real weakness for me in some work settings." Of course, your weakness also needs to be an *honest* weakness.

Computer skills are almost always a great choice when looking for a weakness that is sincere without being fatal. No matter how much you know about technology, there is *always* going to be a long list of computer skills that you lack. Even better, many will be completely irrelevant to the prospective employer. If you're an arts and sciences major, you could tout your MS-Office skills but acknowledge that you have never done any Web design or programming. If you're a computer science major applying for a programming job, you could talk up your Java background while admitting that you know little or nothing about network administration. As long as you aren't dwelling on a skill that might be valuable to the employer, this is a safe option.

Remember that you aren't expected to know everything. Perhaps the easiest way to deal with a question about your weaknesses is to acknowledge what the employer already knows about you: that is, admit that while you have a strong foundation of knowledge in your field of study, you still have a great deal to learn before you could be considered an expert in finance or computers or accounting or whatever. As long as you are enthusiastic and can convince the interviewer that you have aptitude for learning new skills, this kind of answer will work for you with most jobs. After all, you're applying for a job as a student or graduating senior who is in the process of learning a given field. As such, employers would expect that your learning is incomplete.

Emphasize what you have done or what you will do to improve your area of weakness. Who would you rather hire? A person who doesn't admit to having any weaknesses, or a person who tells you about a weakness and how he or she has worked to overcome it? This is a good strategy for anyone, but especially for students who struggle with the English language. Just saying that you're weak in English won't help you. However, if you explain that you have only been in this country for two years, and that you have been taking courses and practicing regularly to improve, and that you enjoy working on your English skills, you will impress some interviewers: most of whom know only one language!

Try to anticipate any concerns or perceptions employers have about your weaknesses as a job candidate. This ties in with the previous example about problems with speaking English. Most likely, an interviewer can tell if English is challenging for you, and he or she may wonder whether this will hurt your ability to do the job. You don't want the employer to be distracted with thoughts like this. So what you can do is bring up the concern yourself—maybe even in responding to a first question such as "Tell me about yourself." If you can anticipate the interviewer's concerns and eliminate them early in the interview, the interviewer is more likely to focus on your strengths.

One undergraduate business student does this very effectively in interviews. Due to a physical disability, this student needs metal crutches to help himself walk. The student knows that interviewers are probably curious about his disability but feel it would be impolite to ask him questions about it. And maybe they're wondering what's wrong with him: Would he be able to get around the workplace, for example?

The student figures that if the interviewer is thinking about his crutches, he or she is not giving *him* the attention he deserves as an individual. Maybe the interviewer isn't really listening to his carefully-prepared questions and answers. So right when the interview starts, the student says, "You're probably wondering why I'm on these crutches." He explains what happened (a motorbike accident), and he assures the employer that the disability doesn't keep him from being able to take a computer apart and put it back together again. Now the interviewer can focus on the student as a job candidate, not as a medical curiosity.

Let's consider some possible answers to "What are your weaknesses?"

Mediocre answer:	*"I don't really know anything about [sociology, journalism, accounting, etc.], and I don't really have any kind of real job experience."*
Ordinary answer:	*"I guess it would be that I work too hard. I forget to go to lunch, and the security guard has to ask me to leave at 10:00 each night, then I just sleep in my car so I can start working when the doors open at 6."*
Extraordinary answer:	*"Although I have done extremely well in my sociology coursework, I would say my weakness is that I haven't yet had an opportunity to work directly in the field. Of course, that's hard to do without an advanced degree. But I hope to build on what I've learned in the classroom by honing my research and analytical skills and by getting some practical job experience in a human services position such as the one at your organization. There's always more to learn, and I can do so quickly."*

8. *"How are your grades?"*

If your grades are good, you probably won't be asked this question because your grade point average will be right on your resume. Obviously, the best solution to this question is to have good grades to begin with! If your grades are not good enough to put your GPA on your resume, though, you'd better be ready to answer this question.

Even though the statistical evidence shows that there is almost no relationship between grades and job success, employers don't necessarily know or believe that. Do employers care about your grades? Generally, yes. Admittedly, some don't care if your grades are mediocre as long as you can do the work. Others, however, may *require* a GPA of 3.0 or better, and others believe that grades are a good predictor of job performance. Therefore, you have to be ready to address this question.

Once again, preparation will help you handle this type of question more effectively. The following strategies that may prove helpful:

- *If your grades are good in the field for which you are applying, discuss those grades explicitly.* In other words, if you have a 2.4 GPA, but your grades in marketing classes are all Bs or better, then focus on those grades if you're applying for a marketing job.

- *If your GPA reflects one or two very low grades in a class outside of your major or concentration and/or in a class that may not relate to your success in this job, then say so.* Just be sure that the class *really* isn't relevant to the job at hand.

- *If your GPA reflects the fact that you need to work a significant number of hours during school to help pay tuition, then say so.*

- *If your grades have improved significantly over the last few quarters or semesters, acknowledge that you got off to a slow start but have improved significantly.*

Here is the range of responses to "How are your grades?"

Mediocre response:	*"Not too good. I have a 2.4."*
Ordinary response:	*"Well, they're okay; they could be better. I've done pretty well in classes in my major."*
Extraordinary response:	*"Given that I've been working part-time while taking classes to help pay tuition, I think my grades are okay. When I take classes outside of my major, it's hard for me to put enough time into them. But my average in my psychology classes is a 3.2, so I think you'll find my academic background is strong in areas that will really count in this job."*

Strategic Interviewing – An Employer's Perspective
by Steve Sim

If I can add any perspective on interviews, I'd have to say one thing: each and every experience you listed on your resume or talked about in an interview should have taught you something. Whether that lesson is how to do something right every time or how to do something right the next time, it's a lesson learned. Be prepared to talk about it.

Steve Sim was a Technical Recruiter at the Microsoft Corporation and is now the
Co-founder & Principal Search Consultant at Envisage Recruiting LLC.

---

9. *"Tell me what you liked LEAST about your job at Organization X."*

This request is basically a check of your attitude and your tact. Don't be tempted to bash your former boss, your co-workers, your lousy job, etc. Doing so will make you come off as a complainer or as someone who dislikes work.

For example, I interviewed a young woman for a medical writing job a few years ago. When

I asked her about her previous job, she was only too happy to go on for a full 15 minutes about her horrible employer. Since this horrendous job was also in medical publishing, I finally put on a very concerned face and asked her "Do you think your previous experience has made you too bitter to continue to work in this industry?" She immediately realized her mistake, but it was too late. She had already been interviewed by our company president, who afterwards dismissed her with a simple sentence: "She's a whiner." We never did discuss her qualifications, which, actually, were quite good.

Instead of harping on the negatives, your best bet is to acknowledge that the job had many good aspects, but that you felt you wanted to broaden your experience and move on to something that would provide you with a bigger challenge.

Here are some sample responses for this request:

Mediocre answer:	*"They made me do all kinds of busywork that any idiot could do. Also, the pay was bad, my boss was totally clueless about how to manage me, and my co-workers were pretty useless, too."*
Ordinary answer:	*"It was an okay place to work, but it got kind of dull after a while. And since I was just a co-op student, I had to do a lot of jobs that other people didn't want to do. Basically, it was just a way to make money for school."*
Extraordinary answer:	*"The job was definitely a good entry-level experience for me; I learned a great deal about _____, which I think will prove useful in my next job. I just believe that I could only learn so much in that job, so I decided it would be in my best interest to pursue something more challenging and interesting. That's why your job description caught my eye."*

10. *"What are your long-term career goals?"*

A variation on this one would be, "What do you see yourself doing in ____ years?" When employers ask this type of question, what they really want to know is many different things:

* *How focused or goal-oriented is the job candidate? Is she or he someone who plans ahead? Is she or he ambitious?* After all, you wouldn't want to hire someone who's just looking to make some quick cash, or someone who isn't achievement-oriented.

* *Does the job at hand really make sense as a match, given the job candidate's long-term goals?* If you're applying for a psychology position in an after-school program, but your long-term career goal is to become an entrepreneur, you had better be ready to explain why you're interested in the psychology job now. "I just really, really need a job" is not the best reason! It is entirely possible to explain the apparent disconnect, of course, but you have to give some thought as to how a job would fit into your career plan *before* you go out for that interview.

* *How mature and realistic is the candidate?* Your answer can reveal a great deal about your maturity and perception of yourself. If you don't have much of an answer, you may come off as someone who lacks focus and maturity. If you say that your goal is

to someday be an administrative assistant, you may come off as lacking confidence or ambition. If you say that your goal is to be CEO of Microsoft, you may be seen as a dreamer, or as hopelessly naive... particularly if you have shown no initiative in acquiring computer skills.

That said, let's look at the range of replies an interviewer might hear to a question about long-term career goals. We'll assume that the student is interviewing for an entry-level bookkeeping job for a small company that manufactures furniture.

Mediocre answer:	*"Well, I'm kind of undecided about that right now... I guess it would be to just pursue a job in my major after I graduate, then see what comes along."*
Ordinary answer:	*"I hope to gain some valuable experience in accounting during my co-op jobs, then I'll pursue my CPA and see if I can get a job with a Big Four firm."*
Extraordinary answer:	*"Down the road, I plan to get my CPA and work for a Big Four firm. I feel that the experience that I would gain from this opportunity would be very valuable, because an accountant needs to build good relationships with companies of all types and sizes. Working here would give me an understanding and appreciation from that perspective, which is essential to success in public accounting."*

What if you don't *know* what your long-term goals are? Don't lie about that; but do give some general sense of your priorities and why the job for which you're interviewing is a good step with that in mind:

> *"Right now I know that I want to have a career in the corporate world, but I think a number of possibilities are plausible in the long run. Regardless of where I land, though, I know that any management professional has to be able to understand financial statements. So I'm excited about this job, as it would be a great first step toward any number of future management careers."*

11. *"What kind of hourly rate are you looking for in this position?"*

The issue of pay can be an awkward matter in an interview. It's natural for you to be wondering about the pay rate or hoping for a specific figure, but your best bet is to not bring it up unless the employer does. Even then, you have to be careful about what you say. You don't want to get ruled out of a job for being greedy, but you don't want to accept $11.50 an hour when they would have been delighted to give you $14.

So how should you handle this question? First of all, always check the job description or ask a co-op coordinator what the pay rate is before you go in for an interview. If the job pays $11.00 an hour, and you can't afford to take a job that pays less than $13.00, it's better to find out ahead of time rather than wasting everyone's time with an interview.

In many cases, the issue of pay in a co-op job or internship is fairly rigid and non-negotiable. Some positions pay a certain figure, period. Others offer varied pay... but the pay only varies depending on your year in school; again, the pay rate is non-negotiable. Although unpaid internships have faced some criticism and scrutiny for employers in recent years, there are still some internships that don't pay at all, depending on the field and the organization.

In some instances, however, the pay rate is a range that can vary depending on your skills, the employer's alternatives to hiring you, and your desirability as a candidate. The co-op coordinator will usually—but not always—have an accurate sense of what the pay range is. Find out before the interview.

If you *do* know what the pay rate or pay range is, you can acknowledge this in response to the question: *"My understanding is that the job pays between $13 and $15 an hour. I'd be comfortable with something within that range."*

This kind of response doesn't pigeonhole you as someone seeking a high or low pay rate and indicates that money isn't the most important consideration for you. For a co-op job, you never want to mention money as the reason you want a particular job, or as the main way you will decide between Job A and Job B.

If you *don't* know what the pay range or pay rate is, your best bet is to reply with a question: *"Is there a pay range that you have in mind for the position?"* Usually, there is, and many employers will provide you with a range. When you are told the range, it is best to not show any surprise, positively or negatively.

If you're pressed for a specific dollar figure, another option is to evade the question until an offer is presented: *"Money isn't the main factor in my decision. But I plan to interview with other companies, and if I get more than one excellent opportunity, then money could be a factor. But once you make me a specific offer, I will give you an answer within three business days."*

This kind of response indicates that money is not the top objective. More importantly, it helps you to project yourself as a person who has options and who considers himself or herself to be an attractive candidate. You want to show that you're strongly interested in the job, yes, but not desperate to get it!

Of course, there are many other possible questions you might be asked in an interview. Several examples can be seen in the following box, which was created by Linnea Basu, a member of the cooperative education faculty at Northeastern University. One accounting employer consistently asks job candidates to "define integrity." Some interviewers may ask candidates to name someone that they think of as a hero. We have heard of one employer who asked a job candidate to tell him a joke! In short, you cannot prepare for every specific question that you possibly could be asked.

When you are asked an unusual question, don't panic: just think, how can I use this question to show that I am THE candidate who is the best match for this job description? Whether you're defining integrity or describing your ideal job, this is something that you can focus on.

OTHER TYPICAL INTERVIEW QUESTIONS by Linnea Basu

1. Why did you decide to attend [name of university/college]?
2. How did you decide to major in [name of major]?
3. What's your favorite class? Least favorite?
4. Why do you want this job? Why do you want to work for our organization?
5. What sets you apart from other candidates?
6. Rate your computer skills on a scale of 1-10.
7. Tell me about a time you had to meet a specific deadline and how you met that deadline.
8. How do you organize your time?
9. How would your friends describe you?
10. How would your boss or professors describe you?
11. What kind of a person do you like to work for?
12. Give me an example of a task or project you had to do which required attention to detail.
13. What motivates you to work hard?
14. What's your greatest accomplishment?
15. Tell me about a time when you had to work with a difficult team or group member and how you resolved the situation.
16. What has been your most rewarding college experience?
17. What has been the most difficult part of college life?
18. What's your dream job?
19. Give me an example of a time when you had to learn a skill or information very quickly and how you learned that skill.
20. If you could change one thing about yourself, what would it be?
21. If you could have dinner with any famous person, dead or alive, who would it be and why? What would you ask them?

DEALING WITH DIFFERENT INTERVIEWER STYLES

Another challenge in preparing for an interview is that you may come across vastly different interviewing styles. Sometimes, students return to the co-op office feeling frustrated because the interviewer never shut up and didn't really give them a chance to sell themselves. Others may have a different frustration: The interviewer barely talked at all, and they felt extremely awkward. So it may be useful to consider how to deal with different types of interviewers.

First of all, keep in mind that many interviewers are NOT experts in interviewing. They may not know the best questions to ask to determine how good a candidate you are. You may find this disappointing, but that's the way it is. You may have to overcome an interviewer's weaknesses or personality if it keeps you from selling yourself. Here are some tips for dealing with several types of interviewers.

Type 1: "The Interrogator"

This interviewer puts job candidates on the spot. The Interrogator asks blunt questions, such as: "Why should we hire YOU for this job?" or "What makes you think you know computers well enough to work here?" Alternatively, he or she may like to pose a challenge for you: "Here's a set of numbers. Figure out the present value of this sum of money if it's invested for 10 years at 8% interest." One interviewer likes to toss a smart phone on the table and ask the potential computer engineering co-op: "How would you go about developing a new app for this phone?" Sales interviewers may pull out a 79-cent pen and say, "You have one minute to sell me this pen."

You should always be prepared for an intense interview. Assume that you're going to be challenged with difficult questions, and that you may be asked to back up your answers with real-life examples.

Interviewer Types – A Co-op Professional's Perspective
by Bob Tillman

I do have some strong upper-class jobs that will only interview upper-class students. They want to know if you've had concrete design, if you've had steel design. Not only that, they'll want to see your transcript. I just had one of my former graduate students come back, and they gave him a test: Here's a beam—analyze it. That's the interview.

Bob Tillman is an Associate Professor and cooperative education coordinator in Civil and Environmental Engineering at Northeastern University.

Most interviewers will not be this tough: particularly with co-op candidates. Still, you have to be prepared for the possibility. And although many job candidates tremble at the thought of facing a high-pressure interviewer, the Interrogator is not the toughest to face. The Interrogator puts you under the microscope and evaluates how you handle tough questions or problems, but this gives you an opportunity to show how you can step up to a challenge and handle it.

Some MIS employers will sit a student down at a computer and have them attempt to fix it. The interviewer sits and notes how the candidate attempts to tackle the problem as much as the result. As the sidebar box indicates, this kind of "on the spot" challenge is not limited to business students.

Type 2: "The Buddy"

This interviewer is very different from the Interrogator. The Buddy will have more of a conversation with you about the job, asking questions in a non-threatening way, showing interest in who you are as a person, etc. Most students naturally prefer this kind of interviewer, but you have to be careful. Some wily interviewers will intentionally take on this friendly tone because they know you are likely to let your guard down. With The Buddy, you might be likely to confide more of your weaknesses, shortcomings, and problems, because their friendliness seems so trustworthy. The Buddy will get you to admit that you got a C- in your accounting class—and will even sound sympathetic—then The Buddy will turn around and nail you when it comes time to pick the best candidate.

If the interviewer is casual and friendly, you should relax too: but be a little cautious. Don't ever forget that you're trying to sell your strengths and show why you're a good match for the job, even if you're doing this with a smile on your face and a more relaxed tone of voice. Friendly conversation can set a nice tone for an interview: Just make sure that your conversation gets beyond small talk.

Type 3: "The Nonstop Talker"

Although The Interrogator may sound like your worst nightmare, The Nonstop Talker is actually the most difficult and frustrating type for most interviewees. You may sit through an interview that feels more like a lecture, barely getting a chance to say anything to this interviewer. At least The Interrogator gives you a chance to say something in your defense!

The Nonstop Talker may not be immediately recognizable. Many good interviewers will begin by telling you a great deal about the job and the organization before asking you questions. The Nonstop Talker may talk about these things, too, in addition to himself or herself, the previous co-op student that worked at the company, and other topics. Applicants for one job came back and reported with some amazement that the manager talked about his ex-wife! The next thing you know, the interviewer has used up all of the scheduled time, and you've done little but nod a lot. Of course, this is a low-pressure interview, but you run the risk of coming across as part of the office furniture: In other words, this type of interview may mean that they like you and have basically decided to hire you, but it also may mean that you are completely forgotten by the interviewer.

When interviewed by The Nonstop Talker, you have to walk a fine line: Don't interrupt, but DO take advantage of any break in the monologue by asking a question that brings the Talker around to considering you as a candidate. During a pause, you might be able to politely say: "Can I ask you a question? I'm very interested in this job. What would be useful for you to know in order to find out whether I'm the best candidate for the job?" Another strategy is to acknowledge and flatter The Talker's talking while changing the focus of the talk: "I've certainly learned a great deal about you, this job, and the organization. In fact, from what you've said, I think this opportunity would be a great match for my skills because...." At this point, you can tailor your response to what you've learned from the nonstop talking... as long as you were listening carefully!

In short, try to get The Nonstop Talker to focus on you. He or she may still talk a great deal, but at least it might be about you and your ability to do the job.

Type 4: "Silent But Deadly"

This interviewer is the opposite of the talker, but this style can be equally frustrating. The Silent But Deadly interviewer will ask very few questions, and the questions may be very vague or general. So why is this interviewer potentially "deadly?" Basically, he or she gives nervous job candidates every opportunity to hang themselves! Consider the following dialogue:

Interviewer:	*"So... tell me about your weaknesses."*
Job Candidate:	*"Although I have a good understanding of basic accounting from classwork and my first co-op job, I need to learn more in order to master accounting: specifically, I'm looking forward to learning more about taxes, which is why the job with your company appeals to me."*
Interviewer [nods slowly]:	*"Hmmmm......"*
Job Candidate:	*"Um, and I guess you want another weakness?"*
Interviewer [nods]:	*"Uh-huh..."*
Job Candidate:	*"Hmmm.... okay, let me think... Um, I guess I'm not that strong when it comes to debits and credits.... I get my ledger entries confused sometimes..."*
Interviewer [nods, says nothing]:	
Job Candidate:	*"And.... I suppose that getting a C+ in my last accounting class wasn't that strong."*

Do you see what can happen in this situation? The job candidate started off with a strong answer but then interpreted the interviewer's silence as a negative: The candidate assumed that he or she failed to answer the question adequately. As a result, the candidate supplied more information. In this case, it was information that can only hurt the individual's chances of getting a job.

Most Silent But Deadly interviewers act this way because it reflects their personalities. But some shrewd interviewers may use this as a deliberate strategy to see if you will hang yourself if given enough rope. This is especially common when asking about weaknesses or reasons for leaving a previous job or situation.

Either way, your strategy is simple. If the length of the silence starts to feel awkward, ask a clarifying question: "Does that answer your question?"; "Is there anything else you'd like to ask me?"; "What else would you like to know about me?" Unless you're asked a specific question requesting more information, have faith in your answer; don't assume that silence or apparent indifference means that you have to say something more.

During my last job search, I was interviewed by a very quiet, introverted gentleman. After each of my answers, he would let a solid ten seconds go by; once, he waited for a good 20 seconds, as if he were curious to see how I would handle that. But I believed I had given a strong, definitive answer, so I simply waited. Finally, he said, "Is there anything you'd like to add?" I replied, pleasantly, "I think I covered everything. Was there something else you would like to know?" Ultimately, I was offered the job. Of course, if I were interviewing for a marketing position, I probably would have needed to be more aggressive in that situation. So it just goes to show you: There is seldom one "right" way to handle an interviewing challenge. It's always difficult to feel that you need to carry both sides of any conversation. But if you can take charge of the situation by offering to explain why you're a good match for the job, what you have to offer the organization, and by asking questions that reflect your research, you may succeed in bringing this interviewer out of his or her shell.

Type 5: "The Big Picture Person"

This interviewer is prone to asking very open-ended, general questions, such as:

- Tell me about yourself.

- What do you want to do with your life?

- What are your career goals?

- What kind of person are you?

Students often *hate* these questions because there seems to be no clear-cut way to answer them. Again, though, remember the rule: When asked about something *general*, answer in a way that shows why you are a match for this *specific* job. What kind of person are you? "I have a great deal to offer to a small medical office like this one. I have excellent grades in my anatomy and physiology classes, and I have solid experience working hands-on with people as a volunteer at the small hospital in my hometown. If you hire me, you will be employing a person who has a solid base of experience as well as someone who picks up new things quickly and does work without complaining." If that's the kind of job description in question, that's the right kind of specific answer to a "big picture" question.

Type 6: "The Human Resources Interviewer"

If you are interviewed by someone in an HR department, you may or may not be asked questions relating to your technical skills. An experienced HR person may have enough expertise to ask you about specific tasks, but it is not uncommon to come across an HR interviewer who knows little about engineering, nursing, or social work. Alternatively, the HR interviewer may have the knowledge but decide that such questions are better left to the person who would be your supervisor if you're hired. Either way, the HR interviewer is more likely to ask the classic interview questions as described in the previous section. The questions may be more "warm and fuzzy," as the purpose of this interview may be to "screen" candidates to determine who will go on to the next phase of the interview process. Be prepared for a structured interview, and don't get too technical in your responses unless the interviewer seems to be looking for that. Save your more technical answers for the interviewer who is a network administrator or mechanical engineer—someone who is an expert in your field, whatever it is.

Interviewer Types – A Co-op Professional's Perspective
by Rose Dimarco

Nursing could be different than physical therapy in that nursing may have people in Human Resources to interview you; they may have nurse recruiters interview you. Part of their skill base is knowing how to interview. In physical therapy, you're more apt to be interviewed by the physical therapist—who may have zero skills in interviewing. So if you're going to probably be interviewed by someone who doesn't know how to interview you that well, what do you want to have them remember about you before you walk out? That means when they're walking you down the hall, and they're showing you all the equipment and all the treatment rooms, how are you going to script what you want to say so that you interject what is it about you that you think would fit? If you're being interviewed by someone in Human Resources, and they're more skilled in interviewing, it might be more traditional questions: Tell me about yourself, What are your strengths and weaknesses?

You have to decide: What three things do I want them to remember about me? It's not: 'Oh, what a cute guy—he's trying to get through school; his mom and dad had three jobs.' It's not that kind of remembrance: It's remembrance about what value you bring, and those three things you have to somehow interject. As they talk about things, don't be afraid to say "That reminds me of when I was in high school, and I had to work under pressure because I had x, y, and z to do, and here's how I dealt with it."

Rose Dimarco is a cooperative education faculty coordinator in Physical Therapy at Northeastern University.

Type 7: "The Behavioral-Based Interviewer"

Some organizations swear by Behavioral-Based Interviewing (BBI), and for good reason: Studies have shown that this style is generally more effective in determining whether someone is a good match for a job. In particular, Big Four accounting firms such as Deloitte and PricewaterhouseCoopers often use this approach. Microsoft and other corporations also use these questions to determine if you have specific "core competencies" that are considered to be vital to success at the organization in question: drive/results orientation; passion for learning; ability to work in a team; ability to handle conflict effectively; good ethical judgment; etc.

The behavioral-based interview features questions that require specific stories in response. This makes it much more difficult for the interviewee to come up with a slick-sounding, canned answer: Instead, he or she must recount something that they really experienced in the classroom or at work. In answering, the interviewee is urged to walk the interviewer through the specific situation and to detail what they were thinking, feeling, and doing in response.

Here are some typical BBI questions:

- Tell me specifically what your greatest accomplishment in life thus far has been.

- Tell me about a time when you had to overcome a challenge or obstacle when working as part of a team.

- Tell me about a time when you felt really successful in something at work.

- Describe a situation in which you faced an ethical dilemma and how you dealt with it.

If you're not too forthcoming or struggle initially, the interviewer may add, "Just walk me through what was going on step-by-step..." or something like that.

The key to these interviews is to have several good, specific stories that you are ready to share. Think long and hard ahead of time about which stories will best showcase multiple positive qualities—some stories are better than others! Describe the situation specifically first, then logically walk the interviewer through how you handled the situation step-by-step, wrapping up with a description of what ended up happening due to your actions.

Practice the telling of your behavioral-based stories. Last summer, my nephew interviewed for an engineering position—his first job out of college. Ahead of time, they gave him a list of core competencies that they seek in applicants and told him that they would be looking for him to share some personal experiences related to those competencies. I told him that this was like going for a test where you have been given the questions a week in advance! However, the first time he told me his stories, they weren't good enough. He had to try out some stories to figure out which ones would be the BEST stories to showcase his strengths. After extensive practice and preparation—and despite limited internship experience—he went in and nailed the interview, and it turned out to be the only offer he got in a tough economy. Without strategizing and practicing for a behavioral-based interview, it may not have happened.

Whether or not you ever have a behavioral-based interview, having extremely vivid and specific examples to share is always a smart idea: It brings alive your ideas and tells employers what you *really* mean when you say that you can learn quickly or work independently or be a strong team player. For a great deal of information on behavioral-based interviewing—including several terrific student examples—check out Appendix E in the back of this textbook.

Type 8: "The Olympic Judge"

The Olympic Judge likes to let you know how you're doing throughout the interview. As you might imagine, this can be encouraging, disconcerting, or both. This interviewer may come out and say, "Good answer!" However, this individual may also shake his head or frown or say, "Well, I don't know about that."

Dealing with immediate negative feedback can be very challenging to your confidence. How can you handle it? Most importantly, *don't ignore it.* If an interviewer reacts negatively to one of your answers, ask a clarifying question: "Is there a concern you have about that answer?" Once you understand why the interviewer reacted negatively, try to acknowledge the concern and address it as best as you can. For example, if you're asked to cite your experience in marketing research, and the interviewer reacts negatively to your response, you might handle it like this:

Job candidate:	*"I noticed that you had a negative reaction to my answer. What is it about my research experience that concerns you?"*
Interviewer:	*"Well, my sense is that your experience is good but extremely limited."*

Job candidate:	*"I think it's fair to say that the quantity of experience I've had is limited. But I feel that the quality of experience has been outstanding. My position at Galvinators Unlimited gave me a great opportunity to gain exposure to research..."*

The candidate could then go on to tout some specifics about this research experience. Would this be enough to turn around the Olympic Judge's perception? Maybe not, but it would at least give you a chance. It shows assertiveness, desire to get the job, and sensitivity to the concerns of others.

A variation on the Olympic Judge interviewer is the person who asks *you* to judge yourself: "On a scale of 1 to 10, with 1 being terrible and 10 being fantastic, how would you rate yourself in terms of...." The interviewer then asks you to rate your communication skills, your analytical ability, your interpersonal skills, etc.

This kind of question tests your honesty, realism, and savvy: Rating yourself uniformly high comes off as insincere or unaware, but who will hire you if you give yourself low ratings? When answering this question, make sure you do yourself justice, but make sure to rate yourself lower in certain areas: particularly those that seem less related to the job that you want. Don't rate yourself as a 1 or 2 in something unless you really know nothing about it (i.e., you're asked about C++ programming, and you've never done anything like it). For most generic characteristics, stick between 6 and 10. Bear in mind that your coordinator would not send your resume out for a position if he or she believed that your skills were not a reasonable match for the given job. Have confidence in your skill level, and show it with ratings that are realistic and positive.

TURNING THE TABLES: ASKING THE RIGHT QUESTIONS DURING AN INTERVIEW

Many job candidates think of interviewing as an audition for a part. This perception has some truth to it, but it's not the whole story. In an interview, you *are* trying to show that you're the best person for the job. Additionally, though, you're trying to determine whether the job is a good match for you. In that sense, interviewing should be a two-way street.

The nice thing about asking questions in an interview is that it helps to achieve both of these goals. Asking smart questions is a great way to show the interviewer that you are:

- prepared for the interview in terms of researching the job and the company.

- excited about and interested in the job.

- determined to find out whether you think this job is the best match for your considerable talents.

Interviewing – An Employer's Perspective
by Mike Naclerio

The goal of interviewing is to determine a "mutual" fit between the company and potential employee. Too often, candidates view interviews as situations where they have to prove to a company that they are good enough to fit in. They often overlook the opportunity they have to "interview the company" to see if the company is good enough for them (i.e., does the company have an appropriate level of ethics, will the position be satisfying, what type of people work there, etc.). So, candidates should not lose sight of this opportunity and ask questions!

Mike Naclerio is the President of Enquiron.

All of these things reflect favorably on you as a job candidate. Likewise, asking questions is a great way to determine whether:

•   the job is what it appears to be in the job description.

•   the job is something that you will be excited about doing for several months (or at least one year if it's a full-time post-graduation position).

•   the job is indeed a good match for someone with your level of skills.

Don't underestimate the importance of determining whether the job is what you really want. *More often than not, individuals who end up disliking their jobs failed to ask the right questions during the interview.* Basically, they didn't have a realistic sense of what the job requirements would be. As a result, they end up being bored or overwhelmed. But isn't it the employer's fault for failing to communicate this to the job candidate, you might say? True, a great interviewer will do this effectively. However, if an interviewer fails to do so, it's the interviewee's responsibility to ask if you want to ensure that misunderstandings are avoided.

What Questions Should I Ask?

Many internship and co-op candidates—even many experienced professionals—struggle to come up with good questions. When they are given the opportunity to ask questions during an interview, they will try to think up some on the spot, then decline the opportunity.

Like so many things in interviewing, this element requires preparation. You should have eight to ten questions ready to ask before you even arrive for the interview. Why so many? Because several questions that you had beforehand may be answered during the course of the interview. Most interviewers won't simply ask questions; they'll talk a little about the company and explain a little more about the job. Thus, you need to have numerous questions ready.

What are the "best" questions to ask? In my opinion, the best questions are the ones that:

•   force the interviewer to imagine you in the job.

•   reflect your attitude and values positively.

111

Let's consider what this means. If you want the job, it is in your best interest that the interviewer envisions you in the position. You can do this by using the words "I," "me," and "my" in your question. For example:

- What would my typical day be like in this position?

- Who would train me when I begin this job?

- Would I receive regular feedback about my performance?

These are good questions, but the very best ones are those that also reflect a positive attitude and strong values. Consider these:

- What could I do between now and the first day of co-op to be ready to hit the ground running in this job?

- It's important to me to get an outstanding evaluation in my co-op job: What could I do to stand out as an exceptional employee in this job?

- I want a job that challenges me and keeps me busy. Given that, can you give me a sense of whether this position would be right for me?

- I would be glad to work part-time after the co-op ends. Do you think that's a possibility?

- If I excel in this position, would I be able to have more responsibilities added to my job description?

Here are some other good questions:

- What would you say is the most challenging part of this job?

- What would you describe as the most rewarding aspect of the job?

- In the research that I did to prepare for today, I noticed that your company is trying to (i.e., implement a new marketing strategy, adopt a new process of providing quality care to patients). How has this development changed things in this department?

- This job involves several different responsibilities: Which do you think would require most of my time?

- Why do YOU like working for this company?

- If everything works out well for this co-op period, would it be possible for me to work here in the future?

- How often do you hire co-ops on a full-time basis after they graduate?

Asking these kinds of questions will show the interviewer that you are serious about the job, and that you value yourself highly enough to know that other options may be more attractive to you than this one. Because this is true, you need to see if the company meets your needs as well as you meet theirs.

One last note: Be sure to *follow up* on your questions. *Listen* to the employer's answer, and *respond* to it positively. Here's an example:

Interviewee:	*"What could I do to earn an outstanding evaluation working here?"*
Interviewer:	*"Well, more than anything we want someone who is willing to do whatever it takes to get the job done—even if that means staying late or coming in on Saturdays from time to time."*
Interviewee:	*"That's great to hear. I have no problem putting in extra hours: I just want to be a productive part of the team, whatever it takes. Actually, if you want to call my previous supervisor, she can tell you about my willingness to work overtime or come in on short notice. I think I would stand out in a similar way here."*

ENDING ON A HIGH NOTE

If you have ever taken a psychology class, you may have heard of a phenomenon called the primacy/recency effect. Research has shown that when individuals are presented with a significant amount of information, they tend to best remember what they are exposed to first and last; the middle tends to get hazy.

We already discussed how to get off to a good start. Now let's discuss how you can cap your interview with a strong ending. Here are a few basic guidelines:

Take charge of the transition from asking questions to closing the interview.

Don't wait for the employer to figure out that you have no more questions to ask. The best approach is to transition from asking questions into closing the interview. After you've had your job-related questions answered, simply say: "I have just one more question. When do you plan to make a hiring decision?"

Ask the interviewer what the next steps will be.

After you learn when the decision will be made, ask the interviewer what his or her preference is regarding next steps: "Would you like me to call you next week about the decision, or shall I just wait to hear from you?" If the interviewer says that you should call, make sure to get a business card, or, at least, a phone number.

Thank the interviewer for taking the time to meet with you.

Even if you're not interested in the job, be gracious and polite. Acknowledge the fact that the interviewer has devoted part of his or her day to talk to you. Show some appreciation for the experience, and mention something specific about your conversation that was enlightening. One possibility would be: "Thank you for taking the time to meet with me today. I learned a great deal about the nursing practices in a geriatric care facility. I look forward to hearing from you."

Shake the interviewer's hand before leaving, and make sure that you haven't left behind any personal belongings.

If you have any doubts about whether or not you handled questions well, write them down soon after you leave. Then you can discuss them with your coordinator.

AFTER THE INTERVIEW: FOLLOW-UP STEPS

To some degree, your follow-up steps may vary depending on the employer's needs or preferences. In all circumstances, respect any request that an employer makes of you, whether it's getting a writing sample to her or additional references to him, calling on a particular day, or not calling at all.

Most people would agree that writing a thank-you note or letter or e-mail would be appropriate at this point. But one dilemma is whether a handwritten card is better than a less formal e-mail. My rule is that if a decision is not going to be made within the next two or three days, then it's better to send a brief card if you mail it by the following morning. But if a decision will be made within 24 hours, then opt for an e-mail.

More than anything, though, make sure that any such note or e-mail is absolutely perfect in terms of grammar and spelling... especially when writing the name of the manager or organization. Sending no thank-you letter at all is better than sending one with errors.

Keep your thank-you note simple and professional. A safe approach would include the following steps:

- Thank the interviewer for taking the time to meet with you on Thursday (or whatever day it was).

- Say something positive about the interviewing experience: something you found especially intriguing to learn about the company, its products/services, the job, etc.

- Briefly reinforce your interest in the position (if you have any) and why you would be a good match for the position.

- Encourage the interviewer to contact you if any additional information is needed.

Here's an example of how one might format a thank-you e-mail:

Subject: Thank you for your time

Ms. Mariano,

Thank you so much for taking the time to meet with me this morning. I very much enjoyed learning more about Deloitte—especially with regard to what would be in store for me if I am hired for a co-op position this January. It sounds like an exciting time for the firm.

I am very interested in the position, and I believe that my bookkeeping experience, attention to detail, and strong academic performance in accounting would make me a strong contributor to your organization.

I look forward to hearing from you soon. Please feel free to contact me if you have any additional questions.

Thanks again,

Cynthia Conrad

A pleasant and timely thank-you note can't turn a mediocre candidate into a great one. But it can make all the difference if the employer is struggling over the decision or believes that several candidates could do the job.

SPECIAL CONSIDERATIONS FOR PHONE OR SKYPE INTERVIEWS

As we noted in Chapter One, everyone has to be aware of what it means to look for a job in the Digital Age. We live in a time where it's all too easy for applicants to apply for jobs, and hiring managers and recruiters get buried with applicants for many jobs. On top of that, people are busier than ever. They often don't want to waste a half-hour or more interviewing someone in person when a five or ten-minute phone interview or "phone screen" can be a big help in ruling someone in—or out—of consideration.

As a result, you're going to have to be ready to deal with interviewing over the phone—or even on video, most likely through Skype. When I coach job seekers—whether old or young—I get asked about this quite often. How do you prepare differently? I've conducted dozens of phone interviews and also have had someone interview me that way a number of times. For the most part, you'll want to prepare and perform as you would for any other interviews. So let's focus on what you should differently. Here are the keys for phone interviews first:

1. *Phone etiquette matters.*
    Usually the call will be scheduled in advance: Don't agree to a time unless it really is a good time for you. You want to be prepared, rested, alert, and set up in a quiet place where you can talk without background noise or interruption. These can be real negatives as distractions. You also need to think about keeping your tone professional and businesslike: Some candidates fall into a chatty, informal style on any phone call, and it hurts them.

2. *Use all the notes that you want...but don't draw attention to them.*
    A phone interview is kind of like an open-book test: You can have any notes in front of you. I usually recommend having your notes laid out flat in front of you on a desk or table, printed out in a large font so you can glance at them easily to remind yourself of any strategic points, stories, research, and questions you may have. I also think it's good to have a pen at hand to check off things you've said as you go. However, you don't want to rustle through papers, as this will be a distraction.

3. *Your voice has to show energy, interest, and attention.*
    One potential disadvantage on the phone is that you have no opportunity to make a positive impression with your eye contact, body language, and attire. Your voice has

to do it all. In advance, practice using your voice in a warm, enthusiastic way. Try to avoid verbal tics ("like" and "you know")—they will make you sound younger and less professional than you want to sound.

4. *Consider your body language.*
   This may sound counterintuitive, but you actually should think about what you're doing with your body. While no one will know if you're in pajamas and fuzzy bunny slippers on the phone, some people find it useful to dress up for a phone interview as if it's an in-person interview. Why? It may help you get in the right mindset. Others may find it helpful to close their eyes and focus intently on listening and speaking. That's a judgment call, but generally I think it's a good idea to sit as you would for a face-to-face interview—leaning forward with good upright posture. It just helps to stay focused.

5. *Practice on the phone.*
   If you have a trusted advisor—ideally someone who is older and who has done phone interviews—try it out first with them. Ask them to focus on your tone—how are you coming across? Getting feedback can help.

With interviews on Skype or some other form of videoconference, it's a little different again. Now your attire will matter, and using notes is possible but trickier. Here are some things that I've seen work:

1. *Download and test the video app in advance.*
   A real easy way to panic is to overlook the fact that you need to download Skype (or whatever app you're using) in advance. It's not difficult, but it's not instantaneous either. Also, you need to test out how it will look in advance. No one enjoys seeing themselves on video, but you'll benefit greatly with a test call. Make sure that you're sitting in such a way that makes it easy for the interviewer to see you filling most of the frame in the shot. Practice with the interface so you won't be worrying about anything but answering the questions when the time comes.

2. *Tape your notes up a little higher than your device's video camera.*
   Usually the video camera on a laptop is up above the screen. As such, it's not so great to have your notes down on the desk. I suggest taping your notes up where they can be easily viewed without needing to have your eyes wander too far from the camera. This helps you connect better with the interviewer, and it also will make you come across as prepared. Printing your notes in large print will help, as well as making sure you don't over-rely on them.

3. *Watch out for distracting backgrounds.*
   Think about what the interviewer will be able to see behind you or hear beyond you. Either a blank background or something like a bookshelf is best for the backdrop. Be sure you're in a quiet place where no one is walking by or talking—especially roommates. Turn off your cellphone and don't look at it at all during the interview.

4. *Talk to the camera.*
   This is harder than it sounds at first. The camera is very tiny, and your tendency will

want to be to look at the picture of the interviewer on the screen. That's fine when you're listening, as you'll want to take note of their body language. But when you're talking, try to look right at the video camera to foster that crucial sense of connection.

It's always preferable to interview face-to-face whenever possible, but that choice won't be up to you in most cases. Keep the above rules in mind as you prepare for phone and video interviews.

USING NOTES IN INTERVIEWS

Although there are some potential pitfalls to consider when using notes in an interview, I believe that almost any student could benefit from using a page of notes—if done properly. The single best thing about notes is that they are a safety net if you are concerned about "going blank" due to negative nervous energy. Your notes will not include word-for-word answers, but they will feature enough words to jog your memory if you blank out. And if you don't go blank at all, nothing says that you *have* to use them just because you prepared them.

Of course, there are some major blunders you could make by using notes. The biggest one would be to write out detailed answers to common questions and to bury your head in your notes page during the interview. That would come across as being *less* prepared or even unprepared for the interview, and it would cause you significant problems with eye contact, natural speech, and connecting interpersonally with the interviewer.

So let's walk through how to create and use a notes page. How should your notes look? One former colleague suggests having your notes on an 8 ½ x 11-inch piece of paper, which is divided into four quarters:

- One quarter features key strategic points you intend to make about why you are a good match for the job. For example: "Excellent ability to work in a team." Beneath each point, you might write words to help you remember a specific example that shows that strength in action (i.e., Example: Crazy day working at Banana Republic on Friday after Thanksgiving).

- One quarter has key notes about the job or company that you learned by researching the position.

- One quarter has eight or ten questions that you might ask, so you can be sure that all of your questions won't be answered in the course of the interview.

- The last quarter is left blank, so you can use it to take notes on what the interviewer says during the interview.

I suggest either writing your notes in large print or—if on computer—printing them out in a large font, so that they are easy enough to read without having them leave your lap or a tabletop. Make sure that you don't wave your notes around. Keeping them on one piece of paper will keep you from fumbling around during the interview to find what you need. A portfolio can be handy when using notes: You can buy one which has a flap for your resume and references on one side, with a clipboard for your page of notes on the other. Hand over a fresh resume and references when sitting down, then fold over the portfolio so your notes page is right in front of you.

Interviewing – A Student's Perspective
by Gabriel Glasscock

As expected, your first few interviews will be a little nerve-wracking. But that's to be expected. It's impossible to know exactly the type of interviewer you will have. So try not to prepare too much for a certain type of interviewer. Rather, invest your time into knowing as much about the job as possible. Find good potential conversation starters. I found it good to start a conversation on relevant job-related topics (where appropriate). This shows the employer that you are not just interested in the job but the field as a whole, and it also eases some of the tension. Look them in the eye, and use good body language.

Expect the unexpected. One time, I was at Snell Library at 8:30 p.m. in the middle of an intense group session. I got a call from a recruiter for an excellent position in Florida with a Big Four firm. We had been playing phone tag for a few weeks and she was to make a decision the next day on whom to hire: I had to interview over the phone outside the library in the freezing cold of December. I knew this would be my one and only 15-minute chance at this job, and I had to sell myself RIGHT THEN, without any preparation at all. Unlike most interviews, this was not pre-arranged: The interviewer wanted to see how well I could think on my feet.

The main thing is self-confidence. They were looking for a trainer in Java. When she asked the infamous "Why should we hire you?" question, I had to be creative. Although I had no prior experience with Java, I convinced her that my experience with Visual Basic would help greatly with learning Java, as both are object-oriented programming languages. Understanding transferable skills—and knowing how to use and express them—is an essential quality for an interviewee and also one of my favorite parts of this guidebook.

Any time an interviewer gives you the floor to ask questions, ASK QUESTIONS. Always have several prepared. I used the "Why do you like working here?" question with the Big Four recruiter, and she loved talking about that. Ask questions that show you have an interest in working there in your specific job and in being a part of their company.

Gabriel Glasscock was an MIS student at Northeastern University, Class of 2002.

A sample of a good notes page can be found on the next page. I'm assuming that the candidate is pursuing a PC support job in a corporate environment.

STRATEGY/STORIES	QUESTIONS
Point #1: Passion for technology Supporting Story: The Week I built new computer for myself at age 15.	What could I do between now and January 2 to hit the ground running in this job?
Point #2: Ability to learn quickly Supporting Story: Day I fixed dad's crashed computer despite no experience with Macs.	How specifically could I earn a great evaluation
Point #3: Customer-service skills Supporting Story: Night I handled eight tables at Applebee's when many called in sick.	Chance of a position after graduation? Any new technological initiatives planned for the coming year?
Point #4: Team player Supporting Story: My role in MIS301 group project on servers.	Opportunity to take on additional work?

RESEARCH POINTS	NOTES
--New investment product, Alpha Edge, just released	
--650 people in Boston office	
--Previous intern said ability to work Saturdays is a plus	
--Intern also said transition to MS-Vista is planned	
--Hiring five co-ops: hardware, software, customer service roles	

Lastly, what if an employer questions you on why you are using notes? The biggest thing is to avoid being defensive about it. If you seem uncomfortable about having a notes page, then it will be perceived negatively. Simply say that it was important to you to feel prepared for this interview: You wanted be sure to articulate your best qualifications for this position.

HANDLING JOB OFFERS

You might believe that the least of your problems is how to deal with job offers. *Getting* a job offer may seem improbable for the time being. However, your job situation can change quickly, and you need to know how to handle job offers. Over the years, I can't believe how many times an employer has called to tell me that they offered a job to someone, only to have the response be a low-energy mumble, indicating only that the person would have to think about it. In extreme cases, I have seen an employer pull back an offer in this situation, figuring that they don't want to hire someone who only wants the job as a last resort.

So don't take this small step for granted! Here are some quick tips:

Be proactive.

As soon as you get home after an interview, you should write down the pros and cons of accepting a job offer with that company. Without thinking about any other options, is this a job that you would accept? In other words, start making up your mind BEFORE you get the offer.

ALWAYS start out by thanking the person for making you the job offer.

If someone is not sure if they want to accept a co-op job, they often quickly state that they'll have to think about it or that they aren't sure. This is impolite, at best. You should be flattered to receive ANY job offer: whether or not you choose to accept it. You also may mention some aspect of the interview that you found enjoyable.

EXAMPLE: *"First, I'd like to thank you for offering me this position. I enjoyed getting the chance to hear what you had to say about working for [ORGANIZATION]."*

AFTER thanking them, gracefully tell them what your situation is.

If you definitely know whether or not you want the job, AND you're clear about the position and pay, this will be easy. The hard part is knowing what to say when you're really not sure what to do or if the job is good but not necessarily your top choice. I suggest handling this situation carefully: You don't want to treat any employer like a second or third choice, but you also don't want to give someone the impression that you probably will take a job when you don't feel that way. Also, you have to be sensitive to the employer's needs. It's not fair to keep an offer dangling for weeks while you decide; if you ultimately say "no," then the employer will miss out on other good students. Most coordinators that I used to work with believed that you should make up your mind within THREE BUSINESS DAYS OF RECEIVING AN OFFER. In other words, if a company makes you an offer on Thursday, you will need to say yes or no by the following Tuesday.

Here is the simplest way to keep an offer on hold without making a potential employer feel like you're shopping around for something better:

EXAMPLE: *"I promised my co-op coordinator that I would discuss things with her (or him) before making a final decision, but I definitely will get back to you in no more than three business days, and sooner than that if possible."*

"Here is another way to keep an offer on hold without alienating a potential employer:

EXAMPLE: *"Let me tell you what my situation is: I'm considering a few other employers right now, and I want to be fair to those other employers and give them a chance to make me an offer. But I WILL give you my decision within three business days, and sooner than that if possible. Is that okay?"*

An employer has every right to ask you to make a decision faster if possible. However, you also have the right to talk to your coordinator before saying yes or no. If you feel that an employer is trying to corner you into making an on-the-spot decision, let your coordinator know. This generally does not happen and should not happen.

Be clear on what you are being offered.

If the employer has not told you what your hourly pay rate would be, NOW is the time to ask or to confirm that. Do so before you accept the job to avoid any misunderstandings. Likewise, you should be clear on what hours and days they expect you to work, your start date, end date, and what your responsibilities will be, so everyone is clear about this.

What's Important to You? Thinking through Multiple Offers – A Co-op Professional's Perspective
by Martina Witt

A recent marketing business student found herself with a nice problem to have: three co-op/internship offers. How to decide? Evaluating the co-op offers, she considered the job duties, location, pay rate, and potential prestige that each company might bring to her resume. One company was a large defense contractor, the other a nationally known online marketer, and the other a small niche technology company. The pay, although comparable for all three, did vary by as much as $3/hour. The type of industry was very different for each offer, and the locations varied by as much as one to 40 miles away from her home. While she confessed it was tempting to take the job with the defense contractor, one mile from home and at the highest pay, in the end the online marketer 40 miles away, with the lowest pay, was deemed the perfect match because the company's brand, culture, and structured rotational internship was most aligned with the student's values, interests, and goals. Knowing herself and looking at the big picture helped her make the choice that was right for her career development.

Martina Witts is an Assistant Director of Cooperative Education in Business at University of Massachusetts Lowell.

Be careful about pay rate issues.

In many cases, the pay rate will not be open to negotiation: You should know whether or not it is before you bring up the matter. And even if there is some room for negotiation, there are good reasons to avoid doing so: Pushing for more pay can send the message that you care more about the money than about the learning experience.

When there is some room for negotiation, you probably should not take matters into your own hands. Talk to your coordinator to find out if there is any latitude regarding pay. In some rare cases, a coordinator may be able to negotiate a higher pay rate. This takes skill and experience, however, as handling this the wrong way can backfire quickly.

The same is true in cases when you are offered less than the job description indicated or less than your coordinator told you to expect. If this occurs, thank the employer for the offer, tell him or her that you need to talk to your coordinator before reaching a final decision, and contact your coordinator immediately. Perhaps the situation has changed, or the company simply has made a mistake. Either way, get your coordinator's advice before proceeding on your own.

If you're not sure what to do, contact your co-op or internship coordinator immediately.

It's hard to predict every dilemma that you may face when getting a job offer. But if in doubt, seek the advice of your coordinator. In some cases, a coordinator may be able to get a faster response from a second employer if you need to make a decision about an offer from a first employer. If it's a matter of being indecisive, your coordinator probably will not tell you what to do: Instead, she or he may try to help you walk through the different pros and cons of the offer or offers. In the end, though, it's your decision.

Follow up with ALL employers once you have made a decision.

After you have made a timely decision, make sure that you communicate that decision to EACH employer that is waiting to hear as well as to each co-op coordinator that you have worked with to obtain the job.

ALWAYS be polite when turning down a job offer.

Usually, people feel awkward when they have to turn down a job. This is understandable: Employers may be very disappointed to hear about your decision. But usually they are understanding if you are professional and gracious about it (see the sidebar box).

EXAMPLE: *"I just wanted to let you know that I decided to accept a job with another company. It was a tough decision: I just felt that this other job was a slightly better match for me in my current situation. But I do appreciate your offer, and I hope that you can find a good candidate for your position."*

Once you have accepted a job offer, you CANNOT go on other interviews or consider other job offers.

There are NO exceptions to this rule. Think of it this way: Accepting a job and continuing to interview is like getting engaged and continuing to go on dates. It doesn't make sense, and it's just plain wrong. Or, if you'd like to think of it another way, how about this: How would you feel if a company makes you an offer on November 1st, you accept the offer and stop pursuing other jobs; maybe you even turn down another good job or two. A week or two later, the company calls you up and tells you "Sorry, but somebody else came along who turned out to be a better candidate." Universities would not work with an employer who behaved in this way, and, likewise, career professionals will not work with you if you treat an employer in a similar way.

Declining A Job Offer – A Co-op Professional's Perspective
by Rose Dimarco

A student who was in her third year interviewed for a job and she got it, but she felt she was more compatible with a very different experience, so she turned it down. But she sent a thank-you note—even though she rejected the offer. She praised that employer—she did not want to burn that bridge.

It turned out that she eventually interviewed again with that employer. It was the same interviewer, and she remembered—very positively—that rejection. So she ended up with a second chance at the job.

Rose Dimarco is a cooperative education faculty coordinator in
Physical Therapy at Northeastern University.

That said, you absolutely SHOULD call back any employer who is interested in interviewing you, even after you have accepted a job. It's professional and courteous to follow up on any interview request, and it is not hard to get across the situation: "I wanted to thank you for your interest in interviewing me. However, I have accepted a position with another employer, so I am no longer available. But I do wish you luck in finding a good candidate, and I will keep you in mind for a future co-op job."

Once you have accepted the offer, make sure to see your co-op coordinator one last time.

Let your coordinator know as soon as you have a job lined up: That's why 24-hour voice mail exists. Your coordinator generally will ask you to come in to complete an agreement form and to go over success factors for your position.

DRUG TESTING

It's important to know that some employers make offers that are contingent upon the candidate's ability to pass a drug test successfully. Though many employers do not require this, drug testing is on the rise. Many large and prominent co-op employers require drug testing for all new hires. Eventually you're likely to encounter this issue.

Why do companies drug test? Generally, it's not a moral issue. People with substance abuse problems can be costly to organizations in terms of absenteeism, tardiness, and turnover. Companies don't want to invest time, money, and energy developing a co-op or new employee who may not prove to be a productive worker.

If you do use illegal drugs—or if you use any prescription drugs *without* having a prescription—you may have time to change your behaviors. Many companies now use hair tests to test for drug use—these tests are harder to fool than urine tests. These tests generally will reveal if you have regularly used drugs over the last three or four months. If you're a fall semester sophomore and stop using drugs now, you likely will be able to pass a drug test for a summer/fall job. If you don't want to limit your opportunities, you should consider this choice carefully.

In some fields, drug testing is not just a part of the hiring process—it's an ongoing part of being a professional employee. See the sidebar box below: It's a good example of a situation in which a couple of good students were wise enough to recognize that they'd better not interview for a position for this reason. These situations should lead you to think about lifestyle choices—unless using drugs illegally is more important to you than being eligible for many great opportunities.

In the past, I had a student get an offer for one of my very best positions—a job that offered an incredible learning experience as well as about $25/hour plus one week of paid vacation. The student failed the drug test because he had smoked marijuana within the last several months. He asked me if the company would let him retake the test in a few weeks—he really wanted the job. Of course, the drug test was a one-shot deal, and he missed out on the opportunity of a lifetime with that employer.

Drug Testing – A Co-op Professional's Perspective
by Bob Tillman

I'm spending a lot more time on drug testing now. Almost all of my field jobs now require random drug testing, and it doesn't happen when you first start, but it happens within a period of time at all of my municipalities. You can get pulled out for testing at any time because you're around heavy equipment. I had two of my best students come in and see me to tell me that they didn't want to interview at a place. One of them said to me, "Yeah, I have a lot of history in my hair."

Bob Tillman is an Associate Professor and cooperative education coordinator in
Civil and Environmental Engineering at Northeastern University.

FINAL THOUGHTS ON INTERVIEWING

Remember, you can't control many aspects of interviewing. You can worry about the quality of the interviewer or the caliber of the candidates who are competing for the job, but that won't change anything. Your goal should be to walk out of the interview feeling good because you did terrific research, employed a smart and thought-out strategy, answered questions honestly and enthusiastically, and asked thoughtful questions to wrap up the interview.

It's a terrific feeling to come out of an interview knowing you gave it your all. If, after that, another candidate gets the job because of superior experience, you should not have any regrets—especially because your effort will pay off for you in the future.

When I helped college students find co-op jobs and internships, we had a grad student working in co-op who applied for a position as a co-op coordinator. In terms of experience, she was ninth out of the nine among the interviewees. This didn't faze her: She interviewed co-op employers, academic faculty, and students, formulated a great strategy, and wowed the five-person committee. Afterwards, she came down and told me, "That was great. Whatever happens, I did exactly what I set out to do."

Did she get the job? Not quite—she was runner-up to someone with more job experience. But within a month another position opened up in the department, and committee members *urged* her to apply and *recommended* her to the chairman of that committee. She used the same approach to ready herself for that interview and completely blew the competition off the map to get the job.

One great fact is that it's remarkable how little the average person knows about interviewing. Even when hiring co-op faculty at Northeastern, I was often amazed at how poor some of the interviewees were. They asked questions that made it obvious that they didn't do one iota of research, and they clearly hadn't begun to think strategically about why they would be good for the job and how they would approach the position. And this for a job in which you must be able to teach students how to interview! In any event, if you can learn and apply the concepts in this chapter, you'll be far ahead of most interviewees.

Lastly, give some consideration to doing a practice interview. At the very least, stop and think about what interview questions you hate answering and why, then see if you can practice them with your coordinator. Reviewing your strategy for a specific interview is something that most coordinators can help you with if a practice interview is not possible. Most importantly do not assume that you have nothing left to learn about interviewing.

EMPLOYER ROUNDTABLE

What advice do you have about interviewing—whether before, during, or after the interview? Do you have any success stories or horror stories that are striking—either from people you've interviewed or from your own interviews?

The most important piece of advice I can offer is to understand that interviews are two-way interactions. Contrary to what you may think, you will not be judged solely on your ability to answer questions. The interviewer will want to know how excited you are at the prospect of working in his or her company. Nothing says that more than you asking questions. For every question you receive, ask one yourself. Remember that everyone likes to talk about him or herself. If you follow this one piece of advice, you will be in the top 1% of all interviewees.

Of course you want to do your homework before the interview. Now that we have the Web, there is no excuse for not arriving at the interview with a solid knowledge of the company. Now that you know that asking questions is a secret weapon, you can ask insightful questions about the company and your interviewer.

Dress for success. No interviewer that I know ever complained that a candidate came to an interview inappropriately dressed in a coat and tie or a business suit. Leave the jeans at home.

Here are some things you want to strenuously avoid:

1. Answering a simple question with a long-winded answer. If you can't answer a factually based question in 30 seconds or less you are an ineffective communicator.

2. Arriving late.

3. Asking about money. (You are an intern, and experience is more important than pay.)

4. Listing too many conditions of employment. If you are unavailable on Mondays because of class that's fine, but telling your interviewer that you have a band and you practice at 4 p.m. every day tells your prospective boss where your priorities are.

5. Being passive.

- Mark Spencer, President, Water Analytics

Even more important than your resume being a reflection of you, the interview is a time where the employer is attempting to get to know you as a person. If you want a job where you will be successful, answer questions truthfully instead of telling the interviewer what you think they want to hear. Spend some time before the interview thinking about and jotting down some of your past experiences in various areas. Interviewers want to hear about specific past experiences you have had, as those are the best predictors of future behavior. Do not exaggerate your experience in any area as doing so could land you a job that you do not have the necessary skills or experience for.

- Ryan P. Derber, SPHR, Segment Human Resources Manager,
PolyOne Corporation

One of the more difficult questions we ask of potential candidates that is hard to answer is: "Tell me about some experience you had that was a real disaster, and what you took away from that experience." Everyone makes mistakes. What separates a great employee from the pack is how they deal with the mistake, what they learn from it, and how it makes them and others they work with better.

- Dennis Tully, President, MTD Micro Molding

Be yourself. Whether the job is right or not right for you, you want it to come out that way. So, no need for nerves either.

- Dennis Burke, Senior R&D Engineer, Depuy Synthes, Johnson & Johnson

You are on the interview from the moment you make contact with a company. Your resume should be in the best condition possible—have someone critique it for spelling and grammar; it's a reflection of your work product. All of your correspondence, whether verbal or in writing, will be considered as you set up an interview, so be sure to conduct yourself professionally.

Arrive 10 minutes prior to your scheduled appointment—even if you have to sit in your car for a while! Arriving too early doesn't show you're eager for the job, it comes across as desperate. I once had a candidate arrive two full hours early; it was rather an inconvenience actually. Members of my firm felt they had to accommodate him and it was disruptive to their schedules.

You hear people say all the time "be prepared" and then a student will show up with obvious canned questions they pulled off the Internet. My advice is to go to the company's website and really find out who they are. Ask questions that interest YOU, not what you think will make you sound good. I like hearing questions like: "What would my responsibilities be?" "What type of training would I receive?" "What is it like to work here?" I've had students ask such complex business questions in the past that I've almost asked them if they really cared about the answer.

The interviewer knows you are entry level; don't try to interview like you are applying for the CEO position. The worst thing you can do is not to have questions and to say "I looked at your website; I have a pretty good understanding of who you are." Really? Last, asking about benefits is the same as asking "How much will you pay me...that is, if you *want* to hire me...." Save it for when they give you an offer. Be professional, be genuinely interested, ask questions, listen, engage in conversation...and say thank you, an e-mail would be fine!

- Donna DeRoche, PHR, Director of Human Resources,
MFA - Moody, Famiglietti & Andronico, LLP.

When interviewing for a new position, do everything within your power to make a lasting impression on the interviewer. Say something that is unique to yourself and will force the interviewer to immediately recall his or her interaction with you over the other candidates. More than likely, you will not be the only qualified candidate for a position; therefore it is critical that something about you stands out from the rest. Most employers will not care if your GPA is a tenth of a point higher than another candidate, but they will remember if you said something that intimately connected you to a position or a desire to work toward a specific goal that is relevant to their mission. Become familiar with a company and the available position before the interview and develop a cohesive answer to the question, "Why do you want this position and why do you want to work for us?"

- Christopher Thellen, PhD, Materials Engineer, U.S. Army NSRDEC

I have been recruiting UMass students since 2010. More recently, I have been working with Ms. Martina Witts and the Co-op program. This past spring, I interviewed several students. Students who participated in the co-op program were better prepared for the interview. From the interview attire to the type and amount of questions asked, there was a clear difference.

The co-op students arrived in business attire; they sat up straight in the chair, engaged in the conversation, asked probing questions about the job, and did ask when a decision would be made.

Students who apply for a position should at least view the company website prior to the interview. Often when asked "Did you review the website?", the glazed-eyed look is accompanied with, "I did not have an opportunity." Review the website, pick specific products or topics, and ask questions about that product or topic in the interview.

Good communication skills are important in all jobs and the interviewer is evaluating how well they communicate. Asking questions helps me evaluate the person's strengths as well as in what area(s) they may need assistance.

Of course, my all-time favorite pet peeve is when asked if they have any questions, they say "No." An employer wants to see an interest in the company and the position. Two-way communication during the interview gives both the candidate and the employer a way to learn about each other.

In today's competitive market, I am also often surprised at how few candidates send a handwritten thank-you note.

- Virginia Salem, Director of Customer Relations,
Applied Science Laboratories

I once had an interviewee ramble on for more than five minutes after each question I asked. (The minutes would have been longer if I hadn't intervened each time.) It was a very unfortunate situation, because on paper the applicant looked like a "rock star." My advice to you would be to keep your answers clear and concise. Know that most answers can be said in 60 seconds.

The most successful interviews I've conducted have been when the candidate came in professionally dressed, enthusiastic about the opportunity to share their knowledge, and passionate about their chosen profession. It was clear in the way they presented their answers, and it was clear in the way they prepared their questions to ask ahead of time. The Internet will only describe so much about a company, so coming up with thought-provoking questions will show you did some research and that you are not just there to interview for the position but are engaged in learning more about the company as well.

- Bethany Burpee, Talent Acquisition Specialist,
Freudenberg-NOK Sealing Technologies

A good portion of a successful interview will come from your preparation and how personable you appear to the interviewer. Preparation comes from getting some background in the company history and what products the company produces. Also, your appearance will play a factor, so dress to impress. You want to come off as someone who can communicate well. When they ask you about your hobbies or things you like to do, chat up the interviewer and try to connect. They don't want to hire someone who is just going to be at their cubicle or office all day and never converse with anyone else. That would not be a successful team player.

During my first internship, I learned one of the reasons I was hired was I did not "BS" them during my first interview when asked a tough technical question. I was complimented for saying, "I don't know." My interviewer said he has rarely heard that as an answer to a question when someone does not know the answer. Don't try to "BS" someone who already knows the answer to the question. Also for this same internship, I was asked to meet for a second interview when my interviewer was talking at a medical device conference at UMass Lowell. What I later learned was that the whole point of that second interview was to see what I wore and how I interacted with my classmates.

- Dan Meunier, Product/Process Engineer, NDH Medical, Inc.

STUDENT ROUNDTABLE

What advice do you have about interviewing—whether before, during, or after the interview? Do you have any success stories or horror stories that are striking—either from people you've interviewed or from your own interviews?

Always research the company and the position before interviewing. Be careful, though! Once I read a whole bunch of job descriptions for co-ops I was applying to. When I went in for my interview, I confused two of the positions!!!! They seemed really confused on why I was dwelling on certain skill sets. Whoops! I didn't get the first job I interviewed for, but luckily I learned my lesson and got a great job somewhere else.

- Mary Beth Moriarty, PhD Candidate, Plastics Engineering,
University of Massachusetts Lowell

Interview preparation is very important. Make sure you have done a lot of research on the company including any news that might have happened that week. If the company issues a big press release the day before your interview, you will want to make sure you are aware of the details and able to work it into the conversation.

In every interview I have ever had I have been asked some variation of the question "what is your biggest weakness?" This is a very tricky one as you want to keep the answer positive but not too cliché (employers see right through "I work too hard"). Thus far all of the jobs I have interviewed for were positions where I did not have direct experience with the responsibilities in the job description. Therefore, I was able to say that my weakness was my lack of direct experience but that I was a very fast learner and had complementary experiences that would allow me to excel in the role.

Try not to be nervous. Remember that the interviewer is a regular person that has been through interviews many times themselves. Although you want to spend a lot of time preparing before the interview, once you are there you should try to think of it as a regular conversation. If you use too many responses that were pre-planned word-by-word you might come off as fake or someone who can't handle being put on the spot. The best advice I ever got was: Remember that no one in the world knows you as well as you know yourself. You are the expert in your past experiences and future career goals. Just be yourself and you will be successful.

Don't forget that you are interviewing the company as much as they are interviewing you. Make sure you have a list of questions that you genuinely care to learn the answer. Make sure you leave the interview knowing if you want to work for the company. Just because you are offered a position does not mean you have to accept.

ALWAYS send a thank-you e-mail after the interview and make sure to include a personal detail from the interview. Try to remember to ask for a business card from each person you meet with so you have their e-mail address easily accessible. If you forget, or they do not have one, it's okay to e-mail the HR recruiter you are working with and ask if they can forward the e-mail address for the person you interviewed with that day. Two mistakes that I have seen recently and must be avoided are: misspelling the person's name you met, and leaving the "sent from iPhone/Blackberry/etc." message at the bottom of the e-mail. Many people use their phones today for sending e-mails, but calling attention to that fact makes the employer think you couldn't take the time to sit down at a computer and write a thoughtful thank you e-mail.

- Rebecca Harkess was a Business Administration/Supply Chain major at Northeastern University, Class of 2009. She is now a Supply Planner at Keurig.

You could call my story "frustrating" rather than "horror." I was interviewed and rejected by six companies before I received a co-op offer. You can shake off one or two rejections, maybe even three, but four...five...six! I was starting to become extremely frustrated; my resume obviously wasn't the problem, and no colleague or potential employer could pinpoint any one particular attribute that was wrong about me during my interviews. It was always the same story, different day, "You did great, but we have decided to go with another candidate."

So what was I to do? "Always the bridesmaid never the bride" was how they described me in the career services department at UMass Lowell. Then there was lucky number 7, my first job offer and, wouldn't you know it, another one from number 8. So just like that I went from having zero options to two options. But what changed? I didn't change my resume, the answers I gave, or the questions I asked: I changed my mentality. I relaxed.

Before, during, and after: RELAX! You are entry level; no one is expecting you to be a hero. On paper, you're almost identical to your peers and competition. One detail on your resume separated you from the pack, putting you in this room. It's in this room where you have to convey you fit within this organization. The person across the table sees you as an investment opportunity. Why? Because you're not a full-time hire, you're a co-op. At the end of the co-op, you and company xyz can part—with no long-term consequences. On the other hand, they can train you, groom you, and fast track you to full-time employment, which is what they're looking to accomplish.

Again, you're entry level, you do not know everything and that's okay. It's you they're interested in—your personality and your potential. Answer each question confidently and more importantly, ask smart questions. They have a position to fill, and you're seeking a job to accept. They need to impress you just as much as you need to impress them.

- Jared Peraner, Market Development Specialist,
Consumer & Electronics, Nypro Inc.;
BS, Plastics Engineering, 2012, University of Massachusetts Lowell

The advice that I hope everyone takes to heart is not to limit yourself. You need to believe that you are great and that every employer should hire you. So often, people read a job description and decide that it doesn't seem perfect or that it may be a reach for their experience level—so they discount the opportunity. I try to look at the job description and think, "*Does this sound like something that I would like to do?*" By changing the mindset from 'whether they want me' to 'whether I want to do it,' I am leaving doors open that may pay off the most. The worst thing that you can get from applying for a job that is a reach is that you simply don't get an interview, and is that really so bad? Conversely, the best thing that can happen from applying for easier looking jobs is that you receive multiple job offers.

In the two co-ops I have had, the job description and the work I have actually done were different. It isn't that I wasn't doing what I signed up for. The employers just tailored what I was doing to my strengths and interests. I ended up applying for a job that I didn't think I was qualified for, and they hired two people for the position and split up the description in half to suit our strengths. The second co-op that I took actually had a very basic and general job description that didn't seem like a challenge on paper. But they hired me for my experience, and my learning objectives ended up being much more intensive and specific. I had the opportunity to challenge myself every single day and create my own opportunities.

I remember thinking when I applied for both of the co-ops I was hired for that I wasn't the ideal candidate. I decided to apply and address any objections that my resume may have in the cover letter. This changed the whole tone of the interview because I answered all of the obvious reasons about why they might not hire me before I even met them. So, we talked more about what I have done in past jobs and what this job really means to the employer. I always saved my best question for last: "What are the measurements that determine my success in the position?" This leaves a lasting impression that I want to succeed and I am already thinking of how to do it.

> *- Matthew Johnson, Business Administration, Manning School of Business,*
> *University of Massachusetts Lowell*

DO RESEARCH on the company's website and take notes to bring with you to your interview. Also prepare questions! Two or three questions are not enough; try to prepare at least a page.

I went into one interview with about five questions prepared and a lot of research notes. I was feeling pretty ready until the interview started, and the interviewer did not ask me one question about myself other than my name. The entire meeting consisted of the interviewer asking me if I had any questions, then answering my questions and repeating the process! Needless to say my five questions ran out very quickly and I had to think on my feet for the rest of the interview, which was very nerve-wracking. Eventually I ran out of questions and she seemed satisfied, but I felt like I had messed up the whole thing. She ended up offering me the job a few weeks later, but it could have gone much worse.

Always keep eye contact and actually listen. When you let your attention slip to other things you don't look intelligent and you can't answer questions. Also, don't spend the entire conversation thinking of responses to what they're saying instead of actually listening to them talk.

- Samantha Hamel, Business Administration, Manning School of Business,
University of Massachusetts Lowell

CHAPTER THREE REVIEW QUESTIONS

1. If you were researching in preparation for an interview, what are two ways in which you can go beyond the job description to learn more about the job and the organization?

2. Which statement most appropriately captures how to approach an interview?

   A. Be able to summarize your strengths as an individual.
   B. More than anything, be sure to tell the interviewer what he or she hopes to hear.
   C. Try to just relax and be yourself—don't get too worked up about it.
   D. Try to make connections between your background and the job description.
   E. Be sure to give the interviewer plenty of personal background about yourself.

3. Think about the kind of job that you hope to get through your next search: For that job, how you would answer a question about your weaknesses?

4. What does the chapter describe as the most difficult type of interviewer for most interviewees?

   A. The Nonstop Talker
   B. The Silent But Deadly Interviewer
   C. The Olympic Judge
   D. The Big-Picture Person
   E. The Interrogator

5. Write a brief but effective thank-you note that would be appropriate to send to an interviewer as a follow-up step.

6. Name at least two great questions to ask at the end of any job interview.

CHAPTER FOUR
Keys To On-The-Job Success

By the time you have prepared your resume, gone on numerous interviews, and finally accepted a job offer from an employer, you may feel like it's time to kick back and relax and let the money come in from your job. However, nothing could be further from the truth: Accepting a job offer doesn't mean you've reached the end of all your hard work. All it means is that you've reached the end of the beginning.

When you have accepted a job, you need to start thinking about living up to your interview... and then some. In other words, anyone can walk into an interview and state that they are punctual, conscientious, hard-working, willing to learn, and happy to help out with some of the less glamorous tasks associated with a job. But it's very different to actually go out and live up to these statements all day, every day, for three months, six months, or longer.

The goal in this chapter is to point out why your performance matters in your first professional job, and to help you get the best possible evaluation from your co-op employer or internship supervisor when it's time to go back to school. Some of the points we make here may seem like common sense, but we have learned that sense can be rather uncommon when it comes to some behaviors in the workplace. If you follow the guidelines in this chapter, you can prevent most co-op problems before they happen... which is infinitely easier than trying to fix something after it breaks.

WHY YOUR PERFORMANCE MATTERS

The best interns and co-op students realize that there is a great deal at stake when you're working in a job. An "outstanding" or "very good" evaluation from an employer means that:

- *You are a person of integrity who remembers your interview and delivers what you said you could deliver.* You come off as a hypocrite if you say that you are punctual, for example, and you start showing up late to work. Right away, the employer might start wondering what *else* might not be exactly true in what you said in your interview.

- *You are intelligent enough to realize that today's supervisor is tomorrow's reference.* Think about interviewing for a future job: It's nice to say "I'm an excellent worker with a great attitude," but it's highly effective and powerful to be able to say "I'm an excellent worker with a great attitude, and I would encourage you to contact my previous employer if you'd like to confirm this." Some employers may even call your previous employer without telling you: You don't want bad performance to come back and haunt you when seeking future employment.

- *If you are asked about a previous job in an interview, you want to be able to say in all honesty that you did a great job.* Interviewers can often tell how successful you were in a previous job by how you describe it. A common interview question is "If I were to ask your previous supervisor about what kind of employee you were, what would he or she say?" You have to be honest in these situations, and you want to be able to mention many positives.

- *You can feel good about yourself.* It's a lot more fun to do things well than to do things poorly. If you can complete your job with a sense of pride and accomplishment, you will have more confidence and will be better prepared for challenging jobs in the future.

- *You'll learn more and get better work to do.* The harder you work—the more you go "above and beyond" the basic requirements of the job, the more likely you are to learn more and gain valuable exposure to more sophisticated aspects of your field. You'll also show your employer that you're capable of handling bigger and better challenges.

The last point merits some more consideration. I always tell my students that there is often a domino effect while on co-op. When you first start work, you may be given low-level work to do. This is rarely because supervisors believe that you're an idiot until you prove otherwise, so don't look at it that way. Rather, employers know that it's difficult to be a new employee, so they want to make sure that you feel comfortable in the early going by giving you work that will be relatively easy.

What happens next? That depends! If you get those simple tasks done efficiently, effectively, and with a positive attitude, eventually this tends to get noticed... and your manager may start giving you better work to do, tasks that weren't even on your job description.

Of course, this domino effect works the other way occasionally. Several years ago, I visited two co-op students at work. When I met with them, they were irritated: "This is a terrible job," they said. "There's nothing to do; they just give us data entry work that anyone could do. This should not be a co-op job."

This surprised me. Many students had worked for this employer before, and the verdict had been that it was a good job. Yes, there was some downtime, but you were allowed to use that time to teach yourself computer skills using resources that the supervisor made available to you. Of course, some good jobs do turn bad, so I approached the supervisor with an open mind. "How's it going with the co-ops?" I asked. He looked at me and shook his head. "I wish we could get these two to *do* something!"

At first glance, this seemed as if it would be an easy problem to solve: Here we had two bored co-ops with nothing to do and a manager who was itching to get them to work. Naturally, it wasn't that easy. It turned out that these two co-ops were *insulted* by the low-level tasks that they initially were given. How did they respond? They did the work slowly and poorly, so the manager assumed that they weren't able or willing to handle anything more challenging. He continued to give them grunt work, and their performance never improved.

Admittedly, maintaining a strong work ethic and an excellent attitude can be challenging in some work environments. When you go on co-op, you're testing out a field as a possible career. As such, you may learn that you don't want to be an accountant or a computer programmer. That's fine, but bear in mind the following: A mediocre co-op can do a great job in a job that she or he loves, but a great co-op continues to do a great job *even after realizing that he or she is working in the wrong field.*

Sometimes you probably will be asked to do work that is less fun, less interesting, and less educational than you had hoped. In fact, one unpleasant fact you have to accept is that almost *any* job you will ever have may require you to do some things that you don't enjoy. But if you can take on *all* work assignments with a pleasant and cooperative attitude, your employer will remember this and often will reward you with better assignments as well as an excellent evaluation.

I have seen first-time co-ops take what seemed to be an entry-level job, only to have them end up making presentations to senior management by the end of their work term! You never know what doors might open to you if you do a terrific job on whatever you're asked to do.

MAKING THE TRANSITION FROM STUDENT TO EMPLOYEE

Don't underestimate the fact that you're undergoing a significant transition when you go from being a full-time student to being a full-time employee. If you're in a parallel program like the new one at DePaul University—working as a co-op while simultaneously attending classes—you will be continually making the transition from your role as student to your role as employee. In either type of format, it's useful to give some thought to these role changes.

As indicated in the sidebar box below, when you're a student, you're a customer of your college or university. You have a right to expect some level of customer service. You also may believe that you have every right to be late to class: After all, it's your money. Likewise, the student lifestyle can be quite different for some individuals. I'm sure that some of my students were staying up till 2 or 3 a.m. more often than not, waking up at the last minute to make a mad dash to their 8 a.m. class, or maybe sleeping through it.

Your role becomes more complicated when you're a co-op. Yes, you're still a student and a customer of the university, but that role is trumped by your most important role: You are an employee and a service provider to your employer. This should be obvious when you're drawing a paycheck, but it's also the attitude that you need to take into an unpaid internship or co-op.

Think about the implications of the fact that your supervisor is your customer. It means that you need to figure out what you must do to be sure that you're not only showing up but that you're arriving rested, alert, and ready to put in a full day's work of good quality.

Another way to think of the transition is an analogy to running: The classroom is more of a sprint, while a co-op job is more of a marathon. In the classroom, you may be able to be very successful with periodic bursts of effort at the right time. On co-op, the individuals who do best are those who are able to sustain a consistent effort for several hours, weeks, and months.

When I worked as a cooperative education coordinator, I had a student with a 4.0 GPA who was fired from her job, and I have seen many other top academic performers fail. Likewise, there have been many co-op superstars whose GPAs were in the 2.0 to 2.4 range. Once you get your co-op job or internship, you have a clean slate... but you also will have to prove yourself day in and day out. Remembering that the employer is your customer and acting accordingly should help you make this transition effectively.

THE FIRST DAY OF WORK

On your first day of work, you'll probably be excited, nervous, and eager to show that you can be a productive employee. This is perfectly normal. However, bear in mind that few workers—whether co-op or otherwise—can be immediate heroes. Be patient. If you're introduced to people, do your best to come across as positive and agreeable. You're going to want to have good relationships with many people besides your supervisor, and you can cultivate those relationships by making an effort to be friendly. This may include going out to lunch with people even if you'd rather be working, and it definitely includes saying "Good Morning" and "Good Night" at the start and end of the day.

You also may have an orientation or training session to attend. Even though you might be dying to dive into the job itself, take advantage of these sessions. They can help you get acclimated and learn what it may take to be successful in that environment. You'll have plenty of time to work before you know it.

UNCOMMON SENSE: WHAT IS AND ISN'T ACCEPTABLE IN THE WORKPLACE

As stated earlier, there are many aspects of work life that internship and co-op coordinators would *like* to believe are common sense: Things that everyone should know without being told. However, we have found that this is not always the case. As a result, here are some critical recommendations regarding how to avoid problems in the workplace. Some may appear obvious; others are less so. HOWEVER, no one should have to *tell* you these things once you have started your job. It is your responsibility to know these things ahead of time!

1. You must be on time to work.

After you have accepted your offer, be very clear about what time you are expected at work. Then make sure you are *always* there at least 15 minutes before that time.

When you become a co-op, intern, or full-time employee, you undergo a tremendous role reversal (see the following sidebar box). As a student, some people may be used to showing up late to classes. This is a bad habit, but you could argue that you're the customer: You have the right to not show up on time for classes. However, when an employer is paying *you* to arrive at a specific time and to work a specific number of hours, you do *not* have that right. Unless an employer specifically tells you that you can come in when you want to, you have to live by that employer's rules. For example, you can't just decide that you'll come in 30 minutes late and then eat your lunch at your desk instead of taking a 30-minute break at noontime.

From Student To Employee – A Co-op Professional's Perspective
by Bob Tillman

When you're a student, you pay the university for services in your role as a student. What are you paying for, and what do you expect to get out of it? How do you know that you're getting what you're paying for? What are the other amenities that you're paying for? It's a good exercise to think about that. Then I tell them that when you go out on co-op, that role will exactly reverse itself. You're being paid for your services now. So let's talk about some of the behaviors that don't work from your perspective as a student: Why do you think they would work as an employee as a part of an engineering team?

Students tend to connect with that pretty well. I want you to shift that role and almost forget that you're a student because it really will bring you down. For example, why do you have to show up on time? Well, if you don't, other work is not getting done; clients aren't getting billed. Let's talk about clients getting the bill, and what that means, as well as all the other people that fit into an engineering environment.

Bob Tillman is an Associate Professor and cooperative education faculty coordinator in Civil and Environmental Engineering at Northeastern University.

Another point to remember is that too many interns and co-op students fail to leave any extra time in the morning to allow for possible traffic, parking problems, car trouble, or whatever. If it takes you 25 minutes to get to work, assuming that you catch every train or traffic light just right, then you probably should allow for at least 45 minutes to get to work. If you have to use this kind of excuse more than once over a six-month job, you need to change your habits: These excuses get old very quickly.

Lastly, remember one critical point: *Just because your co-workers arrive late, don't automatically assume that it's okay for you to do the same.* I recall one memorable student who had been given a warning by his employer because of repeated tardiness. His boss also told me that he sometimes came in by 9 but other times it was more like 10. When I talked to the co-op student about it, he thought that he was being unfairly singled out: "I see quite a few full-time people coming in at 10 or 10:30 every day!"

When I looked into this, it turned out that my student was missing a few key facts: For one, he didn't know that these people were software developers. They had an understanding with management that they could come in late because they often stayed until 8:00 or 9:00 p.m. at night, well after my student left at 5:30! Secondly, the student had misinterpreted something his manager had told him when he was hired. When she said that it was possible to have a "flexible schedule," she meant that you could work from 7:30 to 4:30 with an hour for lunch, from 9 to 6 with an hour for lunch, etc. She did NOT mean that you could change your schedule every day, or that you could start your day later than 9:30. Lastly, I had to tell the student that sometimes policies are not always fair. Sure, the manager could have done a better job upfront about communicating the "unwritten rules" of that workplace, but she didn't. That simply means that the student needed to step up and be sure that his assumptions were correct.

2. If being late or absent is absolutely unavoidable, give your employer as much advance notice as possible.

There may be rare situations in which being late or absent is absolutely unavoidable. These primarily include car accidents, serious illnesses, or deaths in your family. These things can't be avoided at times. However, you need to call your employer *before* the official workday begins. That may mean leaving a voice mail or answering machine message early in the morning before you show up: not in the late morning or afternoon, when everyone has already been wondering where you are for several hours. If you have a flat tire on the way to work, for example, you need to find the nearest possible phone so you can call in and give your estimated time of arrival. Always carry your supervisor's phone number in your wallet just in case something like this happens.

Unless you are completely incapacitated through illness or injury, YOU should be the one to call in: not your roommate, your mother, your roommate's boyfriend's sister's cousin, or anyone else. And if you don't say how long you will need to be out, and you remain sick or otherwise unavailable the next day, you need to call your supervisor *again*.

3. Keep smart phone use to an absolute minimum.

Over the last several years, smart phones have become ubiquitous. As you have undoubtedly noticed, many people don't hesitate to use their smart phones in any place, under most any circumstance. This includes while walking down a busy street, in classrooms during a lecture, and even in restrooms! According to a former colleague in cooperative education, recently he's had to address this issue with a couple of his students who each cluelessly pulled out their phones to check their text messages during an interview! This is an obvious mistake!

Co-op Job Success – A Student's Perspective
by Ted Schneider

- Meet as many people in your workplace as you can. And I do not mean this in only the superficial, "networking" type of way. If your co-workers are willing, do social things with them outside of work. I found that working closely with good friends on co-op was not at all distracting. I actually think that I performed much better when I worked for people who I liked and respected.

- An old one but still so true: Do not ever go to work late if you can help it. I knew people on co-op who were very good at what they did, but would fail to be promoted due to their tardiness. I also find that managers are much more flexible about giving time off if you are on time in the morning.

- Wear the right clothes. Wearing questionable or even semi-questionable attire makes you look like a fool. Enough said.

- Make sure to find a balance between asking for too much help and asking for too little. It's a difficult skill to master - I certainly haven't yet.

Ted Schneider was an Accounting/MIS student at Northeastern University, Class of 2002.

You may even have seen news reports of unsuspecting texters who have walked into parking meters or found themselves careening down an open sewer grate. Don't let this be metaphorical for mistakes you can make on the job! The consequences of using these devices are not limited to tripping on curbs or colliding with an oncoming pedestrian. The problems caused by split attention can also lead to embarrassing slips in the workplace; but these slips don't leave you with a twisted ankle but rather a drastic decline in the quality of your work. When the human brain tries to do too many things at once, efficiency decreases. We like to *think* that we can multitask, but, if you think about it, no one can do more than one thing at a time. And when we try to alternate our focus between several things at once, our efficiency will suffer.

It's important to remember that when you are on company time, you owe it to your employer to give your work your full attention. Don't be a "smart phone zombie," and unless you specifically need to use your phone for job-related purposes—which is not uncommon with PC support jobs, for example—you generally should turn it off before you walk in the door at work and keep it off until the end of the day. Save your personal communications for your lunch break, or better yet, for after work hours. If you absolutely must make a personal call during work hours, watch what you say—even during your lunch break. Most office spaces are open with little privacy. Some employers have accidentally overheard co-op students say the darndest things (e.g., "personal" comments from boyfriend to girlfriend or vice-versa) when the student/caller thinks no one is listening.

Many people have their phones programmed with personalized ringtones, and they often make a variety of sounds to indicate that they receive texts, tweets, e-mails, etc. Remember to turn these off while you're at work since they can be disruptive to those around you. Likewise, some smart phones are set up so that texts, tweets, and photos appear on the screen immediately when they are received. I once had a student who left his smart phone on his desk when an embarrassing picture and caption popped up. Unfortunately, and much to his mortification, his boss and another colleague were standing over his desk at the time.

141

Remember when you are on the job, it is best to "cut the cord," so to speak, and leave your phone off and out of sight.

The same rules apply in the office if you have your own phone at your desk; do not use it to have extended conversations with friends, family, and significant others throughout the workday. One good way to avoid temptation is to not share your work number with anyone besides your parents, your spouse or partner (if applicable), and your co-op coordinator. If you do need to make a five-minute phone call once or twice a week to contact your physician, cooperative education/internship coordinator, a family member in the event of an emergency, or to arrange for plans after work, that probably would be acceptable in most workplaces. But generally, you should avoid it whenever possible.

4. Use your computer for work-related activities only.

Like a telephone, a computer on your desk can be highly tempting to some interns, co-ops, and full-time employees. Most computers have at least some games, and more and more computers have Internet access, which can be an irresistible on-line temptation to some—especially those with e-mails accounts through Gmail, Yahoo, or Hotmail. More recently text messaging has become the communication method of choice for many people—many students are glued to their smart phones almost around the clock, so it's a habit that can be hard to break when you're starting a job. However, it's very important to do so. If you want to juggle doing homework with e-mailing and texting your friends for hours on end, that's up to you. But when you're role has changed from student to employee, and you're generally being paid to be at work, you shouldn't be using personal e-mail or texting on company time. You aren't being paid to take care of personal business or chat with friends, after all. Even in an unpaid internship, this sends the wrong message to your co-workers and supervisor.

Unless your supervisor tells you that it's okay for you to explore the Internet as part of your job, you should avoid using it. If you really want the opportunity to play around on the Web, you could ask your supervisor if it would be okay to come in early or stay late in order to navigate the Internet or send e-mails with a clear conscience.

Instant Messaging at Work – A Co-op Professional's Perspective
by Sandhya Balasubramanian

Instant Messaging at the workplace is fast becoming the norm for communicating among team members. Students familiar with IM and texting as a way of life can oftentimes perceive workplace IM as casual conversations. The truth is that they would need to approach these quick exchanges also as a medium of professional communication. While on co-op, students often work in cross-generational teams and need to use prudence based on the person with whom they are exchanging messages. Though poor IM etiquette may not cost students their co-op job, good IM manners can certainly validate their professional preparation!

Sandhya Balasubramanian, MBA, GCDF, is an Assistant Director of Cooperative Education in Sciences at University of Massachusetts Lowell.

I heard of several students getting fired from co-op jobs a few summers ago, primarily because of using the Internet frequently and spending a great deal of time writing e-mail to friends during the work day. In late 2006, a colleague of mine had had her first—but probably not last—students fired for managing their fantasy football teams on their work computers. Try explaining that to a future employer. Believe it or not it's relatively easy for a computer network administrator to be able to see what applications anyone on the system has open, and it is completely legal and easy for organizations to monitor the e-mails that their employers send and receive to determine whether they are appropriate. Entertaining yourself on the computer during work hours certainly doesn't say very much about your initiative, drive, and judgment. Don't take chances—surf the 'net and text when you're "off the clock" at home or on campus!

Refrain from using any technological activity that is not work-related. Even if no one sees you doing it, I guarantee that your decreased level of productivity will be noticed eventually if you're unable to curb your technology addiction at work.

I will discuss the specifics of professional e-mail etiquette later in this chapter.

Although this behavior is not excusable, these problems are most likely to arise when there is not enough work to do in a given job. Therefore, we will address that next.

5. If you don't have enough work to keep you busy, talk to your supervisor as soon as possible.

If your supervisor needs to come around and see you playing a game, staring at the ceiling, or talking on the phone in order to find out that you don't have enough work, you already have made a significant mistake. If you anticipate running out of work, try to give your supervisor as much notice as possible. It's perfectly fine to ask your supervisor what you should do if you run out of work: Especially if your supervisor isn't always readily available. Asking for more work when necessary shows that you are mature, that you take initiative, and that you have a good work ethic. All of these things reflect positively on you as an employee. Basically, *learn* from your work environment. Something ALWAYS needs to be done. Be proactive. Say something like, "I've finished 'X'; should I move onto 'Y'?" Your supervisor may be too busy to find a project for you and may be appreciative if you offer suggestions.

One challenge with such a conversation is to make sure that you don't come across as a whiner. Even if you're bored because of a lack of work, it probably won't be productive to go in to your supervisor and say, "I'm bored; I have nothing to do." Try to frame it positively by emphasizing your ability and willingness to take on more challenges on top of your current responsibilities.

As noted earlier, many first-time professionals have begun a job with relatively low-level responsibilities but managed to end up with much more demanding jobs—simply by getting the easy stuff done quickly and correctly and then enthusiastically requesting more work to do. Show that you're hungry for a challenge.

6. If you consistently have MORE work than you can do and do well, you should discuss this with your supervisor.

Most good jobs will keep you very busy all day and all week. But if you find that you are working so hard that it is affecting the quality of your work, your health, and your enthusiasm for the job, you need to discuss this with your supervisor *before* it becomes a major problem.

Obviously, the best way to deal with this problem is to avoid these situations in the first place by using your interview to ask the appropriate questions about workload and expectations. But you can't always anticipate this problem. If talking to your supervisor doesn't improve the situation—or if you're unsure about whether you really are being asked to do more than what could be considered reasonable—call your co-op coordinator and get his or her input. Together, you can determine the best course of action.

7. If you're confused or unsure about how to do one of your assigned tasks, say so. When you are assigned a task or given specific instructions, take careful notes so you won't have to request the same information again.

The worst thing you can do if you're unsure about how to do a task is to just forge ahead and hope for the best. Usually, people are reluctant to ask questions because they are afraid of appearing stupid or ignorant. But remember: appearing ignorant is MUCH better than demonstrating your ignorance by doing your job poorly. Making mistakes on the job can be very costly to a company. Good employers expect you to ask for help when you need it to avoid these costly mistakes. Don't be afraid to ask a supervisor or co-worker to repeat or clarify instructions if you didn't understand the first time.

From Student To Employee – A Co-op Professional's Perspective
by Bob Tillman

I tell students that if you only learn two things when you go out on your first co-op, it's going to be a huge success: If you learn when to ask a question when you should, and when to keep your mouth shut when you should, you're really light years ahead. When you figure out, "This is a problem that I ought to be able to solve on my own" and know "What are the resources that are going to help me do it?" you're way ahead.

Another thing you learn out there is that there's a whole language out there that you haven't been exposed to, and you have to learn it. And the last thing is, "What are the other learning opportunities that are going on around you that aren't directly sitting on your desk?"

In engineering, if you can't do the routine work—checking calculations, adding numbers, checking drawings—you're never going to get more advanced work.

Bob Tillman is an Associate Professor and cooperative education faculty coordinator in Civil and Environmental Engineering at Northeastern University.

A corresponding point relates to what you do with information or instructions when given to you. A smart employee shows up on the first day of work with a calendar for marking down due dates, deadlines, and meetings. A smart employee also brings a notebook and some writing materials so he or she can jot down specific instructions, guidelines, job requirements, computer procedures, and anything else you need to know. Nothing frustrates an employer more than a student who claims that he or she doesn't need to write things down, and then winds up making mistakes or sheepishly asking for the same information sometime in the future.

8. Always keep your desk and/or work area reasonably neat and well organized.

This means keeping food and drink to a minimum in your work area. Keeping some mints or granola bars in your desk and a coffee cup on your desk is okay, but leaving food wrappers or food in plain sight at any time other than lunch is something to avoid.

Also try to keep items on your desk well organized. If asked to produce some paperwork, you shouldn't have to do a scavenger hunt in your desk or office to find it. If you're unsure about ways to organize your work materials efficiently, ask your co-workers for advice.

Co-op Job Success – A Student's Perspective
by Mark Moccia

In order to get the most out of your job, you must bring a strong work ethic to the table. Once your employer sees you are willing to work hard, they will be impressed. Then, after you have shown the ability to work hard, you can polish your "working smart" skills: By this I mean getting things done quickly AND more efficiently for the company/department.

It is also important to learn the preferences/personality of your boss immediately. It is important to know whether your boss is the type that wants assignments done in five minutes or 30 minutes. A question I still ask to this day is, "When do you want this done by?" This avoids any confusion as to when you are supposed to finish an assignment and also avoids potential conflicts.

Speaking of conflicts, if you encounter one at work then it is important to alert your immediate supervisor. While fellow co-op students might lend an ear to your problems, they might not always have the best solution because they are just as inexperienced as you. If the conflict is with your supervisor, bring it to the attention of your co-op advisor quickly. I have heard stories of co-op students who feel invincible because they are only on assignment for three or six months and imagine that the company cannot fire them because it would look bad for the company. This could not be further from the truth; if you have direct conflicts with your supervisor or are not performing to your potential, you can be fired just as easily as a full-time employee. I encourage co-op students to use their best judgment in these situations and avoid "blow-ups" at all costs. If you can do this, work hard, and bring a positive contribution to your time on the job, a good reference and evaluation will follow.

Mark Moccia was an Accounting/MIS student at Northeastern University, Class of 2002.

---

9. Always use good judgment regarding attire and hygiene in the workplace.

You need to convey a professional image every single day that you are employed. The standards may differ from one workplace to another: Some places allow "business casual" attire, for example. But be careful in how you interpret dress codes. Casual attire generally still means that you should wear a collared shirt and nice pants: not blue jeans or shorts. Sometimes you can get away with dressy black sneakers, but not always white sneakers. Women should avoid low-cut blouses, halter tops, and tank tops. Open-toed shoes or sandals are a bad idea for men and may or may not be okay for women, depending on the particular office. You should always wear clothing that is clean, wrinkle-free, and without any holes in it. For men in casual environments, you should still shave each day. It's not a bad idea to look at how your co-workers dress, but you want to err on the conservative side— don't assume it's okay to dress a certain way just because one or two co-workers choose to wear extremely informal attire at work!

Another point here: You may think nothing of wearing an eyebrow ring or a nose ring or a tongue stud, but an employer may find these items to be unprofessional. Save your unusual jewelry for after-hours and weekends.

10. Don't misunderstand the meaning of the words "casual work environment."

As stated above, you may be able to wear more comfortable and informal clothing in some work settings. But don't think that "a casual work environment" means that *everything* is casual. Just because the company president wears jeans and jokes around with you when he or she visits your desk or cubicle, it doesn't mean that it's okay for *you* to pop into his office and joke around with him or her. Likewise, a casual work setting is not a place where work is done in a casual, laid-back manner. In fact, there are many very intense organizations that allow casual attire. Remember, casual work environments are just like all other jobs in one important way: You still can get a poor evaluation or get fired by not living up to your interview and by not living up to the company's expectations and standards.

Another point about casual environments: It is *never* acceptable to wear headphones in any workplace unless your boss specifically *suggests* it. This is true regardless even if you are working on your own, doing boring, monotonous work. Wearing headphones on a job sends a clear message that you're not really paying attention to what you're doing and that you don't care if you look unprofessional. Even if co-workers wear headphones, don't make the same mistake.

Co-op Job Success – An Employer's Perspective
by Steve Sim

There are two things to keep in mind when coming for an internship/co-op at Microsoft:

* Know your limitations. This is a fact at MS. There will always be someone who knows more about business, technology, marketing; etc. than you here (especially technology). Knowing your limitations also makes you aware of how these people can help in your development.

* Don't be afraid to fail. You're here to learn about how we do things. MS is a place where we do things, if anything, for the right to learn how to do that thing better. You'll always be challenged to do something right the first time, and possibly, you do it right the first time. Or did you? Have you tried <u>everything</u> possible? Who's to know that better than you?

Steve Sim was a Technical Recruiter at the Microsoft Corporation and is now Co-Founder & Principal Search Consultant at Envisage Recruiting LLC..

---

11. When asked to do something that you don't enjoy, do so without complaining or sulking.

I visited one employer who was Director of MIS for a prestigious organization in Cambridge, MA. He mentioned that a co-op student from another university complained when he was told to do a fairly monotonous and time-consuming task with the computer system. The employer told me, "The thing that I asked him to do is something that I have to do pretty often, and I'm the Director of the whole department! And he tells me that he shouldn't have to do it?"

There's a valuable lesson here: Sometimes students are quick to assume that they are given boring tasks to do because they are "only students." This can be an erroneous assumption at times. Sometimes, you may be asked to do something simply because it has to get done, and it doesn't matter who does it. Employers appreciate *any* employee who does routine, unglamorous, necessary tasks without complaining, whining, or sulking.

If an employer asks you if you enjoy doing a certain task, be honest but be pleasant about it. If you don't like doing a given task, you might say, "Well I don't mind doing it, but it's not my favorite part of the job..." Be ready to point out some other tasks that you would be excited about doing.

12. Go above and beyond your basic duties.

One reason some students fail to get great job evaluations is because they basically show up at 9, do their job in a competent, acceptable way, and go home as soon as possible. If you want to get a very good evaluation, you need to go beyond this. You need to be willing to put in extra hours if necessary. You need to show some pride and excitement in what you do: If you're asked to do something, give them even more than they expect in terms of effort, ideas, and attitude. Always think about ways in which you could do your job more efficiently, whether it involves helping your supervisor, your co-workers, or just the tasks you do on your own. The following sidebar box is a great example of this phenomenon.

Above and Beyond – A Co-op Professional's Perspective
by Ronnie Porter

We had this co-op job that on paper didn't look very exciting. It was doing some computer work for a company that manufactured an instrument that allowed anaesthesiologists to know if a patient undergoing surgery was getting to a level of wakefulness. So there was a lot of data entry—looking at the data, reviewing the data, etc.

What this person ended up doing was taking this information and learning a tremendous amount about what kinds of drugs were used on what kinds of patients for what kinds of surgeries. He really came to understand the sleep patterns and how all that interrelated. He actually had so many conversations with his co-workers that he got to go to an open-heart surgery and witness an eight-hour surgery along with the person who was teaching the anaesthesiologist how to use this device. He came back and said, "You need to rewrite this job description! It's the most exciting position, and there are so many things you can learn in this job. I didn't really realize that, looking on the surface."

Ronnie Porter is a cooperative education faculty coordinator in
Biology at Northeastern University.

---

13. Understand what an employer's expectations are regarding time off from work.

Before you begin any job, you should make sure you have total clarity regarding your start date and end date as well as time off from work. In many cases, co-ops and interns—or full-time hires for their first six months on the job—have NO vacation time coming to them! So don't assume that it's going to be fine to take a Spring Break if it falls in the middle of your work term; don't imagine that there will be no problem if you want to take a week off in the middle of the summer.

What days do you get to take off? Any days that are official holidays for your employer (i.e., Memorial Day, Labor Day). Technically, that's all that an employer is required to allow you to take. But can there be exceptions to this? Sometimes, yes, but you shouldn't count on it. For example, a student who works in a position that is far away from his or her home may *ask* his or her employer if it would be okay to conclude a work assignment prior to Christmas rather than going home and coming back for three or four days before the assignment technically ends. The employer may or may not grant this request.

What can you do to improve your chances of having a request for unpaid time off granted? Do the following:

- Keep such requests to an absolute minimum. If you know you're going to ask for time off after Christmas, for example, don't press your luck by looking for additional time off earlier in the work period.

- Only ask if you have an excellent reason for requesting time off. Besides Christmas and other religious holidays, it may be reasonable to ask for a day off to attend an out-of-state wedding, for example. Or if you've been working 12 hours a day for a month during tax season in an accounting job, it may be reasonable to ask for a day off when things slow down once again. Generally, though, you don't want to ask unless it's an absolute necessity. You never know when you might really need the time off.

- Do such an outstanding job during the work period that your employer will be willing to give you time off. An outstanding worker definitely has a much better chance of having requests for time off granted when necessary. In some cases, an employer even raises the subject to offer a reward to an extremely productive worker.

Look at it this way: If a worker has a bad attitude, is late or absent frequently, does mediocre work, and constantly needs to be supervised, an employer is bound to look at a request for time off as the final insult.

14. Keep your internship or co-op coordinator informed about any major problems, dilemmas, or unpleasant situations that arise.

The majority of students will not have any major problems arise during their work experiences. However, there is always the possibility that you might face problems that are beyond what you are expected to handle without help. Please call your coordinator as soon as possible if you are:

- the victim of sexual harassment or other abusive behavior from your co-workers or supervisor.

- laid off from your job, regardless of the cause (i.e., budget cuts, buyouts).

- given a warning about being fired.

- fired.

- being paid less than promised.

- having problems with your supervisor that are difficult to discuss.

Additionally, call your coordinator if you have brought up any of the following problems with your supervisor, and the conversation has not produced a change:

- You are given far too much or too little work to do on a regular basis.

- Your job is not what you were led to believe it would be, and you are not having a good learning experience.

- You are stressed out due to the work, your co-workers, or your customers.

Sometimes a problem can be easily fixed if addressed quickly, while it can become a huge issue if ignored. When in doubt about the seriousness of a problem, contact your coordinator.

Co-op Job Success – A Student's Perspective
by Gabriel Glasscock

Don't sit back and say to yourself "I'm just an intern." This is your job, and you have the ability to make the most of it. Some jobs will have downtime; it's just a fact. You can spend that time surfing www.espn.com, and www.boston.com, or you can go to your boss and say "Hey, I have some downtime, is there anything I can do?" In one such situation, I went to my boss, and she ended up shipping me off to a very expensive class on Web development in which I learned an immense amount, and thus had more responsibility at work.

If there is a problem at the job, don't be afraid to talk to your manager. If you're not doing anything stated on your job description, don't go silently. Remember: it's up to you to take charge. Your advisor or boss can't do anything unless they know about it.

Gabriel Glasscock was an MIS student at Northeastern University, Class of 2002.

---

15. When faced with ethical dilemmas, make sure that you always act in a way that allows you to maintain your self-respect, integrity, and clean record.

We hope that you won't face too many ethical dilemmas during your practice-oriented work experience. However, any job that you will ever have potentially can present you with tough situations. For example, would you cheat on your timesheet: even if you were sure you could get away with it? Sadly, I have had students caught for falsifying their hours, and they were terminated immediately—all those potential references and resume-building experiences permanently ruined or severely damaged, just for the possibility of a little extra money. This kind of offense also may lead to suspension or expulsion from your college or university.

What would you do if you became aware that another employee was stealing money, supplies, or equipment from the organization? If you make a potentially critical mistake and become aware of it later, should you tell your supervisor or simply hope that no one notices your error?

A few years ago, a student of mine faced a major dilemma. He had been asked to do the back-end work involved in getting antivirus software ready to go on the desktop computers of a big department. A full-time worker was supposed to take the final steps to get the software operational. When my student followed up with him to see if it was completed, his co-worker said to him, "I had trouble getting it to work, so I basically just decided to forget about it."

My student agonized about whether or not he should go to their mutual boss to report this. If he spoke up, he knew he would feel that he had "squealed" on a co-worker. But if he kept his mouth shut, and a new virus ended up causing significant problems, then he could be getting himself and others in trouble as well. What would you do?

I think he handled it very well. He went to his supervisor and told him about it, but he did so in a way that *assumed the best* of his co-worker. He told his boss that his co-worker had not completed the task, but he also said, "He might have been intending to get back to finishing up once he solved the problem." His boss was grateful, pointing out that the people in that group downloaded things all the time, and a major virus and worm problem would have reflected badly on the whole group.

Ultimately, every individual has to decide for himself or herself how to act in situations when no one—not your coordinator, your supervisor, or your parents—is looking over your shoulder. Basically, it's simple: Do the right thing, and you will save yourself a lot of guilt, fear, and worry about the consequences. If you're not sure about what the right thing is in a given situation, contact your coordinator.

16. Sit down with your manager during the first week of your job to set goals for your co-op work period.

If your program uses a standard work evaluation, you and your manager should review the entire evaluation upfront to know how you will be judged at the end of the work period. Additionally, though—whether or not your program requires it—you should write at least three goals for your work assignment, and you should do this in the first few weeks of your work experience.

Setting Learning Goals – A Co-op Professional's Perspective
by Erin Doyon

This is an important aspect of a co-op that many students avoid, or forget to do. In the beginning of most events and relationships everything seems wonderful and smooth, but by chance that things get a little rocky later on goals can be what help you manage challenging conversations. I tell most of my students to think of their co-op work experience like another class that they want to do well in. In any class you have a syllabus, this will tell you what books to read, when the exams are, and essentially how to get an A. Setting learning goals with your supervisor in your first month is like creating a syllabus for your work experience, you will know what is expected of you and be able to ask questions about how to accomplish those goals. If you have any challenges throughout your experience you can reference your goals that you set together with your supervisor to initiate these conversations, essentially you will know what you need to accomplish to be successful, how to get an A.

Erin Doyon is an Assistant Director of Cooperative Education in Engineering at University of Massachusetts Lowell.

What might your goals be for a given work assignment? They could vary dramatically depending on your major, the job, and your level of previous experience. For some first-time student employees, one goal may simply be to learn how a corporation works and how to perform effectively day-in, day-out for six months in a professional environment. Some goals may relate to refining soft skills, such as improving presentation skills, proving to be a dependable employee by arriving at work early every day, or perhaps learning how to multitask or to prioritize in the face of deadlines or multiple responsibilities. Other goals may be more advanced and/or more geared to specific job skills: "I hope to find out if I'm comfortable working hands-on with patients of all backgrounds as an aspiring physical therapist;" "I intend to learn how to use ASP to make database-linked dynamic websites," or "I want to be immersed in the activities of this cat hospital so I can learn if this veterinary environment is right for me."

With goals in place, you and your manager will have a better mutual understanding of what you are supposed to be accomplishing in your role, and you can both do a better job of tracking your progress toward these objectives as the work period progresses.

17. Do everything you can to become part of the work team and not "just a student."

To make the most of your job experience, make an effort to integrate yourself as fully as possible in the workplace. This is especially important if you work at a company that employs more than one student. Some students have the tendency to go to lunch with their fellow students, socialize outside of work only with fellow students, and generally avoid significant contact with full-time employees. This is understandable—in a new and strange situation, a person may be tempted to cling to something or someone who is familiar or similar. However, if you fail to make some connections with full-time employees, you're missing out on one of the great things that co-ops, internships, and other practice-oriented roles have to offer.

Once, with the best of intentions, a few students started an e-mail thread that enabled their fellow students to be aware of social plans for after work and other such events. Over time, though, it became obvious that some people on the list were spending a significant part of their work day reading and responding to these "co-op group" e-mails! Inevitably, many of the students started getting perceived as an outside group of co-op students rather than blending in with the full-time employees. That made it harder for the co-ops to be looked at as true equals at the office.

On-the-Job Success Tips – A Student's Perspective
by Daniel Brooks

Do not hesitate to network. Seize networking opportunities with people at work. Find common interests outside or work and get to know your "peers."

Work strategically on your projects so as not to step on anyone's toes. This may mean visiting stakeholders of your projects even when you have nothing to request or get input on. Just being personable, building a relationship, and asking how their work is going will help them build trust with you. Knowing that you understand their work challenges will make them more likely to help you when you are in need. They will also not see you as a timid kid, but rather a part of the team.

Daniel Brooks was a Plastics Engineering major at University of Massachusetts Lowell, Class of 2012. He is now in the Commercialization Leadership Program at SABIC Corporation.

Initially, talking to full-time people at work will help you learn the "unwritten rules" of that particular workplace regarding what is and is not acceptable and appropriate. Ultimately, your experience can become a chance to rub elbows with people who work professionally in your field as well as other areas of possible future professional interest. Simply joining these people for lunch or for a bite to eat after work, you may pick up invaluable information about:

- how to succeed in your job.

- whether or not you have much in common with people who work professionally in the career that interests you.

- what kinds of coursework, job experiences, or self-study projects will help prepare you for a great career after graduation.

- how people perceive the pros and cons of their own career choices.

Another benefit of getting to know full-time employees is that they will be more likely to think of you as part of their group or team, and therefore more likely to give you tasks to do that are appropriate to your interests, experiences, and skill levels.

Becoming Part of the Work Team
by Marie Sacino

Our computer information systems interns at the Queens Public Library work on the client side, providing 24/7 functionality, troubleshooting, changing hard drives, and ghosting as ongoing support tasks. Interns also work in the field on new PC rollout projects—2,000 new PC installations at branches throughout Queens this past summer.

What does it take to be a successful IT intern? Philip Darsan, Director of Information Technology at Queens Public Library, has some good thoughts. "An intern needs to begin to understand their working environment, to ask more questions, to utilize the department's organizational chart, to be cognizant of naming conventions—firewalls, deployment, DNS, IP," Darsan says. "We need serious students who really want to learn and don't watch the clock. Most IT personnel work 50 to 60 hours a week.

"I try to give the students an opportunity to open their eyes to the technology," adds Darsan. "Just how wide they choose to open them is up to the student. I'm interested in students who have a technician's perspective and who are customer-service oriented. I'll ask a student, 'How well do you communicate?' Without solid communication skills—interpersonal, reading, writing, speaking—there will be little growth for a technical support person."

Marie Sacino is Professor of Cooperative Education at LaGuardia Community College.

---

18. However, be careful about mixing business and pleasure.

Sure, you want to be part of the work team. This can mean going out for lunch with co-workers or going out after work. It's great to fit in and be part of the gang, but you need to be careful when it comes to drinking with co-workers or getting romantically or sexually involved with people at work.

First, let's talk about alcohol. In some organizations, drinking is very much a part of the culture—you may be encouraged to drink at lunchtime before going back to work for the afternoon. In some offices, going out for beers after work is routine—or even having beer or wine brought into the office on a Friday afternoon by the organization itself! What should you do? You have to decide for yourself, but remember a few things. If you're underage to drink in your state, it's simply a bad idea to drink with co-workers—even if they urge you to do so. I had a student years ago who got fired from a prestigious firm because he drank at an office Christmas party. His boss had been proactive—telling him in advance that he could come but he could not drink. At the party itself, though, co-workers twisted his arm and got drinks for him: His boss found out, and he was fired.

Even if you are legal to drink and enjoy doing so, you should be discreet about doing so. I would never recommend that you take the initiative in ordering a drink if you're out with a colleague. If you're with several people who are drinking, it might not be a big deal to have a beer or a glass of wine—but be very moderate at most.

The same goes with getting romantically and/or sexually involved with people at work. In particular, it's never advisable to date a supervisor or someone who works for you. Even if someone is a fellow intern or a co-worker of similar age, you need to proceed with caution. What will you do if you break up with someone, and then you need to keep working closely together? Not a fun situation for either party. At the minimum, the best bet is to wait until after you complete your job before considering any relationship with a co-worker. Remember, also, that making unwanted advances can lead to embarrassing disciplinary issues as well.

One other reminder: When are student employees most likely to forget that it's not such a great idea to get involved with co-workers? You guessed it: When they've been out drinking at lunch or after work! If you're not careful, this issue can be double trouble, and it can affect how people perceive your professionalism at work.

19. If you're on a full-time job, your job performance should be your highest priority.

When you're in classes full-time, that should be your top priority. But when you're on co-op or on a full-time internship, you need to focus the bulk of your energy on performing your co-op job to the best of your ability.

Two factors can interfere with your job performance if you're not careful: First, some students choose to take classes while on co-op or an internship with long hours. To do so, you may need the permission of your co-op employer and your co-op or internship coordinator. Before seeking their permission, however, be honest with yourself: Can you take on one or two classes without jeopardizing your job performance or your academic performance? If in doubt, it is best to avoid taking classes on co-op or to keep them at an absolute minimum. Of course, if you're in a parallel program, you'll have to master the ability to be a student and employee at the same time without compromising your performance level in either role.

Another situation may arise for seniors: Naturally, seniors are concerned with getting full-time jobs after graduation. Sometimes, seniors may be interviewing for full-time jobs and co-op jobs simultaneously. However, once you've started a co-op job, you should keep any full-time interviewing to an absolute minimum. To go on one or two interviews through your Department of Career Services during your co-op job—with your co-op employer's permission, and with the understanding that you will make up for the missed hours—may be acceptable. To miss significant time from work to go on numerous interviews is not acceptable. For that matter, it's not that smart: Many seniors get full-time job offers from their last co-op employers IF they are outstanding performers. Don't jeopardize your co-op job—and a possible future offer—by looking elsewhere for full-time jobs during your work term.

20. If you're working part-time while attending classes full-time, you need to manage your time very effectively.

There are a few possibilities here. In some programs, students regularly juggle a co-op or internship with full-time classes. Likewise, some full-time co-ops opt to stay with their co-op employer on a part-time basis when their co-op experience officially ends. Either way, working part-time poses several challenges. I have had some full-time co-op superstars who absolutely destroyed their reputation with their employer because of their failure to adapt to being a part-time employee.

Effective Internships – A Co-op Professional's Perspective
by Ronnie Porter

I think in addition to the skill sets, there's a professionalization/socialization piece that doesn't occur as much when you're working on a part-time basis, ten hours a week, as opposed to doing it full-time when you're a member of a team and equally counted on.

I think the important thing is that at the outset you really set some goals for the time period of the job. I think that's really critical in any situation—that students have goals and that employers agree as to what those goals are. I think it's even more critical when you're there on a limited basis—when you're going to have to pick and choose what you do or what you want to learn and still have that coincide with what's needed at the organization. Otherwise, anything could happen. Things might turn out okay, but in other situations they might turn out to be very disappointing with people feeling like they've wasted their time.

Ronnie Porter is a cooperative education faculty coordinator in Biology at Northeastern University.

Here are a few tips to avoid this pitfall:

- *Don't over-commit.* Some students ambitiously promise to work 25-30 hours per week part-time. The employer counts on this resource, only to have the student start to realize that it's too much to balance—so he cuts back to 18 hours.... Then 15. This is all very annoying to the manager. Better to under-promise and over-deliver—don't commit to more than roughly 15 hours of part-time work per week while in full-time classes unless you really, really know you can handle it.

- *Set a regular schedule and stick to it as much as possible.* Committing to 15 hours a week generally doesn't mean that you go in whenever you feel like it in a given week. Look at your course schedule and block out some times that you can regularly do. Maybe one whole day and a couple of half-days; maybe two whole days—it doesn't really matter as long as your supervisor is comfortable with the arrangement and you generally stick to it. If you have voice mail and e-mail at work, make sure to include a message that informs everyone about your hours and what to do in your absence. Likewise, if you have a desk, office, or cubicle of your own, prominently post your part-time schedule so people will know when you will be working next. In scheduling, also remember that coming in for just an hour or two here and there seldom works well.

- *Plan ahead.* As soon as you get your syllabi, note the dates of exams and major due dates on your calendar. Maybe you have a week in which you have three midterms. In that case, you can approach your boss with plenty of notice to let her know that you'll need to be out for a few days. There is really no excuse for calling in the morning to say that you can't come in because you have an exam that day.

21. If you are relocating for a job, be careful about how your situation can affect your perceptions of the job.

If you take advantage of an opportunity elsewhere in the country, you may end up living with other students who work for the same employer or with a different employer. As a result, students sometimes end up comparing notes about jobs, employers, supervisors, co-workers, etc. If both students are having a good experience, this is fine. But if one student is having a bad experience, everyone in that living situation needs to make sure that they continue thinking for themselves. In other words, decide for yourself whether or not you are having a good experience: Don't let anyone tell you what you should or shouldn't be thinking about your unique situation. This is true of any roommates who live together while working, but the negative effects can be magnified when you're living a long way from home and perhaps eating, breathing, and sleeping your practice-oriented experience every minute of the day. It's a powerful experience, so you have to make sure you maintain some objectivity.

Working in a different part of the country can be an excellent idea. In a sense, you're guaranteed of having a "double learning experience"—you'll learn on the job, and you'll learn off the job about what it's like to live in a different region. At best, you may find a place you enjoy more than your home city. At worst, you'll appreciate your own region, campus, or home more when you return.

22. Learn to master "cubicle etiquette" if necessary.

Many work environments feature cubicles or other arrangements that blur the lines between what behavior is public and what is private. Basically, a somewhat contradictory but useful rule of thumb is to assume that all of your own behavior is on public display... but also that you need to respect the privacy of others despite the lack of doors.

First, here are some good reminders relating to the fact that your own behavior is quite visible and public:

- Keep your phone ringer on a low volume and your speaking voice relatively low as well. Obviously, avoid speakerphones.

- Be aware that most phone conversations can be overheard.

- Turn off your phone ringer—or forward your calls—when not in your cubicle.

- E-mail or even instant messaging can be useful in this context to communicate to co-workers without unnecessary noise.

- Keep computer sound levels low.

- Try to avoid eating hot food at your desk. The aromas may distract those who are hungry or disgust those who are not hungry or who don't share your food preferences.

When it comes to respecting the privacy of others in a cubicle environment, here are some more good tips:

- Act as if your co-workers' cubicles have doors. Don't just barge in and start talking: Knock on the cubicle's wall.

- Don't be a "prairie dog," peering over the tops of cubes to see if someone is in or to talk.

- If you go to see someone in their cubicle, and they're on the phone, leave and come back later. Don't hang around where you can readily overhear their conversation.

- Here's a really challenging one: You may overhear a question or comment occasionally and be tempted to respond because you know the right answer. Unless the question is directed to everyone in the area, don't do it! It will bring attention to the fact that you've been eavesdropping, intentionally or not. Wait until someone asks you directly.

- If you have to share a cubicle or workspace with a colleague, you might want to suggest arranging different breaks or lunchtimes so each person gets at least some privacy regularly.

23. Don't assume that no news is good news.

One of the toughest things about being an employee is that people are often reluctant to give you honest feedback—especially if it's negative. In my current job, I even hear of executives who have any number of bad habits that are affecting how others perceive them... but no one tells them.

Basically, it's human nature for many people to avoid conflict. Thus, it can be very hard to know how you're really doing—whether people are REALLY happy with your work, or if they are uncomfortable because of how you dress, what you say, what you do, and so on. At times, people may smile and laugh at something you say—while quietly taking offense and thinking less of you in the process.

This is not always fair. Sometimes one individual can make comments that border on inappropriate, and everyone accepts it... while someone else repeats those comments and is taken to task.

What to do? Don't assume that no news is good news. On the whole, it's best to err on the slightly paranoid side: Avoid subject matter that might be deemed offensive—even if others talk freely about similar topics. It can be very hard to read how it's going over. Along these lines, it's also good to seek feedback from trusted advisors at work to find out what you're doing well and what, if anything, you could be doing better.

24. Return to school with a network of new contacts.

Lastly, don't miss the golden opportunity of co-ops and internships: When you're working in any position, make sure that you have acquired a network of new contacts before you complete the job! You have the opportunity to earn the respect of many people in your field during your work period. That's great, but make sure you capitalize on that by collecting business cards and/or contact information before you leave. You never know who might be in a position to help you out when you're networking for another job in the future. If you only know one or two people at your worksite, you might be out of luck if those people move on and can't be located.

Assuming you've done all you can to make a positive impression, having plenty of names can pay incredible dividends in the future when it comes time for another job search. Even if those individuals can't directly hire you, they may be in a position to recommend you for other jobs or to give you valuable career advice. Don't miss the boat!

Networking – A Co-op Professional's Perspective
by Bob Tillman

Who did you network with? Can you tell me ten new people who you know now, who know you? People who you could talk to down the road about a job? Because if you didn't, you wasted your time. That was the freebie out there. That's the value added that you don't get someplace else.

Bob Tillman is an Associate Professor and cooperative education faculty coordinator in Civil and Environmental Engineering at Northeastern University.

E-MAIL

I started working with co-op students and interns in March of 1995. Without question, the biggest change I have seen over the years is the degree to which e-mail has come to dominate business communication. Likewise, the average person is far more likely to be much more familiar with this form of communication. People love e-mail because of its speed, ease of use, and relative informality. However, all of these characteristics also can lead to blunders in the workplace. So let's review what every professional should know about e-mail.

The 'E' in E-Mail

Most people know that the "e" in e-mail literally stands for electronic. However, it's important to remember that 'e' stands for many other words as well: embarrassing, everlasting, eternal, evidence.

Because an e-mail seems to disappear into cyberspace, it's easy to imagine that it's less "real" than a hard copy. However, the opposite is true. E-mails have lives of their own, and there is always a chance that once they are sent that they will never go away. Maybe you only intended to send it to one person, but who's to say that they won't forward it on? Perhaps you sent something confidential to a friend... but what might happen if that relationship turns sour? You never know when e-mail you sent might reappear at the worst possible moment.

One terrific student that I had in my class a few years ago recently had an experience that showed how 'e' can be embarrassing. While at work, she fired off a hasty e-mail to her boyfriend, basically implying that she was looking forward to spending a very passionate Sunday with him. But with a few unsent messages open, she accidentally e-mailed the steamy message to her supervisor!

What happened next was rather amazing. The supervisor thought it was funny and forwarded the message to six or seven colleagues in the Boston office, adding a little joke about how he seemed to be making quite an impression on his intern. Those six or seven colleagues passed it along to others in that office... and to colleagues at *another* office in another city. By the time I saw the message, it had been forward to over 60 employees in five cities!

To the student's credit, she owned responsibility for her part in this embarrassing fiasco. Interestingly, though, her manager was reprimanded for passing along the message instead of quietly confronting the co-op to make her aware of her mistake. Still, the co-op could not have enjoyed knowing that her private feelings were now known across the company.

Remember, anything you send as an e-mail is NOT private. I once had an IT co-op whose job was "sniffing" e-mails. As a senior, he spoke to my class of first-time co-op students, describing how part of his job was to look through e-mail messages. He often came across porn, illegally downloaded music and videos, and many other incriminating messages. I'll always remember how horrified the class looked as he described what he found and how he reported it to his supervisor, who in turn went to Human Resources. I think that the students were shocked to know that their electronic communications at work were fair game for scrutiny.

Basically, you should be careful about what you send from your home computer... and maybe even a little paranoid about what you e-mail from your work computer. Don't think you can beat the system by sending questionable communication from a Gmail or Twitter account: Any of these can be traced back to the computer from which it was sent!

If you stop to reflect that e-mail and any electronic communication really is everlasting, embarrassing evidence, you'll go a long way toward avoiding problems.

Preparing to Send an E-Mail

Before you send your first e-mail as a new employee of a professional organization, there are several factors to consider and steps to take:

1. *Become familiar with your organization's culture regarding e-mails.* Every organization is different when it comes to communication. I deal with employers who almost never use e-mails to communicate internally, favoring the telephone or face-to-face interaction. On the other end of the spectrum are companies like Microsoft, where employees routinely e-mail individuals who are in the office next door!

    In your early weeks in a new job, pay attention to who e-mails who and for what reason. You may need to e-mail less or more frequently than you ordinarily would to fit in with the new culture. If you're not sure, ask your co-workers or manager how to proceed.

2. *Set up your e-mail account to ensure that your name is obvious to message recipients.* At times in my career, I have routinely received 50-75 e-mails daily during the busiest times of the year. As a result, I ended up scrolling through dozens of messages all day long. One minor annoyance is when it's not possible to deduce the sender from the

name on my inbox. It may say something like jg1967@gmail.com, which gives me no clue as to the sender's identity.

Avoid inflicting this minor bit of inconvenience by setting your e-mail properties up so your name is readily obvious to the recipient. Then that message will appear as coming from Jill Gómez <jg1967@gmail.com> in the message itself.

3. *Fill in the "To:" field LAST when sending any e-mail message.* Depending on the e-mail application you use, it can be surprisingly easy to send a message before you've finished writing or proofreading it. Therefore, it's a good practice to leave the recipient's e-mail address out until you're definitely ready to hit SEND. Because once you do, that message is not coming back!

4. *Always use a concise, descriptive subject for each e-mail message.* This is another problem area for many young professionals. It's not unusual for students to use problematic subjects when e-mailing me. I had one young man who seemed to think it appropriate to use a complete sentence as a subject: "Mr. Weighart I have some things I need to discuss with you." Another student simply used to write "IMPORTANT" for almost every message... and, believe me, the subject matter never turned out to be all that important. That almost feels like a Spam e-mail tactic—using a vague subject that conveys some sense of urgency.

Keep your subjects concise, but also be sure to give some sense of what the message concerns. Here are some good and bad examples:

Good e-mail subjects	Bad e-mail subjects
Question regarding Munze account	Call me ASAP!
Agenda item for Monday's meeting	Hi!
Quick update on JTC project	This is Henry.
Expense report – January 2014	Hey, how's it going?
Dentist appointment tomorrow	John can you answer these questions for me?
Following up on yesterday's meeting	<no subject>

5. *Don't abuse the "high priority" or "high importance" options.* This e-mail option can become like the story of the boy who cried wolf. If you abuse it in an attempt to get a quick answer to a less-than-urgent question, people will resent it. It leads people to question whether your judgment is good... and eventually they may not take it seriously when something really is high priority!

If you're looking for a quick answer to a simple question, you might just indicate that with an e-mail subject that reads "Quick question." Save the high-priority option for

159

situations that truly are emergencies. For example, I would use it if a student was at risk of being temporarily withdrawn from the university quite soon due to a paperwork issue. You may never need to utilize this option at all, and consider it carefully. If the matter is all that important, you might want to just pick up the phone.

6. *Use an appropriate salutation.* Surprisingly, some of my best co-ops and interns have struggled with this one. I had a top student at Microsoft recently, and she had to e-mail a group of about 50 people with a project update. She knew that introducing the e-mail with something like "Hey guys" would be inappropriate, but a better alternative didn't come to mind immediately.

First, though, let's consider the easier situation. When writing an e-mail to an individual, there are several options that may be appropriate:

> Dear Charlie, -- This is a little more formal but fine.
> Hi Charlie, -- This is a bit more informal but also acceptable.
> Charlie, -- Perhaps a bit more of a down-to-business salutation, but it's fine, too.

If you're writing to someone you don't know as well, go a little more formal, avoiding the assumption of being on a first-name basis:

> Dear Mr. Bognanni,
> Hi Ms. Shumbata,
> Ms. Brady,

It also can be acceptable to not including any salutation at all—just launching into the body of the message. However, some research shows that people are less likely to respond when there is no personal salutation.

Above all, avoid the salutations that you might see in e-mails from a friend:

> Hey Charlie!
> Hey, how's it going?

When writing to a group, I would recommend something like this:

> Hi everyone,
> Hi all,

There are probably other things that would work there—including no salutation at all—but this seems to be the simplest and most effective.

7. *Be wary of the cc and bcc options.* There are times when it's appropriate to use the cc function, which sends an extra copy of your e-mail to another person. Maybe you're updating a colleague on some issue but feel that your supervisor also should hear about it—but more as an FYI rather than as an action item. That's a good time to use the cc function. It can be a good way to keep people informed while also implying that you don't necessarily expect a reply from them.

Unfortunately, though, people get carried away with sending a cc of their e-mails. There are those who overestimate the importance or interest level that their news will generate, and—even worse—there are those who send a cc to show a third party how dumb the original message was and/or to escalate the intensity of the problem. As we'll see when we consider "flaming" e-mails, this can get out of hand in a hurry.

Then there is the bcc, which technically stands for "blind carbon copy." In this case, you're letting a third party see the e-mail without the primary recipient being able to see who else is allowed to see it. There are times when this makes a great deal of sense. Sometimes I write to groups of people but want to make sure that others don't see the individual e-mail addresses, which may be considered private. For example, if ten students were late in getting something done for me, I would e-mail them all at once to save time... but I would also bcc them all, as it would be potentially embarrassing for each student to know who else is not getting things done. It's also no one else's business.

But I try to avoid bcc in most cases. Some feel that it's rather unethical—I have heard of a bcc recipient being referred to as a "blind co-conspirator." However, the biggest risk is that the bcc recipient will accidentally hit REPLY TO ALL, and then the primary recipient will become aware that others saw the initial message. If I do want others to see an e-mail that is somewhat sensitive, I may just forward a copy from my Sent folder AFTER sending that initial message.

8. *Beware of REPLY TO ALL.* This connects to the previous point. It's all too easy to click "reply to all" instead of simply "reply" when you receive a group message. What is the impact? At best, you end up sending information to a group that has no need whatsoever to read your response. For example, sometimes invitations to events go out on work e-mails, and recipients are told to reply to the sender to RSVP. Instead, the person hits REPLY TO ALL, and the whole group gets a message indicating that, say, that person will not attend the event because of a dentist appointment. Not a horrible thing to share with a group, but it's basically just another message that needs to be deleted.

However, there are other situations which can lead to serious embarrassment, bad feelings, or even disciplinary action. A few years ago, I received an e-mail on a nationally distributed list-serv that reached thousands of individuals. One person sent a perfectly fine message to the group. But then a colleague at her own organization hit REPLY TO ALL and informed the e-mail sender that the toilet in their building was clogged yet again! The exchange went back and forth a few times before a recipient finally wrote to say "Do we all really need to read about your bathroom issues?" A mortified apology followed.

Even worse, though, is another possibility. Let's say that Tom sends an e-mail to his entire work group, noting that there will be a farewell party for Jane, a co-worker who is leaving the company. Then Jack—a very close friend of Tom—intends to send a message back to Tom that is for his eyes only. But he accidentally hits REPLY TO ALL. There are any number of things that he might say that could have terrible consequences. He could ask Tom if he thinks the boss will make another of his stupid speeches at the event, or he could express delight that Jane is leaving the company at last. He could talk about a "hot" co-worker who he plans to ask out for drinks after the event. The possibilities are almost infinite.

The moral of the story is to think twice before you put anything in an e-mail which will reflect poorly on you if others see it—either due to it being forwarded, intercepted by someone in IT, or accidentally shared through REPLY TO ALL.

9. *Don't open file attachments unless you're very sure that they can be trusted.* File attachments often contain malware including computer worms, ransomware, Trojan horses, and more. Even if a friend or co-worker sends a file attachment, look out for vague messages with file attachments. They may be the result of a virus, worm, or Trojan horse that's infected their machines. More obviously, don't open files from people you don't know.

10. *Don't forward virus threats, offensive content, or chain letter e-mails.* Sometimes e-mails *claiming* to warn people of virus threats actually contain viruses or worms. Let your IT department stay current on such threats.

Offensive content is very much in the eye of the beholder. What's funny to one person might offend someone else. In general, stay away from forwarding jokes—especially when you're new at an organization and probably not clear about what people will find humorous or even how they might feel about you spending time at work forwarding jokes. If you're just there temporarily for a co-op or internship, I would say that you never should send e-mails to co-workers that have nothing to do with work.

Many people get sucked in by chain letter e-mails. Periodically you may receive emotional pleas in which, say, a warning of a terrorist act is passed along or a child dying of cancer wants to see how many e-mails he can receive from around the world before he or she dies. Sometimes there is a claim that the American Cancer Society will donate a few cents to cancer research for everyone who receives the e-mail.

While such appeals may bring out your humanitarian nature, don't be fooled. More often than not, these e-mails are hoaxes. Sometimes I go to www.snopes.com to see if e-mails are true or not, as this site reports diligently on "urban legends." Most of them are hoaxes, so you're often just wasting your time and that of your friends and co-workers by passing along such nonsense.

11. *Don't reply to spam e-mail messages.* You may receive quite a few annoying spam messages, offering everything from discount drugs and loans to elaborate scams promising you massive amounts of money for helping some overseas widow get access to a massive inheritance. Unless your organization has a spam-reporting mechanism to follow, the best thing to do is to simply delete such messages. Responding to them or clicking on a link—even when doing so supposedly removes you from a mailing list—actually can help a spammer *confirm* your e-mail address and may lead to getting viruses.

12. *Strike when the iron is cold.* Never reply to an e-mail when you are angry, frustrated, or otherwise not prepared to write a professional, businesslike message that you can live with forever. I call this "striking when the iron is cold"—exactly the opposite of the expression "strike when the iron is hot." As a professional, you want to respond with a rational, constructive response—even when you are agitated.

It's very easy to blast someone when you are angry, saying things that you never would say face to face. Sometimes it's best to resist the urge to fire off a response when you first receive an emotionally charged e-mail. Take a walk, talk about it with someone, maybe sleep on it if you can. Ask yourself what kind of response will reflect on you best as an aspiring professional. Then write back when your frame of mind is more positive. Better still, it's best to just meet with someone or call them if it's an emotional topic. If you send a message in the heat of the moment, you'll have a long time to regret responding in the heat of the moment.

The E-Mail Message Itself

Now that we have considered everything that should go into preparing to e-mail, let's go through the writing of the actual message itself. Here are several pointers that will help you write effective e-mails:

1. *Be concise.* Limit your professional e-mails to "need to know" information. Be quick to describe why you are writing, what you need to tell or ask, and what steps, if any, the respondent needs to take in response. Then thank them and end it.

It's also a good idea to take a moment to reflect on whether an e-mail really is the best way to convey your message. If you can't convey the information in a few short paragraphs—or if the information is complicated and requires additional input—it may be best to use the phone or have a brief meeting. Most managers will get impatient with any e-mail that is longer than five or ten lines. If there is no other option, you may have to send a longer message... but try to avoid that if you want your message to be read.

2. *Create templates if you find yourself writing identical or highly similar e-mails on a regular basis.* Depending on your job, you may need to write highly similar messages repeatedly. Why waste time rewriting them from scratch every time? I keep a Word file of messages that come up constantly. If I get a request for information or about how to set up an appointment with me among other things, I can paste in the appropriate response and add the appropriate salutation on top. That saves hours and hours each year.

3. *Use blank lines to separate paragraphs as opposed to indenting.* Just as in any piece of writing, you want to avoid massive paragraphs with no visual or conceptual break. Getting a 25-line e-mail with no spacing just makes the recipient groan. Try to limit each paragraph to no more than five or six sentences or lines, and hit ENTER twice at the end to go to the next paragraph without indenting.

4. *Understand that e-mails are one-way communication.* When you have a face-to-face conversation with a co-worker, you can infer a great deal from the speaker's tone of voice

and body language. In a regular conversation, you also can adjust your message based on how the listener reacts to what you say as the conversation progresses.

Naturally, all of these helpful cues go out the window in an e-mail message. It can be very difficult to grasp the writer's tone. Sometimes it's hard to tell if someone is angry or just in a hurry as well as whether they're joking, serious, or sarcastic. As a result, it's good be cautious in drawing conclusions. Ask clarifying questions if need be, and avoid emotional topics.

5.   *Use "smilies," "emoticons," or "emoji" sparingly in professional e-mails.* Smilies and emoticons are small symbols that are sometimes used to compensate for the one-way nature of e-mail and IM communication. There are literally hundreds of them out there, but here are some common examples:

:-)	Happy
;-)	Winking
:-(	Sad
:-o	Surprised

Experts differ as to whether such symbols have any place in professional e-mails. Some believe that it can be helpful to add an emoticon in order to make sure that there is no misunderstanding about whether you're joking. For example, an intern who receives an e-mail informing her that she is going to have much more responsibility going forward might write the following text in response:

Looks like I'll have my hands full for the next month.

If the message is left like that, we're not sure whether her reaction is an expression of complaint, anxiety, or enthusiasm. So writing it this way makes that very clear:

Looks like I'll have my hands full for the next month. :-)

The best advice is to use these emoticons sparingly. There are quite a few that will baffle e-mail recipients who don't use them at all. For example, can you even guess what these represent?

:C

*

{}

'\'-)

Respectively, they are supposed to indicate astonishment, a kiss, no comment, and tears of happiness! But you'll baffle most co-workers by using these, so stick with the common ones if you use them at all.

6. *Capitalize appropriately and avoid text message slang.* Many young professionals are experienced e-mail writers and texters and they bring their highly informal e-mail and texting habits into the workplace. I cringe when I get a professional message in which someone writes something like this:

    can i meet with u 2day? maybe 4 lunch?

    Occasionally, I'll get e-mails using other abbreviations, such as LOL (laughing out loud), FWIW (for what it's worth), or IMHO (in my humble opinion). I use these sometimes in m personal e-mail but not in professional e-mail. For the latter, I think it's fine to use FYI (For Your Information) and maybe BTW (by the way), but generally these acronyms should be avoided.

    This issue *can* be confusing. You may receive e-mails or texts at work from very senior people who opt for punctuation-free e-mails with plenty of slang and no capitalization. However, even though it's obviously faster to ignore capitalization and use "shorthand slang," it can come across as unprofessional. And when you're new to an organization, it may underscore the fact that you are young and inexperienced.

    Also understand that it's not just texting slang that is a problem. I had a student who made a serious mistake at work. When I encouraged him to apologize, he wrote an e-mail that included this sentence: "That definitely was my bad." You might say "my bad" when you make a bad pass in a pick-up basketball or football game, but you would never use such an expression in any form of professional communication. Basically, if it's not the kind of word or expression that you would use in a term paper, don't use it in an e-mail.

7. *Avoid attaching large files unless absolutely necessary.* Sometimes you may need to forward a Word, Excel, or PowerPoint document at work. That's fine. However, it can get annoying to get massive audio or video files in one's e-mail account—whether they are humorous or actually have some work relevance. Generally, avoid sending large files. They can be especially annoying if someone is accessing their e-mail account from a slower home computer.

8. *Use threads and quotes sensibly.* Many e-mail applications give you the option of simply hitting "reply" or "reply with history." So what should you do? It depends, but including at least some of that history may be very helpful to your e-mail recipient. Not infrequently I get a response to an e-mail *without* that history. Sometimes I know what the writer is talking about, sometimes not. If the message says, "Yes, it would be great if you could do that for me" and nothing more, I may have to dig through my Sent folder to figure out what the heck the person wants me to do—especially when I have looked at 50 or 100 e-mails in between the new message and the previous one!

    Keeping the "thread" of previous responses allows the recipient the luxury of scrolling down to remind himself of what had been said previously. That can be very helpful... and it also can get a little out of control. If you've exchanged many previous messages— including some with file attachments—the e-mail can get to be quite large. In that case, you may want to cut and paste the last two or three exchanges into a new message. Another option would be to just cut and paste small bits of text so the person can see what you're talking about. This can be indicated with a > sign as follows:

> When can you meet on Tuesday?

Any time from 9:30-11:30 works for me.

> Do I need to bring anything?

Just bring your hard copy of that report.

9. *Don't write "flaming" e-mails or respond in kind if you receive one.* A flaming e-mail is a message that is intended to provoke with inflammatory comments. An example might be the following:

> *I CANNOT BELIEVE THAT YOU FAILED TO INCLUDE THE COST OF GOODS SOLD ON THAT SPREADSHEET. WHAT WERE YOU THINKING???*

Writing an all-uppercase message is something to avoid in general, as is the emotionally charged tone of the e-mail. Faced with such a communication, it may be tempting to get defensive or to go on the warpath in response. Don't engage in the same behavior, though, or you'll regret it. Sometimes it's best to not respond at all via e-mail but to call or see the individual to deflate the tension. Bashing the person in reply may be momentarily satisfying but will not win any points for you in the long run.

10. *Prepare an automatic electronic signature for the end of your e-mail.* It's relatively easy to set up an electronic signature that automatically appears whenever you compose a new e-mail or reply to an existing one. The signature should include your name, title, organization name, phone number, and e-mail address, which may not be obvious from the e-mail itself. Your mailing address at work may be included as well if that will be helpful to your recipients. If you are often not at your desk due to the nature of your job, you might include a cellphone number too. It's a professional courtesy to include this data when e-mailing, so someone can have ready access to your contact information.

Some people include brief quotes with their signatures. These can be nice but also could create problems. They certainly aren't something you need to include in an e-mail signature.

11. *Proofread and spellcheck.* Many e-mail applications can be set up to proofread messages automatically before they are sent. While this can be useful, remember that spellcheckers are far from foolproof. They often fail to find missing words or words that really are words... but that are not the correct word for that context. So use your spellchecker, but also proofread messages carefully before sending them. This is especially true for those who are prone to spelling errors and typos.

I have an employer who hired a terrific interviewee, only to be horrified at the quality of her e-mails. Now the employer always includes a writing component in the interviewing process. After having his department embarrassed by unprofessional e-mails, he came to realize how important it was to avoid them. I hope that this section will help you do the same.

After You Send an E-Mail

After the e-mail goes out, there are just a couple of things to bear in mind:

1. *Don't "recall" a message.* What if you do send a message that includes a mistake—whether a factual error or a bad typo? Many systems now have the option of allowing you to "recall" an e-mail. This may give you the impression that you can "take back" an e-mail that you now regret for whatever reason. Instead, what happens is that the recipient finds both the original e-mail message in his or her inbox along with another e-mail notifying him or her that the message has been recalled. Being human, I know that the recall makes me immediately curious about what dumb error is in the first e-mail. In other words, it effectively draws more attention to it.

   If you do make a factual error, it's best to send out a correction. In some cases—when you have incorrectly named a time or place for a meeting—you might have an e-mail with an explanatory subjection: CORRECTION on meeting location. Don't profusely apologize—just explain the mistake and clarify what the message should have said.

   If a small typo or other stylistic error is made, it's probably best to just let it go. Drawing more attention to it might make it worse.

2. *Be responsive to any e-mail messages that require a reply.* At work, you will receive many group messages that require no reply at all. However, when a message is sent to you individually, it's good to acknowledge receipt of it, briefly. For most professionals, the rule of thumb is to reply to any personal e-mail message within 24 hours if it's a message that requires any sort of response. Responding faster is better if possible and potentially critical if it's a more urgent question.

   Failing to respond quickly to e-mails may start to create unfortunate negative perceptions. Your manager or co-workers may believe that you lack attention to detail, organizational skills, or the ability to manage your time effectively. Responding efficiently and effectively will reinforce the notion that you *do* have these qualities.

THE EMPLOYER'S PERSPECTIVE

All of the recommendations listed in this chapter generally reflect the expectations of most managers and organizations. HOWEVER, remember: *Every manager and organization is different.* One of the most important survival and success skills in any job for the rest of your career is to pay close attention to the written and unwritten rules of each workplace. Don't make assumptions about what is or is not okay!

Find out what drives your supervisor crazy and what makes her happy, then make any adjustments accordingly. Some bosses really don't care what time you arrive as long as you do a great job—others are upset if their employees don't arrive *early* every day! In some environments, wearing jeans and a t-shirt is acceptable; in others, wearing anything other than business formalwear is a major mistake. In some organizations, how you dress, speak, and act may have very different rules depending on the department. I visited a small software company in Cambridge a few years ago: The software developers wore ripped jeans and t-shirts and were playing chess at 2:00 in the afternoon. Meanwhile, the marketing personnel were wearing suits and working hard from 9-5 with a brief lunch break, while the accounting personnel were wearing business casual clothes and working fairly flexible hours.

On-The-Job Performance – An Employer's Perspective
by Mike Naclerio

Students can get the most out of their jobs by taking the initiative. Many co-op positions in the business field have heavy administrative functions built into them. Do the administrative part thoroughly and without resentment and find additional opportunities to contribute in the organization. Do not get stuck in the gossip and pity trap of how bad my co-op and/or supervisor is. It is all what you make of it. Ask for more work and if your supervisor doesn't have anything, come back to them with a proposal to fix a major problem they may be facing or overlooking. Do not wait for the company to provide you with the opportunity because many organizations are just too busy to focus. If you come to them with a well thought-out plan that addresses a key problem, you are sure to stand out.

As far as dealing with conflict, just deal with it. If you are having a problem with a supervisor or co-worker, ask them if they have a few minutes to talk, go somewhere private, and clear the air. There is no time for drama in the workplace and most people should respect the directness.

Mike Naclerio is the President of Enquiron.

All of this was happening in a company of about 40 people. Any co-op student entering that environment would have to be very careful in figuring out what was and was not appropriate behavior.

Regardless of your position, you must begin to think and act like a professional. Professionals remain on the job until a project is completed in a timely accurate manner.

Figuring out what is and is not okay with a given employer can be much trickier than you might imagine. Just because you see a couple of co-workers take a two-hour lunch, you can't assume that it's okay for you to do the same. If you see someone wearing shorts at work, that doesn't mean that this should be your dress code as well. On the whole, you need to keep your eyes open: Don't make the "lowest common denominator" at work become your standard. There are many co-op students who prove to be more motivated and productive than their full-time counterparts. Make sure that you're doing whatever you can to exceed expectations, whether the issue is attire, breaks, effort, or anything else.

Don't worry whether you are being compensated or not for extra work. A marketing manager recently calculated what his salary worked out to be on an hourly rate, only to discover that he was making just a few more dollars per hour than his co-op students!

SPECIAL CONSIDERATIONS FOR HEALTH SCIENCE PROFESSIONALS

If you're majoring in one of the health sciences—nursing, physical therapy, occupational therapy, pharmacy, athletic training, and cardiopulmonary science are some examples—you may do clinical assignments as well as co-op jobs. In both cases, you're working in the world of practice as opposed to the classroom. However, there are some key differences between the two experiences. The following sidebar box addresses them. As you'll see, the contrast can be ironic—some behaviors that are extremely appropriate for a health sciences co-op can be quite out of place on a clinical!

Clinical versus Co-op – A Health Sciences Co-op Professional's Perspective
by Rose Dimarco

Clinical affiliations in the health care professions are a place in the world of work where students have to demonstrate clinical skills that they've learned in the classroom as well as some professional behaviors that are appropriate for that level of student. There is a curriculum; there are objectives that the student must fulfill in the out-of-classroom experience. They are graded on it, and they are supervised by someone from the university—typically in all the health care professions. Co-op is driven by a job description: Opportunities for learning are there in co-op, but they're not the first thing.

In most cases, clinicals are assigned—there's no interview. But approaching it? Well, I'll tell you a quick story. One of my better students on co-op came back and said, "I'm having a hell of a time on my clinical." And I said, "Abby, how can that be? You just shine in everything you touch." And she said, "Rose, I don't know how to delegate. As a licensed therapist, I have to demonstrate that I know how to delegate to appropriate personnel, and I do it all! As a co-op, I was delegated to, and I don't know how to get out of my own way! So if I need towels, I go get them. If I see a linen closet that needs organizaging, I organize it. I make time for it—I stay after work. My clinical advisor at the site would say, "Abby! That's what you should have given the aide to do!"

So that transition is more of a challenge than anything—getting out of that mindset. So a clinical is more student objective-centered, based on a curriculum.

Rose Dimarco is a cooperative education faculty coordinator in
Physical Therapy at Northeastern University.

FINAL THOUGHTS REGARDING ON-THE-JOB SUCCESS

Getting on top of the many details in this chapter obviously has an enormous impact on the job experience. Perhaps the biggest key is owning the responsibility for your own success. Sooner or later in your career, you'll have to contend with a poor manager, a difficult co-worker, or a problematic or uninspiring work environment. I've dealt with some high-level managers at Microsoft who like to say, "It's not the situation: It's how you handle it."

One senior manager at Microsoft told me the following: "When I interview people now, I mainly try to weed out the whiners, complainers, and moaners," he said. "Years ago, I sometimes interviewed people who told me that they were held back in their old jobs because of poor managers, a negative work environment, or a lack of resources. I hired some of these people, because I believed that once they got to Microsoft—where we have great managers, a very achievement-oriented work environment, and plentiful resources—they would shine. It didn't happen. Instead they found new excuses. I've learned that good people just learn to overcome obstacles."

By adhering to the principles discussed in this chapter, you will learn to be solution-oriented, preventing problems from arising and building a foundation of success in the workplace that will help you get your next job and excel in it. Above all, if in doubt about what to do and how to do it, ask someone. Then you'll find out how to live up to your interview.

EMPLOYER ROUNDTABLE

What can interns, co-ops, or new hires out of college do to be successful DURING their first job? What are the must-do tips and/or must-avoid blunders? What might surprise students about adjusting to a professional environment?

When you snare the job, behave like every day is an interview. (It is.) Become engaged with more than just a task you've been given. Find out why you are doing that task and where it fits into the broader company strategy. Initiative is a keyword every employer, including myself, uses to describe the ideal employee. We are always listing that as a top trait because we experience it in an employee so infrequently. If you are given an assignment to do "X" do "X+1." In other words, 100% of a task will win praise but 110% brings adoration.

You will find that the skills you learned at school give you less than 50% of the skills you really need. As an intern or co-op, you are not expected to know everything. The bargain that we employers strike with interns is one in which we pay you less than what you would earn as a graduate but, in return, we give you the freedom to learn new skills. Take advantage of every learning experience you can. If you are employed in a small company this is easy. Offer to do production or assembly work. Man the technical support line. Take a webinar. Visit a vendor. Organize the work area. If you work for a large company, these opportunities are more limited, but no one will ever turn you down for going outside your comfort zone.

That said, remember that you have been hired to make the company more profitable. I once asked an intern to determine how much water pressure a glass electrode could handle before it breaks. He was excited about using material from his hyrrodynamics course and he started to set up a complex system of equations using MATLAB to model the process. It was going to take days. I told him to set up a plastic tube with an inexpensive flow meter and blast the bulb until it broke. It took two hours.

Out of sight is out of mind. If you bury yourself in your cubicle or lab space and your boss rarely sees you, then you're letting him (or her) form opinions of you using his imagination. Make a point of sitting down with him/her about once a week. Summarize everything you've done that week and determine what you will be working on next. This should take less than a half-hour but, if you do it, you will do something that 95% of young workers are NOT doing. That sets you apart.

Here are some activities that tell your employer you are not keeper material:

1. Spending ANY time on Facebook, YouTube, or any other website not connected to work.

2. Dressing like a college student. Look around at your co-workers and make sure you are as well-dressed as any of them.

3. Arriving late.

4. Leaving early.

5. Keeping a messy work area.

6. Hiding in a cubicle or lab and not engaging with other workers or your boss.

Go beyond the boundaries of what you believe an internship, co-op position, or first job should be and you will be a star.

- Mark Spencer, President, Water Analytics

Pay attention to your surroundings. It's important to pick up on the norms of the organization. If everyone in your department stays late, you should stay late, too. Your first job is not the time to set yourself apart as an individual. Do as much as you can to make yourself a valuable part of the organization by offering your assistance to those around you whenever possible. The more you reach out to help others, the more likely they will be to help you out by giving you tasks that will lead to further development of your skills.

- Ryan P. Derber, SPHR, Segment Human Resources Manager,
PolyOne Corporation

The expectation for interns, co-ops, or new hires is that they know how to figure out things on their own. The other important thing is to demonstrate that you can work with others in a team. One of the key things for me is how the individual shows their eagerness to learn and demonstrates dedication to the position.

- Wentao Wang, ETP Engineering Manager, Pfizer Global Supply

The most important thing you can do at your new job is to act like you want to be there. By that I mean, you show up early to work and stay longer. Just by being there longer shows that you are committed to the job. You will also want to ask questions. Questions show you are engaged in what you are doing. You will also want to keep your desk organized and take notes when people are asking you to do things, you can't remember everything. Lastly, take pride in the work you do because what you do reflects not just on you but on your company.

- Dan Meunier, Product/Process Engineer, NDH Medical, INC

STUDENT ROUNDTABLE

What can interns, co-ops, or new hires out of college do to be successful DURING their first job? What are the must-do tips and/or must-avoid blunders? What might surprise students about adjusting to a professional environment?

Mental stamina becomes much more of a real thing. As students we are used to throwing ourselves 100% into three or four hours of morning classes or a caffeine-aided lab report, and then taking a break to digress with a workout or some video games requiring pretty much zero responsibility. The workday however, is more drawn out at a slower pace with eight hours of dedication. If college consists of quick spurts of grilling, the workday is a simmering barbeque. Maintaining high energy levels and an upbeat demeanor throughout the day is a challenge, especially when 2:30 rolls around, and it has been a busy day. A good night's sleep, spaced out snacks, and correctly spaced coffee consumption are things I found to help.

Here are three more tips:

1. Set up a LinkedIn account before your co-op and add people as you meet them.

2. Unless asked to check in with your supervisor right away, give him or her some time to settle in for the day before reporting for duty. A simple "Hi ____" is good as you pass his or her office on the way in, but give him or her a chance to drink some coffee and settle in. Have everything ready to go for when you meet though – graphs, reports, etc.

3. Don't be afraid to strike up a conversation

- Andrew Sanginario, Biological Sciences major,
University of Massachusetts Lowell

Make sure you always have a notebook and pen with you during your first few months (I still try to do this even after two years at my job) because you never know when someone may share important information that you will want to reference later. Remember it's always okay to ask questions if you don't understand something, but try to write down the answer so you don't have to ask twice. Volunteer to help with any project or task, no matter how small or annoying it may be, and do so without complaining. Even if your co-workers are complaining about something, try to stay positive—especially when you first start. Having a positive attitude goes a long way.

Don't forget that you are in a professional environment and should act accordingly. This can be especially difficult if the company has a large number of interns or co-ops that may want to be friends with you. Try to remember that you are there to do a job, not to make friends. Try to differentiate yourself from the other interns by socializing (having lunch, talking at the coffee station, etc.) with full-time employees as well as the interns.

- Rebecca Harkess was a Business Administration/ Supply Chain major at
Northeastern University, Class of 2009. She is now a Supply Planner at Keurig.

You are entry level, the bottom of the flow chart and in this fast-paced, "real world" everyone is busy, making it easy to be overlooked. Ask your superior for anything and everything you can to work on. Bury yourself. Learn. Learn about the company you work for, but most importantly learn about the people you work with. You'll accomplish two things by learning about who you work with. First, you'll know who you need to talk to when you need something; this makes your life significantly less stressful. Second, it builds your network. You absolutely cannot do it alone, especially as a new hire. Your success will be attributed to your network. As the saying goes, "It's not always what you know, but who you know."

- Jared Peraner, Market Development Specialist, Consumer & Electronics,
Nypro Inc.; BS, Plastics Engineering, 2012, University of Massachusetts Lowell

---

Never use your cellphone at work. No matter how covert you think you are being your employer knows when you are texting, and they will not be pleased. During my last internship, one of the other interns was actually fired because she was texting instead of working and she thought that the owners wouldn't notice. It's just not worth it, and it makes you look really bad.

Always try and remember the names of people that get introduced to you. Repeat their name back to them to be sure and make the mental effort to remember. You never know who you will need to ask for help and it gets more difficult, if you don't know their names.

Ask a lot of questions. Your co-workers' experience is a really great resource for you because they have been where you are, and they worked to get where they are today. Their insights are invaluable.

Keep a journal and take notes about your experience so you will remember lessons and learn from mistakes.

Build your network while you're at a company. You never know who you will meet later in life or who will have the right opportunity or connection to jumpstart your career. Record e-mails or phone numbers, and keep in touch. Don't be the intern that worked for one summer that everyone has forgotten about a month later.

- Samantha Hamel, Business Administration, Manning School of Business,
University of Massachusetts Lowell

On the job—always be busy. If you have downtime, ask your boss for feedback and for more projects. Don't be afraid of criticism. If you don't know something, ask. I strived for open lines of communication with my boss and other employees to do the best job possible. As I got to know people at a company, I would add them on LinkedIn. That way, I would keep those connections for future job searches, and references. I have a hard time not taking criticism personally, and that is the biggest adjustment I have had to work on in the professional environment. It's all about becoming the best that you can be and any input should be, and is, appreciated.

- Mary Beth Moriarty, PhD Candidate, Plastics Engineering,
University of Massachusetts Lowell

My greatest challenge was overcoming my mindset of "being just a co-op." It prevented me from interacting with co-workers unless I had questions. I was able to overcome this because I was lucky enough to work with really friendly, outgoing people. I also realized that although my role was small it still made an impact and was needed. From this, I learned the importance of professional relationships. Since I had regular conversations with my co-workers, they introduced me to people from other departments that I would not have otherwise met—including VPs and Presidents. I still stay in touch and catch up from time to time. Because of this, I know who to look to if I ever need a referral. So beyond doing a good job with the projects you are given, maintaining professional relationships with your manager or coworkers is very important because it makes you memorable even after you complete the co-op.

- Lynn Le, Finance and Marketing Major, University of Massachusetts Lowell

One of the most important things you can do on your first co-op is stay adequately productive. In my experience, employers are ready for you to start. Sometimes early on, you may complete tasks faster than expected and have some free time. Sometimes you may have to wait on others to approve what you were working on all day, and you need something else to do while they work on it.

If you don't have something to do, ask to help on more projects. If you have to constantly ask for more work, find something that you should be doing and propose to your boss to do it. In some fields, this may be easier than others; in marketing, it is a must. By asking to pick up the ball on a project or help to relieve the burden of a task from a co-worker (only so they can be more productive where they are the most accountable), you show initiative and aptitude that may get you hired afterwards. My work would be much less important to the department if I just let the workload come in. There is always something else to do. Just don't bite off more than you can chew. Take on new responsibilities in small pieces and work your way up to the big picture.

- Matthew Johnson, Business Administration,
University of Massachusetts Lowell

CHAPTER FOUR REVIEW QUESTIONS

1. List three different ways in which performing well on your job or internship will benefit you.

2. Depending on traffic or public transportation issues, let's say that it could take you anywhere from 30 to 50 minutes to get to work. If you absolutely have to be at work by 8:30 a.m., what time should you leave?

3. Give three examples of specific goals that you would like to be able to set for your next internship, co-op job, or full-time job.

4. Name four on-the-job situations in which it would be highly advisable to contact your internship or co-op coordinator.

5. Describe three common mistakes students make when trying to juggle a part-time job or internship with full-time coursework.

CHAPTER FIVE

Making Sense of Your Experience

Eventually, your job will end, and you will return to the classroom. Whether your experience was terrific, terrible, or anywhere in between, it would be a missed opportunity to just put it behind you when you return to the classroom. At this point, you need to take the final steps toward getting credit for your co-op as well as figuring out what comes next in your career. At Northeastern, this process includes a) turning in an evaluation and b) completing a reflection requirement. Make sure you find out what's required in your program.

Receiving an evaluation and fulfilling reflection requirements offer you a chance to make sense of what happened while you were on co-op. Because the primary goal of co-op is to learn from anything you experienced at work—whether positive or negative—the evaluation and reflection processes will help you gain some perspective on how you did and what you can take away from the experience. This will help build self-awareness—including a sense of what you need to do to keep growing and improving as a professional in the future. It's not uncommon for a student to emerge from a co-op or internship with a greater sense of urgency about the classroom. For that matter, it's not unusual for students to improve dramatically in their coursework after co-op. In addition to seeing the practical relevance of the material in the "real world," taking classes sometimes feels pretty easy after a demanding work experience!

As the following sidebar box indicates, internships and co-op jobs don't only answer questions about career fit that you may have—they also may raise new questions regarding about what comes next.

YOUR EVALUATION

As your co-op job comes to a close, you generally will receive an evaluation. Most programs have a standard form that employers can complete and return to the program coordinator. Often you will be asked to summarize the job and your sense of how it was as an experience, while your supervisor will write up her or his thoughts on your responsibilities, strengths, areas for further professional development, and on your soft skills: interpersonal relationships, dependability, judgment, etc. You also may be given an overall rating, such as outstanding, very good, average, marginal, or unsatisfactory.

Some employers will give you an evaluation form that is typically used for all employees in their organization. These forms can be several pages long and are quite detailed. At some organizations, the format involves asking you and your manager to reflect briefly in writing on how successful you were in reaching your job-related tasks and objectives.

Whatever your evaluation looks like, keep a few things in mind when receiving your first performance evaluation:

1. *Don't take it too personally.* You and your manager may not see eye to eye on how you did in your job—and it won't always be because your supervisor has a higher opinion of your performance than you do! You may receive criticism that you believe to be inaccurate or unfair. Regardless, you want to end your relationship with any employer in a gracious, classy manner—don't blow it because of an impulsive, emotional reaction to evaluation comments.

2. *View the evaluation experience as a learning opportunity.* If you have communicated consistently with your manager throughout your co-op, you should not be too surprised by your evaluation. In any event, your evaluation gives you things to think about and talk about with your co-op coordinator—it can lead to specific goals for personal improvement and success in your next co-op. No one is perfect, and no one is perfectly self-aware of all of her or his strengths and areas requiring further development. Use the evaluation as a tool in your professional development.

3. *If you feel your evaluation is unjust or unfair, take the initiative to discuss it with your coordinator.* Getting evaluated on co-op is hardly an exact science. Some employers may rate students higher than they deserve because they fear that a negative or neutral review will cause undesirable conflict or impair your academic progress. Other employers may have impossibly high standards or just believe that most employees should receive average reviews unless something really astonishing was accomplished. In other situations, you may have a change of manager midway through your co-op, or perhaps you reported to numerous people or maybe even to no one at all. Obviously, any of these developments will affect the fairness or accuracy of your review.

    Discuss any of these concerns with your coordinator. We know that these things happen, and it also can be quite challenging for us to figure out the truth amidst many different perceptions. Your coordinator should be able to provide you with a more objective and balanced view of how you did if you're not sure what to think about your review.

4. *After a few months have gone by, review your evaluation again.* It's easy to lose your objectivity when you're immersed in a job for 40 hours or more per week. After you have been out of that specific work environment for a good while, you may find that it's easier

for you to consider the positives and negatives of your review more openly and less emotionally. It's also good to reconsider your performance before you begin your next job search, so that you are ready to discuss how your job went with a future employer. This is a good opportunity to show self-awareness and graciousness. Even if you have lingering bad feelings about a previous job or supervisor, you need to move on and take the high road when discussing past events with a potential new boss.

While most co-op students and interns get anxious about their initial performance evaluation, in my experience, the great majority of well-prepared coop students do very well in the eyes of employers. Probably at least 90 percent receive very good or outstanding evaluations. Still, everyone always has ways in which they can improve, and it's generally very helpful to get feedback from an experienced manager in the professional world.

Returning To The Classroom – A Co-op Professional's Perspective
by Ronnie Porter

In my program, students sometimes realize what the theories really meant when they were put into the practice—or sometimes the other way around: They've done things on co-op and then studied the theory and figured out why things were done a certain way. Either way, it just naturally flows into the academics and into thinking about how they want to do things next time around on their co-op.

Through their co-op experience, they may know that they need to take courses to enhance their expertise in a certain area. In Arts and Sciences, the question should not be, say, "Can you give me a list of all the philosophy jobs?" We say, "That's not the right question." We're interested in "Why are you interested in philosophy and what do you want to do with it?" So it's a different approach. There's no list of jobs, rather there are a lot of conversations around what the person wants to do and what their hopes and expectations are about how they're going to use this information that they're learning.

Ronnie Porter is a cooperative education faculty coordinator in
Biology at Northeastern University.

PURPOSES OF REFLECTION

As co-op, internships, and other forms of practice-oriented education become a bigger piece of the learning puzzle at many colleges and universities, more schools are beginning to require some form of reflection requirement for students returning to school following co-op. Why do co-op programs require reflection? There are numerous reasons:

1. *Making connections between classroom and the world of practice.* One purpose of co-ops and internships is to give students a practice-oriented element to their educations, making learning "hands-on" instead of just learning about theories. Reflection often requires you to think about how a work experience brought classroom concepts to life, or how practical work experience changed an understanding of something you thought you understood in a course. In return, your job experience gives you raw material that you bring with you to class to help you understand new concepts and theories in your field.

Integrating Practice With Coursework – A Co-op Professional's Perspective
by Rose Dimarco

I find that as an undergrad student in health care, you learn quickly when to do something and how to do it. The why you are doing it—why you are doing that range of motion or stretching exercise or providing certain pharmaceutical drugs—comes in the classroom. So it's up to you to take the where and when and connect it with the why. Now you're slowly going to evolve from studying nursing to becoming a nurse—that's going to come from that interchange.

Rose Dimarco is a cooperative education faculty coordinator in
Physical Therapy at Northeastern University.

2. *Having an opportunity to compare your experience with those of others.* Going to reflection seminars gives you a chance to hear about where your classmates worked, what they did, and how it all went. It can be useful to hear about how others dealt with challenges that they faced and to hear the thoughts that upperclassmen have about the job experiences after going through the process repeatedly. At best, you may be able to learn from the successes and mistakes of others.

3. *Learning about future job options.* Hearing about other students' experiences may give you some added perspective about where you might want to work in the future as well as jobs or organizations that you may wish to avoid. HOWEVER: Be careful about drawing conclusions from the experiences of others! Just because one industrial engineering student complains bitterly about her internship at Amalgamated Suitcases, does that mean that YOU wouldn't like the same job? Maybe, maybe not. In the same reflection seminar, you may hear another engineering student praising his supply chain management job at an organization called www.advancedlogistics.com—does that mean this job is great for everyone? Of course not.

Exploring Job Options – A Co-op Professional's Perspective
by Bob Tillman

The discussion now is going to be, "Tell me more about what you're looking for the next time. Are you looking for more of the same but just at a higher level? Is it a new challenge? A career exploration you're looking for? Skill development? Are there certain projects you want to work on? What's the itch? Let's identify that.

Bob Tillman is an Associate Professor and cooperative education faculty coordinator in
Civil Engineering at Northeastern University.

Whenever I started my reflection seminars, I would usually tell the tale of two students who did the exact same job at the same time with the same employer. In one reflection seminar, the first student said, "My PC support job was fantastic—I'd recommend it to anyone. The day goes by really quickly because there's always something new to handle—you're not stuck behind a desk; you're going all over the company to troubleshoot problems. When you go to see end users, they're usually upset about their computer problems, but when you fix the problem, they are SO grateful! What a great job!"

At the next reflection seminar, that student's co-worker complained bitterly about his job: "Don't ever work in PC support! What a bunch of headaches—you come in and try to get a project done, and you keep getting interrupted constantly by end users. They're generally pretty clueless about computers, and they're in a foul mood when you go to see them. Every day I went home with a headache."

Which student is "right"? Both... and neither. The quality of a job experience is very much in the eye of the beholder. When students describe their previous jobs, listen more carefully to their descriptions of the job duties and the reasons why they liked or disliked their jobs. Make up your own mind as to whether that job would be good for you.

4. *Having the opportunity for a more detached and objective appraisal of one's experience, after the fact.* Working at an organization full-time is kind of like being in an intense relationship. Whether you're in a romantic relationship, living with a roommate, or working in a job, it can be easy to lose your perspective when you're immersed in the situation. Positively or negatively, you might do things you wouldn't ordinarily do—and then wonder why that happened, after the fact.

   Reflection gives you an opportunity to make sense of your experience in a more detached, open way, after you are no longer in the situation. This may lead to new insights and a new appreciation of what it all meant.

Reflection also can be quite surprising for both students and coordinators. One time I was running a reflection seminar for entrepreneurship/small business management students. One student reported that he had worked at a small restaurant but found it frustrating because the entrepreneur was highly secretive about the financial affairs of the business. "My guess is that he didn't want to show me the books because he was cheating on his taxes," the student said. "But I guess that's what you have to do to make it as an entrepreneur."

I managed to hold my tongue and asked if anyone else in the room had another perspective on the situation. A second student raised his hand, "My family has run a business for several generations, and my grandfather *went to jail* for basically having the same mindset as your boss." It was a powerful moment and a great chance for the group to reflect on the challenges and ethical dilemmas that entrepreneurs face—as well as considering the potential consequences of running a business that is engaged in illegal activity.

FORMS OF REFLECTION

Generally, there are many ways in which you can fulfill your reflection requirement. Which one will you end up doing? It depends partly on what works best for you and partly on what your coordinator finds most advisable given your circumstances. All reflection methods have pros and cons, so let's consider briefly the different forms of reflection.

1. *Small-group seminars.* Most Northeastern students participate in a reflection seminar in a small group—usually no more than 15 students. Many students are required to go

to one 60-minute session with their coordinator and a group of students in their field. On the positive side, this method is fairly quick and painless for most students and coordinators. It also gives students a chance to exchange ideas and experiences with classmates. On the negative side, it's hard to go into serious issues in great depth in a one-time, one-hour session. Also, some students may feel awkward or uncomfortable sharing their job experiences—especially if something unpleasant happened at work. For these students, another reflection method may be preferable.

2. *Writing a reflection paper and/or keeping a journal.* This is another common form of reflection. Your coordinator may provide you with some questions or topics that can be addressed in a paper. Alternatively, you may decide on your own that it just would be a good idea to keep a journal. In the summer of 2012, the intern who worked for me at Bates Communications kept his own journal—taking a few minutes at the end of each day to reflect on what he was doing and what he was learning. I was so impressed!

Often the focus of a journal is not so much on a plot summary of your work experience: instead, the idea usually is to try to make connections between the real world and the classroom and to get across what you learned about yourself and the organizational world while on an internship or co-op—-even if that included getting fired from your job! Some students even write weekly journals reflecting on their development through the job experience—it can be quite remarkable to look back at a list of your anxieties and concerns before day one at the end of a six-month full-time co-op.

Here are some questions that might be considered for a paper or journal:

- How has this job experience helped you understand concepts that you previously learned when taking classes in your major? Has this experience changed your attitude toward being in classes and your ability to perform since returning to campus after completing your job? How have liberal arts classes helped you build useful transferable skills for the professional world?

- What was the purpose of your job? How did your job fit into the overall organizational mission?

- How did you learn how to do your job? Formal training? Personal instruction by your supervisor? "Peer-to-peer" learning—did you pick things up from co-workers? Figuring things out for yourself? Break down the various ways you learned about appropriate behaviors as well as work tasks or products.

- What differentiates an excellent manager or supervisor from a poor or average one?

- How and why did your job confirm or change your career direction?

- Describe the organizational culture of where you worked and whether or not this culture is the best for you as a worker.

- What were the norms or "unwritten rules" regarding what was and was not acceptable where you worked? Was it difficult to learn these norms and adjust to them?

- How would you rate the quality of your job as a learning experience?

- What did you learn in this job that had nothing to do with your technical skills or your major/concentration?

- How would you rate your performance in the job, regardless of the job's quality?

- Now that you have had this experience, what are your plans for your next job, whether co-op, internship, clinical, or post-graduate?

Journals and papers are advantageous in that they provide a chance to really go into depth about what you learned, and they also are a more private form of reflection. The downside is that they are more time-consuming and don't allow you the chance to hear the perspectives of fellow students.

3. *Reflecting via e-mail, online message boards, and the Web.* Some coordinators may set up electronic ways of helping you reflect on the job while you are still working. You may have questions e-mailed to you for your consideration and response. Sometimes programs like Blackboard, online message boards, or the Web are used in order to create places where students can connect with other students and their coordinator despite being far away from campus. The best thing about these methods is that they help you have opportunities to reflect when there is still time to make changes in your performance or address problem areas at work. The negatives include the time involved and the risk of information getting into the hands of those who are not meant to see it. Additionally, the technology is a hurdle for some co-op programs.

4. *Taking a work-related class DURING your co-op.* Some Northeastern students have had the opportunity to take a one-credit course during their co-op. The students who took this course on ethics in the workplace were allowed to have this count toward completing their reflection requirement. The class generally meets only a few times in the early evening, though there are also online assignments and discussions. In addition to getting reflection credit for this course, many students found this to be a great opportunity to discuss ethical issues or concerns while they were in the midst of them in the workplace.

5. *Having a one-on-one meeting with your coordinator.* Occasionally—most often in special circumstances—a coordinator may find it acceptable to meet one-on-one with a student to complete the reflection requirement. This is not typical, as it is a very labor-intensive method for a coordinator who may have over 100 students returning to classes after co-op. If something particularly difficult happened on the job, though, this may be an important and useful option in order to confront problems, learn from mistakes, or to determine if the coordinator has issues that must be addressed with the employer.

GETTING CREDIT FOR YOUR WORK EXPERIENCE

For most students, getting at least an average evaluation and completing a reflection requirement means that they will get a passing grade for their work experience. (Most co-ops and internships are graded on a pass/fail basis, if at all.) Sometimes, though, the outcome is in doubt. Any of the following can jeopardize your ability to get a passing grade for your work experience:

- failing to notify your coordinator about your job before it begins

- accepting an offer from one employer, only to renege on your agreement to accept an offer with another employer

- quitting a job without getting your coordinator's permission first

- getting fired (or getting a poor evaluation)

- failing to turn in an evaluation in a timely manner

- failing to complete a reflection requirement within two months of returning to school

In the end, your coordinator will determine the grade you receive for your work experience. Make sure you understand the grading criteria. Make sure that you're never in a borderline category by doing a great job and completing all steps with your coordinator! After all, failing your work experience doesn't look so great to future employers who will be reviewing your transcript.

FINAL THOUGHTS ON CO-OP SURVIVAL AND SUCCESS

After reading this much of the guidebook, you should have a good foundation when it comes to understanding workplace survival and success. If you can apply the concepts that we've covered in these pages, you will emerge with greater self-awareness, a sense of accomplishment, and a set of experiences that will entice employers looking to hire new graduates. You also will have a new appreciation for how, why, and where learning happens as you go from one job to the next as well as from the classroom to the world of experience.

For a co-op coordinator, internship director, or career services professional, the most satisfying part of the job is seeing students come in with retail stores and restaurants on their resumes and graduate as professionals with a keen sense of who they are, what they want, and what they are capable of accomplishing through hard work. I have seen students who were barely able to get a low-level administrative job on the first co-op who ultimately graduated with incredible experience and a very attractive job offer. I often tell students that internships and co-op jobs are not sprints: They are marathons that reward those who display persistence and consistent effort over the months of a co-op position.

But perhaps I should let some of top students tell their stories to give you a better sense of what I mean.

Making Sense of Your Co-op – A Student's Perspective
by Ted Schneider

There is nothing like co-op for turning inexperienced freshmen into successful professionals. The constant transition between class and work is painful, tiring, and repetitive but also extremely exciting, rewarding, and invaluable. After four co-op positions in four terrifically different locations, I "know" that I have had a college experience that cannot be matched by experiences had by those at traditional universities.

When I go home for the holidays, I laugh about my high school friends' nervous questions regarding the interview process. Since freshman year, I have had approximately 25 interviews for "professional positions." Interviewing has become such a commonality for my peers and myself that most of us look forward to it almost as if it is a fun challenge - not to see if we could do well, but to find out if we could do even better than the last time. NU students—or co-op students anywhere I guess—are so far ahead of their traditional-program counterparts when it comes to professionalism that we have a reason to be a little proud.

Ted Schneider was an Accounting/MIS student at Northeastern University, Class of 2002.

Here's another one:

Making Sense of Your Co-op – A Student's Perspective
by Mark Moccia

To be honest, I did not know what to expect from co-op. I heard mostly positives about co-op. However, I was still unsure of how I was going to be treated, the relationships I would have with management, how much work I would receive, and other job-related concerns. The most surprising thing I learned about co-op is that you are, in fact, treated just as a full-time employee. You are expected to work standard hours (and overtime if needed), take your job seriously (and not as a temporary assignment where you can "goof off" for 3-6 months), and contribute in a positive manner. The co-op program is the main reason I attended Northeastern: I would have been making a $100,000 blunder by not getting the most out of co-op. The other amazing advantage of co-op is that if you perform well enough, you have the inside track on a full-time position with the company!

I have always been a great student. However, the co-op program has made me realize that it takes more than excellent grades to be successful. Co-op has taught me that you need to have good transferable skills, such as communication, multitasking, time management, and the ability to interact with all levels of the organization. Working with corporations has taught me to take my focus on schoolwork and apply it to the business world, specifically through the co-op program. Without the co-op program, my grades would be just as strong but I would not have the skills and savvy to match it.

Mark Moccia was an Accounting/MIS student at Northeastern University, Class of 2002.

Here's one more!

Making Sense Of Co-op – A Student's Perspective
by Gabriel Glasscock

When I began my co-op career, my expectations weren't high. I expected to be exposed to the corporate climate and have minimal responsibilities at a few companies, graduating with my foot in the door at a few places. Before I knew it, I was in Tampa, Florida, standing in a classroom in front of 80 over-analytical recent college graduates, giving them lectures on the Java programming language. The most surprising thing I've learned is that you can ride this co-op roller coaster as fast as you want to if you're not afraid to take on challenges.

Co-op has humbled me but also made me aware of my capabilities. It tests your resilience, and helps you realize what you really want to do with the rest of your life. It has helped me mature and exposed me to many things. I now know what it's like to have 12 friends laid off on the same day!

Co-op prepares you mentally for the reality of working and dealing with life after college. I truly consider myself lucky to have had these opportunities. In some areas, I consider myself 100% different, and for the better. Typical four-year programs? Heck no! CO-OP!

Gabriel Glasscock was an MIS student at Northeastern University, Class of 2002.

The rest of the book features appendices that may or may not be useful to you right now. Appendix A covers the job search process through the Co-op Learning Model.

Appendix B is a Skills Identification Worksheet that you can complete and tally up. I've found that this is a real confidence builder when used shortly before beginning work on your first resume. Many fledgling co-ops believe that they have nothing to offer a prospective employer. This exercise will help you realize that you probably have at least 20-30 soft skills that are going to be attractive to employers.

Appendix C details how to write cover letters—whether for obtaining an internship, a co-op job, or your first job after graduation. Generally, you won't need to write a cover letter if you're applying for a job through a co-op or internship program, but sooner or later you will want to learn how to write a cover letter that is every bit as strategic as the interviewing approach described earlier in the book.

Appendix D includes a "bridging" exercise that will help you make connections between your resume and a specific job description. Doing this activity will help you realize how you need to change gears and emphasize different strengths and skills based on the job description at hand. I originally created this exercise several years ago, but my counterparts at the University of Massachusetts Lowell improved on my version considerably. As a result, I've included their version in this edition.

Appendix E has more in-depth information on behavioral-based interviewing, including several excellent student examples. Being able to rehearse specific, vivid stories that can be used to prove that you really do have a given skill is a great way to prepare for *any* kind of interview, not just a behavioral-based one.

Appendix F is written by my former colleague at Northeastern University, Charlie Bognanni. It's his special guide for international students who are looking to do co-op jobs or internships in the United States. This is "must reading" if you're an international student. While all of the material in this book applies to all students, international students sometimes face different challenges because of cultural issues. A careful read of this section can help international students avoid problems and get the most of their experiential learning opportunity.

Appendix G is provided by my friends at University of Massachusetts Lowell. It features their helpful tips on informational interviewing. This advice is very helpful, especially if you're not sure about your career path or if you're simply looking to add new connections in the field of your choice.

Appendix H features some handouts that I liked to use in my Introduction to Co-op course. Some may be useful in helping to fine-tune your resume or interview, while others are thought-provoking scenarios that can be a good basis for written reflection or in-class discussion.

Good luck with your co-op career, and remember: The goal is to shine and not simply survive!

CHAPTER FIVE REVIEW QUESTIONS

1. Why do many students start getting better grades in classes after completing a co-op or internship?

2. What are three benefits of attending reflection seminars?

3. Think about the last job that you held. What was the *purpose* of that job? How did it fit into the goals of the organization that employed you?

4. Name three situations that could result in a student not getting credit for a co-op or internship.

5. From the three lengthy student sidebar boxes at the end of the chapter on the benefits of co-op, which one resonated the most with you? Why?

APPENDIX A
The Co-op/Internship Process

In this book we have covered a great deal of information about co-op. Nonetheless, you may very well be wondering "what do I do next?" Every program has its own rules, regulations, and idiosyncrasies, causing difficulty in making generalizations about the job search process across universities. However, there are enough commonalities to make it worth our while to review them here.

More than anything, though, I want to make sure to preface this information with a warning: *The job search process is always evolving and changing over time. Universities are continually revising the job search process, making changes to computer systems and student requirements such as deadlines for turning in resumes, creating e-portfolios, and changing ways to get referred to employers.* **As such, ALWAYS stay in touch with your coordinator to be sure of the requirements and deadlines for your specific program!** If in doubt about when you need to get started, make contact and find out sooner rather than later. Failing to do so could make all the difference between success and failure in your job search.

CO-OP LEARNING MODEL

The Co-op Learning Model is a simple but useful way to understand the three primary phases of the co-op process: preparation; activity; and reflection.

The Preparation Phase

The preparation phase includes all of the activities that you undertake to get ready for your co-op or internship. Contrary to the opinion of a few misinformed students, most programs are not job placement services. In other words, you can't just waltz into your coordinator's office a few weeks before your scheduled work period begins and—just like that—get "assigned" to a job. The system doesn't work that way. Why not? The most important reason is that we want you to own the responsibility of your job search, so you will understand how to do everything you need to do to get a job for the rest of your professional

189

career! Therefore, most co-op professionals won't write your resume for you, don't tell companies who to hire, and require an employer evaluation to help determine if you should get a passing grade for your work experience.

Because of all of this, preparation takes time! Generally, you will be asked to revise your resume more than once, and some students may go on more than a dozen interviews before getting and accepting an offer.

The Activity Phase

After you get a job, you start working regularly with your employer; the work period is the activity phase. During this phase, your focus should be on understanding and meeting your supervisor's expectations regarding everything from work hours to job responsibilities, setting goals together to ensure that you have a mutual understanding about your level of job performance.

During this phase, it also may be advisable to check in with your coordinator back at school—especially if any concerns or problems arise. The objective is to return to school with the best possible evaluation and reference.

The Reflection Phase

After you return to classes, you need to complete the reflection phase to get credit for your co-op. Basically, you will need to make sure that your coordinator receives your evaluation and find out if any reflection requirement needs to be fulfilled. It's also advisable to update your resume, while the job is still fresh in your mind.

Now that you have an overview of the co-op process, let's take a closer look at the details that may be involved in each step.

WORKING WITH YOUR INTERNSHIP/CO-OP COORDINATOR

As mentioned briefly in Chapter One, it's critical to build a good working relationship with your co-op coordinator—and with other co-op faculty if necessary. Here are some key pointers:

Stay On Your Coordinator's Radar Screen.

Given that your co-op or internship coordinator works with hundreds of students each year, you can't expect him or her to hold your hand through the process. It's absolutely critical that you own the responsibility for finding out and remembering how early and often you need to come in and what you need to accomplish each step along the way. If you're not sure, call or send an e-mail. "I just didn't have time to get in touch" just doesn't cut it—not when it takes all of one or two minutes to send an update by e-mail or voice mail at whatever hour of the day or night. If you're not in touch regularly—especially during the months before you're scheduled to start your job—your coordinator will assume that you're really not that interested in working.

Know How To Determine Your Co-op Coordinator's Availability.

Find out if your co-op coordinator can be seen individually either by appointment or by going to walk-in hours. But how can you find out when a given co-op coordinator is available? See if your coordinator has a calendar—either online or just outside the door of his or her office.

If you have trouble finding a time to meet with your coordinator, you should e-mail or call your coordinator to see if additional times are available. If your coordinator don't know that you're trying to get in touch, she or he can't help to accommodate you!

Here are a few other helpful hints about working with co-op and internship coordinators as well as career services professionals. With a little thought and communication, you can avoid considerable frustration.

1. *If you are on a tight schedule in general, try to schedule appointments.* Some students have limited free time available due to classes, part-time jobs, clubs, and varsity sports. If you fit this description, you need to be proactive, scheduling appointments ahead of time and asking your coordinator for ways to ensure regular meetings. Most coordinators and career professionals will schedule meetings at irregular times if a student has legitimate conflicts and is proactive and polite about addressing the situation.

2. *If you prefer to come to walk-in hours, try to come first thing in the morning and/or bring homework or reading material if you must come when it's busy.* During the months leading up to the beginning of a work period, coordinators can be very busy seeing students. Some students end up frustrated because they haven't really thought about how to avoid the walk-in logjam. There are many ways to minimize your waiting time. First, come in early—early in the day and early in the process. Many college students are not early risers, so most coordinators tend to have shorter walk-in lines during the morning hours. Anytime after 11:30 tends to get really busy during the peak times of year. Likewise, if you come in several months before your co-op for that first resume review, you will beat the rush and be in good shape the rest of the way.

   Sometimes, though, you can't avoid a long wait—especially during peak months. With this in mind, bring some homework or reading material. That way you won't sit around feeling impatient if you do need to wait a while.

3. *If you really can't come in every week or so during referral period, you need to stay in contact via e-mail or voice mail.* Some students keep popping by during a busy afternoon walk-in hour time... only to find that there is a long line. If they get discouraged and leave, the coordinator has no idea that the student has made any effort to get in touch. Thus, you really need to stay in touch by voice mail or e-mail—even if it's just to give a quick update regarding your job search or to let your coordinator know that you're having difficulty coming in during the available times. If you fail to communicate that you're having a problem, then no one can help you!

4. *Be reasonable about what you expect your coordinator to be able to do for you in person, on the phone, or by e-mail.* In person, don't expect your coordinator to write or rewrite

191

your resume for you or to describe numerous available jobs to you. You need to do many things for yourself. As for e-mails, bear in mind that they should not replace individual meetings. One of my frustrations was when students e-mailed their resume to me and asked me to critique it or correct it. It's incredibly time-consuming to edit a resume this way, as it results in extremely long e-mail replies: "On the fourth line of your second job description, three-quarters of the way across the line, add a comma before the word 'demonstrated.'" Ugh! There may be situations in which long e-mails are unavoidable—for example, when you are facing a major problem at work and can't openly talk about it on the phone or come into the office because you're on the job full-time—but resume reviews are generally not one of those situations. Many situations just require a personal meeting.

5. *When faced with frustration or uncertainty, assume the best of your coordinator.* If your coordinator doesn't reply to your call or e-mail as quickly as you like, assume the best in this situation. It may be because you wrote your e-mail on Monday night, and the coordinator was out visiting companies on Tuesday. Then that coordinator may be welcomed back to the office with a few dozen e-mails, 15-20 voice mails, and a long line of students filling up the whole morning of walk-in hours. It doesn't mean that you have been forgotten or that your coordinator doesn't care. If more than three days go by without hearing back—or sooner if you are facing a real emergency—follow up politely and professionally: "I'm sure you're very busy right now.... I just wanted to follow up to make sure you got my message and to see if there was anything else I should be doing right now. It would be great to hear from you when you get a moment. Thanks!"

This is good practice for when similar situations arise with managers and co-workers on co-op. In either situation, this kind of message goes a long way in terms of getting a quick and professional response.

THE STEP-BY-STEP PROCESS

Preparation Phase

Step 1 – *Become Aware of ALL Deadlines and Requirements As Soon As Possible.*

If you're a first-time student—and especially if you are a transfer student, meet with your coordinator as soon as possible to learn about your options regarding when to start co-op. *Don't assume that you can start your co-op or internship whenever you feel like it!* Co-ops and internships are not guaranteed for all students—if you blow off meeting with your coordinator, the consequences generally will be severe. If you miss deadlines, you may not be allowed to use the resources of the co-op department in finding a job. The student who does this will end up seeking his or her own job and risks getting a failing grade for co-op.

Step 2 – *Have a One-on-One Meeting with your Co-op Coordinator.*

This is a mandatory step in most programs. You will identify and discuss your short-term and long-term co-op and career objectives with your coordinator. You also will bring a hard copy of your resume to your co-op coordinator, so he or she can critique and edit it. Save these edits, and use them to revise your resume accordingly. Bring a hard copy of your revised resume to your coordinator along with the edits, so your resume can be proofread quickly and effectively. It may take a few rounds of corrections, but eventually your coordinator may ask for an electronic copy of the finalized resume to e-mail to employers.

Step 3 – *Review Co-op Job Descriptions and Rank Them.*

Once your finalized resume has been approved by your co-op coordinator, you generally will be allowed to start pursuing jobs. Make sure you understand your school's system—including how to work with computerized job listings.

Study the description and requirements and try to determine which jobs represent good learning experiences for you as well as being within your reach. If you're not sure, ask your coordinator. Many coordinators will require you to print out job descriptions that are of great interest to you—this will help you and your coordinator to determine if the job is a good fit and if you meet the qualifications. Keep the job descriptions in a folder.

Step 4 – *Meet with your Co-op Coordinator to Review your Job Rankings.*

The next step generally is to review your job rankings in an individual meeting with your co-op coordinator. Find out how early you can do this, and also if there is a deadline for making this happen. Bring your folder of printed job descriptions to your co-op coordinator.

Your co-op coordinator will review your rankings. In all probability, he or she will have additional suggestions and also may determine that a given job might be too much of a reach for you. Don't be discouraged—it's part of the process, and sometimes seeing your "reach" jobs can help your co-op coordinator suggest other jobs that are steps in the direction of your "reach" jobs. In many but not all programs, coordinators will limit how many jobs you can pursue simultaneously. Coordinators definitely do not want students to just fling dozens of resumes at employers—they want you to be more selective. This also means that you should really know each job description when you come in: Don't just look at a company name or job title and print out the job description without really thinking about how you match up with the job duties and requirements.

I can tell you that students vary *dramatically* in how they interact with a coordinator. I have had students interrupt a meeting with another student—or a phone call—by walking into my office regardless and saying "Send this to Gillette for me for the such-and-such job." Such behavior says a great deal about a student's professionalism—it's never a good idea to treat a coordinator as if she or he is your servant or administrative assistant.

On the other hand, there have been any number of times when I have been absolutely wowed by a student. If someone comes in and is upbeat, professional, and polite, I'm going to try that much harder to help them. There have been many occasions when such a student came in asking about a job that was already filled—and I was so impressed by them that I encouraged them to apply for other good jobs... and even recommended them to an employer!

Step 5 – *Stay in Touch with your Coordinator Regularly throughout the Process.*

After your rankings and referrals have been completed, your resume will start going out to employers. Most coordinators e-mail resumes out at least once per week. At this point, there are many different possibilities. Some students get a few interviews out of their first batch of resumes to go out to employers; others don't get any—especially less experienced students.

If you get an interview, let your coordinator know—even if only by e-mail or voice mail. Ask your coordinator how often you should check in. At some point, your coordinator may be able to fill you in a little. You may be told that a company has not contacted any candidates yet, or you may learn that you are not one of the candidates chosen for an interview. In any case, your coordinator will suggest sooner or later that you select some more jobs and then come in again to discuss the new selections.

The worst thing you can do is to get discouraged by not getting interviews or by getting interviews and no offers. These developments don't always come easily! Some students start on time and do everything right—but then disappear completely after they send a batch of resumes and get no reply! Other students definitely intend to stay on top of things, but then they get distracted by mid-terms or other academic responsibilities. *You have to stay in touch*—even if it's just to say that you haven't received any calls and aren't sure what to do next.

Repeat the process of ranking jobs, getting referrals, and going on interviews as many times as you need to in order to get a job. In a job search, you never know if you're ten percent of the way to getting a job or whether you're incredibly close. But you always have to assume that you're really close and that with another push of effort it will happen for you.

Step 6 – *Responding to a Job Offer.*

Remember these key points:

- Unless you are in a dire financial situation, money should not be the deciding factor in which job you accept. Money is NOT a motivator! That's been proven in many studies. What WILL motivate you? A job with the following characteristics:

  —You like the work itself
  —You have opportunities for growth and advancement
  —You have opportunities for achievement and recognition

  If you're choosing between a great learning experience that is an unpaid internship, or a mediocre experience that pays $8/hour, which will you choose? Depending on your field and other alternatives, you very well may be better off taking the unpaid position. On the other hand, there's nothing wrong with taking a great job that pays $14/hour over a comparable job that pays $10/hour.

  For most students, my advice is to go after the best learning experience at this point in your career. If you focus on your career development now, the financial rewards will come sooner or later—and you'll be happier in the meantime going to work every day.

- If you are offered a job that is not your first choice, you can ask the employer for a short time to consider the offer—no more than three business days. Chapter Three details how to put an offer on hold gracefully.

- Once you have accepted a job, meet with your coordinator to do an agreement form and any other paperwork. **If you are an international student (here on F-1 and J-1 visas), it is absolutely critical that you receive work authorization BEFORE starting ANY job in the United States.** After 9/11, the government became incredibly strict about international students who are working without formal authorization. Deportation is becoming much more common. For all students, though, meeting with your coordinator is a good opportunity to discuss success factors for your co-op job, including how to avoid problems and get the best possible evaluation and reference.

- REMEMBER—do NOT accept a job unless you are prepared to honor your commitment no matter what else happens. It is completely unacceptable to renege on your acceptance if you get another offer later—even if the other offer is a much better offer for significantly more money. Students who don't honor their agreements risk getting a failing grade for co-op. If in doubt, ALWAYS talk to your coordinator before you accept a job offer.

- That said, be careful about being too fickle when it comes to job offers. Increasingly, students have been waffling about accepting a perfectly good offer—merely because "I really hoped to have several offers to choose from." Applying for a job is not like applying to college, where you might apply to eight or ten and then have weeks or months to choose between three or four who accept you. You need to make a prompt decision in fairness to other candidates who might accept if you decline.

- Re-read Chapter Four of this guidebook before starting your job, as this chapter has many good ideas about on-the-job success.

Developing Your Own Job

Chapter One goes over the guidelines for developing your own job, so you should re-read them if you have any questions about how the process works. Most importantly, remember that students developing their own jobs still need to be in regular contact with their coordinators. You can't go off and do a job without getting it approved beforehand by your coordinator.

Activity Phase

You are expected to complete the entire work period once you have accepted a job. In other words, you can't do a job for a few weeks and then decide you don't like it and just quit. There may be rare occurrences in which a student may be released from their commitment— for example, if the employer misled the student about the nature of the job, or if harassment is going on. HOWEVER, it is the student's responsibility to bring any problems or concerns to the attention of the co-op coordinator instead of just quitting as soon as a problem arises. Send an e-mail, make a call—anything—just let the co-op or internship coordinator know what's going on and get her or his advice before taking action.

Note that most co-ops and interns rarely get vacation days during their co-op work period: There is no "Spring Break" for students working winter and spring, for example. Likewise, students can't end a full-time co-op job in early December to get an extra long Christmas break: At best, your co-op will end a few days before Christmas. Likewise, students working winter/spring may end their co-op on a Friday and start classes by the following Wednesday!

You are expected to work on any days that the organization is open—meaning that some students will get a day off on Columbus Day, while others will not. Organizations have different policies regarding paying students for holidays, but most often employers simply pay you for whatever hours you work.

Contact your coordinator with any problems that arise on the job.

Reflection Phase

Most of the whys and wherefores regarding reflection can be reviewed in Chapter Five. To get credit for co-op or an internship, most programs require that you:

* complete your co-op job successfully.

* turn in a relatively good evaluation form.

* complete a reflection requirement or some other follow-up activity.

APPENDIX B

Skills Identification Worksheet

Instructions: This worksheet is designed to help make you aware of how many skills you already have—probably more than you realize! Put a check mark in every box that reflects a skill that you have as well as WHERE you have demonstrated that skill. Then add up the total number of skills in each column.

COMMUNICATION	Job experience?	School experience?	Other experience?
Sales/Marketing			
Teaching/Training			
Explaining/Listening			
Public Speaking			
Total # of Skills			

ORGANIZATION	Job experience?	School experience?	Other experience?
Anticipating/Planning			
Attention to Detail			
Prioritizing			
Researching			
Time Management			
Multi-tasking			
Total # of Skills			

INTERPERSONAL	Job experience?	School experience?	Other experience?
Working in a Team			
Advising			
Resolving Conflict			
Negotiating			
Total # of Skills			

CREATIVE	Job experience?	School experience?	Other experience?
Designing/Inventing			
Developing Solutions			
Out of the Box Thinking			
Conceptualizing			
Total # of Skills			

LEADERSHIP	Job experience?	School experience?	Other experience?
Owning Responsibility			
Setting/Reaching Goals			
Delegating			
Managing/Supervising			
Total # of Skills			

QUANTITATIVE	Job experience?	School experience?	Other experience?
Bookkeeping			
Budgeting			
Calculating			
Collecting			
Estimating			
Recording			
Total # of Skills			

COMPUTER	Job experience?	School experience?	Other experience?
Data Entry			
MS Word			
MS Excel			
Databases			
Programming			
Web Design			
Total # of Skills			

SOFT SKILLS	Job experience?	School experience?	Other experience?
Ability to Learn Quickly			
Positive Attitude			
Work Ethic			
Dependability / Reliability			
Flexibility			
Good Judgment			
Total # of Skills			

SKILLS IDENTIFICATION SUMMARY

SKILL	Total Number of Skills
COMMUNICATION	
ORGANIZATION	
INTERPERSONAL	
CREATIVE	
LEADERSHIP	
QUANTITATIVE	
COMPUTER	
SOFT SKILLS	
Grand Total:	

Questions

1. What area would you most like to improve before starting co-op?

2. Name two ways in which you could improve some of these skills before starting your first co-op:

APPENDIX C
Writing Effective Cover Letters

If you're looking for a co-op job with the assistance of a co-op program, you may not need to write any cover letters. It may be enough to submit your resume through a co-op coordinator in order to obtain a job interview. Sooner or later, though, you will need to write an effective cover letter in response to a job listing. I have read thousands of cover letters over the years, and it never fails to amaze me how bad they can be—and how good they can be.

The most common mistake made by job applicants is to write a cover letter that really doesn't say anything useful... or not to write one at all. The bad cover letter will be extremely short, often saying no more than this:

> In response to your listing [in The Boston Globe, on www.monster.com, etc.], I am writing to be considered for the position of Accounts Payable Coordinator [or Financial Analyst or Desktop Support Manager]. As you can see on the enclosed resume, I have a degree in business. I am a hard-working individual who would be a good fit for a company in any number of different accounting and finance roles.
>
> I am excited about the possibility of working for your organization. If you wish to arrange an interview, please contact me at... .

What's wrong with this approach? It breaks the cardinal rule of cover letters: You need to think of the cover letter as a bridge connecting your resume to a specific job description. For the letter to be an effective connection between your resume and the job, it needs to do more than explain you're interested in the job and to refer to your resume. An effective letter "sells" the employer on the idea of hiring you. It allows your personality to come through while also painting a picture of how you can help the employer meet his or her goals.

The Digital Age also has greatly changed the process of applying for jobs. In many ways, it is now too easy to apply for jobs. Years ago, submitting an application required reading through tons of job descriptions in the newspaper, then producing hard copies of a resume and cover letter on good paper, and then getting to a post office to mail the whole thing.

Today, job seekers can set up search agents on various job boards to automate the process of trawling through jobs, and it's possible to see many more than those that were listed in the local newspaper. Applying is much easier, too. It's all too easy to just copy and paste a cover letter into an e-mail or attach it as a step on an applicant tracking system.

I say "all too easy" because job seekers often take the easy way out: They write a simple cover letter that is so general that it can be modified quickly to send to another employer. While this has the advantages of being efficient and convenient, there is no question that this is a short-sighted perspective. As it's so easy to apply for a job these days, a recruiter or manager may receive 100-300 applications. Inevitably he or she sees quite a few cover letters that are completely generic. Fairly or unfairly, the reader of the quick and general cover letter will make several assumptions about the candidate. It's easy to conclude that the applicant is probably flinging his resume at dozens of jobs—maybe even sending out a hundred cover letters and resumes in the hopes of getting a small handful of interviews. The potential interviewer has to question whether the applicant has even given any serious consideration to whether he really wants the job in question. It's certainly hard to believe that the candidate really wants this specific job, and why would you ever want to hire someone who doesn't really want the job at hand—even if they have a terrific resume?

THE SEVEN DEADLY SINS OF COVER LETTERS

After leaving my job at Northeastern in 2010, I became a consultant. One of my first projects was to handle all of the recruiting steps from A to Z for a start-up company. I needed to fill four positions and ended up reading hundreds of cover letters as a result. I was amazed at how few of them were tailored to the jobs for which I was screening candidates. Most remarkably, I noticed several candidates who apparently had copied and pasted their generic cover letter from their application to another job. In other cases, there was no question that this is exactly what had happened, as the candidate even left in the name of the other company and its job title in their cover letter. Here is one of my e-mail responses to such a candidate:

> Joe,
>
> Your resume came to me through the LinkedIn job application process, but I believe that this represented some sort of error on your part. Your cover letter refers repeatedly to the fact that you are an ideal candidate for "Student Advisor." That may be the case, but you submitted your resume and cover letter to an organization seeking a Director of Marketing.
>
> I thought I should let you know, so you could be sure to submit your application materials to that position if you have not done so already.

The candidate responded to apologize for his mistake, adding "Geez, what a way to make a first impression!" He said that he would resubmit his application but never did, obviously recognizing that the damage had been done.

After reviewing hundreds of cover letters with a great variety of mistakes, I devised these Seven Deadly Sins of Cover Letters:

- *The first date analogy:* If you went on a first date and your date became furious with a waitress over some minor issue, would your assumption be that your date is just having a bad day? I doubt it. You'd probably run screaming in the opposite direction, figuring that an individual is probably on their best behavior during a first date... so why wait to see the *rest* of their behavior! With a cover letter, the equivalent is submitting a cover letter that is fraught with typos, spelling errors, and incomplete sentences.

- *The copy and paste nightmare:* This was described above with poor Joe, the "ideal candidate" for the Student Advisor job. I saw others make the identical mistake, most notably someone who submitted her resume for a job with a bra manufacturer, touting her expertise in marketing a physical product. That was a problem, given that I was trying to fill a marketing job that didn't involve a physical product at all!

- *It's all about me:* Some candidates go into extensive detail about why the job is great for them without describing why they are good for the job. *"This job would really build my understanding of marketing and give me exposure to working with MS-Access, a skill that I very much want to learn."* Sure, we want to hire people who are excited about the job, but we don't want to pay someone purely to fulfill their professional development needs.

- *Right person, wrong job:* In some cover letters, the candidate does a terrific job of touting their strengths, experiences, and competencies. The problem is when these qualities bear little or no relationship to the job at hand. I literally have seen someone talk about their skill, experience, and preference in working for a team for a job description that strongly emphasized that the individual would be working very independently. Not too smart a position to take.

- *The cliché fits like a glove:* If I had a dollar for every time someone referred to themselves as the "ideal candidate" for the job, I could fly from Boston to my favorite country: Iceland! Likewise, so many people provide a list of admirable qualities that they possess: hard-working, eager to learn, motivated, etc. While soft skills are important, the cover letter needs to talk about experiences and qualities that *differentiate* you from the many other candidates. What's special and unique about *you*?

- *Instruction Manual needed:* When posting my first job description on LinkedIn and Craigslist in July 2010, I noted that candidates should send a resume and cover letter. Many couldn't manage to follow that instruction, sending only a resume. Others did send a cover letter, but it was completely generic. So when I posted another job a few weeks later, I made sure to note "Be sure to submit a resume and a cover letter *that specifically describes why you would be a good match for this particular position.*" The results? A higher percentage of people wrote customized cover letters, but most did not. I guess it just seemed like too much work. It probably *is* too much work if you're applying for 50 jobs per week instead of focusing on those that are really a good mutual fit. Whatever the reason, I reached the conclusion that a) the candidate wasn't all that interested in the job, and/or b) couldn't follow a simple instruction. Those are not qualities that an employer is seeking.

- *Let's see what sticks:* Some cover letters definitely give the resume reviewer the impression of someone who is throwing a handful of spaghetti against the wall to see what sticks. In other words, they send a very abrupt cover letter that doesn't mention the company or the job at all. Maybe they don't even send a cover letter. Without even looking at the resume, the recruiter figures that there is an 80% chance that the candidate's experience does not remotely align with the job qualifications. It's very easy to ignore these applicants.

So a cover letter can result in ruling yourself out of a job almost immediately. On the other hand, a great cover letter will not get you a job—but it can get you in the door for an interview, even if you're not a perfect candidate on paper. At best, the cover letter can make the interview much easier by covering the fundamental, strategic reasons why you are a good match for the job. So let's take a look at what comprises an effective cover letter before walking through some specific examples.

ELEMENTS OF AN EFFECTIVE COVER LETTER

Yes, writing a cover letter is more time consuming than you might like because of the need to tailor each letter individually for each job that you're pursuing. The good news is that there are numerous elements that can be applied to all cover letters. While you can never reduce cover letter writing to a formula, you'll find that they become easier to write because the style issues are quite consistent. Here they are:

Start off flush-left with the date you are sending the letter. Create a flush-left heading two lines underneath the date that gives the appropriate name, job title, and address of the cover letter's recipient. Usually this would look something like this:

Nov. 15, 2014
Ms. Lenora Fritillary, Human Resources Manager
Schlobotnick Products
123 American Way
Roanoke, VA 33547

You then would begin your cover letter with "Dear Ms. Fritillary,".

At other times, you may not have a name and may have to use a job title:

Network Administrator
Byte Size Products
1200 Easy Street
Walla Walla, WA 94239

If the job is one that you are pursuing without any contact name, call up the main number of the organization and ask for the name of the person who is doing the hiring for the position. If you're told it is the human resources department, ask to speak to the office staff there and see if you can get the name of the individual responsible for hiring for the position. It can be very effective to tell the office staff person you just need the name because you are sending them something in the mail. It's always better to have a real live person listed as the cover letter's recipient unless the ad obviously indicates that the employer prefers to avoid a personal contact.

If you are simply unable to get the name of a person, use a greeting that omits a person's name. Some experts suggest using the company name in the greeting as in "Dear Oregon Detailers." Here are some additional suggestions for greetings: "Dear Hiring Manager," "Greetings," "Hello," "Good Day," "Good Morning," or "Good Afternoon." All of these greetings are effective however they are less formal and may not be considered appropriate in your area of the country or in your career field. On the west coast, the use of "To whom it may concern" is considered very formal and somewhat old fashioned and therefore not typically recommended. On the east coast, the greeting "To whom it may concern" is more acceptable. Check with your co-op coordinator or career professional for his or her recommendations. Briefly state how you learned of the job opportunity (if there is one) or simply express your interest in potential employment. Just as you always want to target a specific individual when you write your cover letter, you definitely want to write a cover letter with a specific job description in mind whenever possible. Otherwise, you face the challenge of writing a cover letter that implies that you're equally excited about any of a wide range of possible jobs. That's a much tougher sell.

This first paragraph should communicate your enthusiasm and convey energy with the language you use. Just flatly stating the name of the job and where you learned of it is boring to read and will not entice the receiver to read further. Demonstrating that you've done your research about the company and indicating how you fit into the organization can also contribute to the opening paragraph. Here are a few ways in which you might describe how you learned about the job at hand and create interest in you as a candidate:

Example 1:

I am writing to express my interest in the Accounts Payable Assistant position, which I saw posted on LinkedIn, and to offer my talents to your company. I understand XYZ Company is dedicated to manufacturing quality widgets. If you seek a dependable employee who has well developed accounting skills and who is willing to work hard to contribute to the success of your organization, than I am the person you want to hire.

Example 2:

Speaking to my friend Patti O'Furnichoor, who works in accounting at your organization, I learned that your organization is looking for a GIS Technician, especially one who brings solid GIS software skills, a positive attitude, and who can be an effective liaison between departments. From my research, I have learned that XYZ Company provides services to planners in both government and industry, and I am confident that my recent GIS education coupled with my solid work history have prepared me to effectively fill this position.

Example 3:

Having completed the majority of an intensive two-year drafting program, I believe I am well qualified to fill the CAD operator position advertised recently on Craigslist. My strengths include solid AutoCAD skills and an extensive mechanical background; these skills should prove valuable to help your company manufacture cutting-edge material handling equipment.

If you have no choice but to submit a cover letter without knowing what jobs might be available, you are forced to write something more general.

Example 1:

If your organization would benefit from a trained office assistant with exceptional interpersonal and organizational skills, please consider bringing me in for an interview. My recent course work in Office Administration has prepared me for a range of positions in your corporate office. I am confident that my well-developed facility with all Microsoft Office products as well as my familiarity with a variety of other office software has prepared me to contribute to your organization's success.

Example 2:

After doing extensive research on the Internet, I know that your company has 600 employees at your Eugene office. With this in mind, I was wondering if there might be opportunities available in PC/LAN support, database administration, or Web development. Through my recent computer information technology course work at Lane Community College, I have demonstrated that I learn computers quickly, and I have the flexibility to be effective in any number of IT functions.

In the body of your letter make several strong connections between your resume and the job description at hand whenever possible. At this point, you need to put your resume next to the job description and read the two side by side. Are there specific job requirements that you definitely have? Why would this employer hire you instead of someone else for this job? Why wouldn't this employer hire you? Making these assessments will help you figure out what your strategy should be—for the cover letter as well as for a potential interview. You need to come up with three or four concrete reasons as to why you are an excellent candidate to interview.

REMEMBER—the goal is to do more than justify why you thought it was okay to submit your resume! Some cover letters come off as a little defensive or apologetic in this way: "Your job description said that you were looking for someone with an accounting degree who also has strong knowledge of advanced functions in Excel. I hope to receive my accounting degree by the end of 2004. While my knowledge of Excel is not advanced, I am certainly very willing to learn..." If you're writing many sentences like these, you probably just aren't a good enough match to merit consideration.

As noted in the Seven Deadly Sins, another common mistake—both in cover letters and interviews—is to talk too much about why the job would be great for you, rather than why you would be great for the job! This ill-fated applicant might write something like this: "Working for your organization would give me a great opportunity to build my knowledge of hotel management. I would be very excited about enhancing my computer skills in this position as well...." Showing enthusiasm about the job is always a good idea, but not if you're only excited about what the job will do for you. You have to imagine yourself as the person reading a big pile of cover letters and resumes—your goal is to find the person who can best help in your organization in this role: not to find the candidate who most needs your help! As such, the hiring manager is going to pick out some number of candidates (probably somewhere between three and ten) who appear to be the most plausible for the job, based on the cover letter and resume.

There are no hard and fast rules about how many paragraphs you should have in your cover letter. Students who move right from high school to college may be fine with three paragraphs—the opening paragraph which we just described, a paragraph describing how you meet the employer's needs and then a closing paragraph describing your availability and asking for the interview.

On the other hand, students who are career changers and those of you who worked for a period of time between high school and college should consider four or more paragraphs—the opening paragraph, a paragraph that describes the skills you gained in school that meet the employer's needs, another paragraph or two that identifies what you bring from prior work experience, and then the closing paragraph where you ask for the interview.

One of the most effective ways to create a letter that sells you is to include testimonials from instructors and employers. Testimonials are a way to "prove" you have skills in a more believable way than just asserting it yourself. Anyone can say "I'm detail oriented" or "I'm a hard worker" but when someone else says it about you, and that person can be contacted to verify it, then it is believable. Here are a couple of examples of testimonials:

Testimonial Example #1

My drafting instructor, Margaret Robertson, is one of my references and would tell you that my drawing assignments in her courses are always error free and turned in on time.

Testimonial Example #2

If you spoke to my supervisor at ASI, he would tell you that I am a very dedicated and conscientious worker who is willing to lend a hand at a moment's notice in order to get the job done on time.

Like everything else you include in your letter, testimonials must be true—you can't make them up or exaggerate. And, I also recommend no more than one testimonial per letter.

We'll consider some full-fledged job descriptions and resumes shortly. In the meantime, here are a few examples of ways in which a good cover letter might "sell" you by making connections between a resume and a job description:

Example 1:

Your job description details the need for candidates to have a strong background in marketing as well as excellent communication skills. I received a grade of A- in my Introduction to Marketing class; in particular, I earned a top grade on an analysis of market segmentation in the automobile industry. Additionally, I have worked in numerous retail positions, honing my customer-service skills and refining my knowledge of merchandising. As for my communication skills, I have obtained considerable presentation experience in my business classes and have augmented this by taking an elective in Public Speaking—a course in which I performed extremely well.

Example 2:

From your ad on www.monster.com, I know that you are seeking a highly trustworthy individual with a solid understanding of accounting principles and Excel for your Accounts Receivable Associate position. Both in the classroom and on the job, I have shown that I possess these qualities. My overall GPA at Lone Star Community College is 3.0 —but my GPA in accounting classes is 3.6. Many of my classmates struggled mightily with Intermediate Accounting in particular, while I received an A- in this rigorous course. While in school I also became proficient with Excel: I am extremely confident and comfortable when creating formulas, charts, and graphs—even pivot tables.

As far as being trustworthy, I would encourage you to contact any or all of my previous employers, whose contact information is available on the enclosed reference page. I am confident that each supervisor will indicate that I was entrusted with depositing considerable amounts of cash after closing for the night and locking up the place of business. Additionally, they will tell you I have developed effective working relationships with team members that resulted in increased sales.

Notice that the education-related information is grouped in one paragraph and work-related information is grouped in another paragraph. This is an effective way to create a smooth flow of information. Also notice the use of a testimonial to make the skills assertion more believable while adding team skills to the content. When discussing previous or current employment, it can also be effective to comment on how you contributed to helping the company make money, save money, or save time, as these interests are common to most employers.

Close the cover letter by reaffirming your interest and noting how you prefer to be contacted.

This is fairly straightforward. And, one other note here: for graphic design students, drafting students, and others in career fields where it is best practice to bring examples of your work to an interview, the closing paragraph is the right place to indicate you'll bring a portfolio or course assignment samples to demonstrate your talent and skills.

Example:

I would welcome the opportunity to interview for the bookkeeping position. To arrange an interview, please feel free to contact me via e-mail at mbrooke95@gmail.com or by phone at 617-555-0000. I look forward to hearing from you soon.

Revise, edit, and proofread your cover letter and resume with extreme care—then find some other competent people to double-check your work.

I can hardly overstate the importance of this point. As noted earlier, remember that "first date analogy." When reading cover letters and resumes, managers assume that they are seeing the very best that you have to offer. Intentionally or unintentionally—fairly or unfairly—an employer will infer a great deal from your cover letter. The potential employer will develop perceptions regarding your communication skills, attention to detail, level of interest in the job, self-awareness, and selling skills based on the quality of your cover letter. Accordingly, your cover letter needs to be perfect grammatically and completely free of any typos. I knew of one employer who would simply circle typos with red pen and return the cover letters to applicants, noting that "you clearly lack the attention to detail that we seek in all potential recruits." Most employers won't be that harsh—they simply won't bring you in for an interview.

From my experience as a recruiting consultant, I've seen some amazing typos and errors on cover letters and resumes. The worst was from an individual who was applying for an executive position. This is how he wrote the last sentence of his cover letter's first paragraph:

I recently sold my start-up in May and looking to work in a

The cover letter then went on to the next paragraph and a new sentence. The rest of the cover letter had three blatant typos. Regardless, he not only submitted that cover letter online, he also submitted the identical message to three other people at the company in his zeal to get an interview. Obviously, he would've been better off putting more energy into proofreading his submission instead of sending in this error-fraught message repeatedly.

A COMPLETE EXAMPLE OF CREATING A COVER LETTER

Remember the resume of Meghan Brooke from the sample resumes at the end of Chapter Two of this book? Because we always must try to match a specific individual to a specific job description, let's use her resume in writing a sample cover letter. As for the job description, let's say Meghan is applying for the following job:

GLAMTONE PUBLISHING

Glamtone Publishing—a leader in the publishing and distribution of medical textbooks and other health-related media products—seeks a PC/LAN Support Associate to assist our 400+ end users with computer-related issues ranging from simple MS-Office issues to Intranet updates and ultimately more technical troubleshooting issues, including assistance with our Windows NT network.

Qualifications: All applicants must have familiarity with MS-Office, strong communication skills, and the ability to learn to use new technology quickly. Exposure to the following technologies is a plus but not required: HTML, Symantec Ghost, Windows NT Server, and Active Directory. Looking for a team player with a great attitude who can handle a high-pressure environment!

Compensation: This position pays $42,000-$48,000 depending on experience.

To submit a resume, please write to Louise Guardado at Glamtone Publishing, 145 West North Street, Southborough, MA 01234. No phone calls please.

It would appear that Meghan has some chance of getting this position: She believes she has all the required skills and at least one of the "plus" skills. She decides to write a cover letter.

The first step in writing this cover letter would be for Meghan to try to be honest with herself regarding her strengths and weaknesses for this position. Here is a quick checklist of some questions for a candidate to ask herself at this point:

1. *Why would this company hire me rather than someone else?* You want to focus on attributes that might make you stand out from other applicants if at all possible. Lots of students have familiarity with MS-Office, for example, so that might not be the best primary selling point. For Meghan, her best bet might be to concentrate on her high GPA as a reflection of the "ability to learn quickly"—not everyone can say that they have a high GPA. Her customer service experience at two jobs—including the ability to learn quickly at Kohl's—would be worth citing as well.

2. *Why WOULDN'T this employer hire me, and can I do anything about that?* When looking at job descriptions, you can't just consider what jobs are attractive to you—you have to ask yourself how you can make yourself most attractive to the employer. You have to be honest with yourself—for example, could Meghan be beaten out by someone who has more of the preferred skills listed in this job description? Absolutely. Can she do anything about that? Maybe. If she really wants this job and has the time to do some additional research, she could take a few days to try to ramp up on the skills she lacks. She certainly could learn enough about Symantec Ghost to be able to mention it briefly in the cover letter and discuss it intelligently in the interview. But isn't that a lot of extra work in light of the fact that she doesn't even have an interview yet? Of course

it is. You have to be judicious about how much time you are willing and able to invest in each cover letter. However, if Meghan is completely sure that she wants a PC/LAN Support job, then doing some extra research on software applications is bound to pay off sooner or later. Doing research on the company also can help—though that would definitely be the kind of extra effort that is more of a one-shot deal.

3. *Is there anything I can reasonably do that will help get me inside information about the job?* If you were referred to the job by someone, you definitely should pump that person for information about the organization. It's also worthwhile to go to LinkedIn to see if someone in your network of contacts has a connection to the hiring organization. With some luck and effort, you may be able to find someone who will be able to tell you some useful facts about the organization's culture, the supervisor and/or interviewer, and the job itself. What do people really like and dislike about this job, this department, this organization? If you know some of these things, you may able to tailor your cover letter accordingly. At the very least, you could check out the company website or maybe drop by the company and tell the receptionist that you intend to apply for a job—is there any general information available about the company. Taking any of these steps can reflect your willingness to go the extra mile as well as your sincere interest in the job.

Once you have made this kind of self-assessment and done what you can do regarding your "fatal flaws," you can write the cover letter itself. On the following page, you can see what Meghan's finished cover letter might look like.

March 24, 2013

Ms. Louise Guardado
Glamtone Publishing
145 West North Street
Southborough, MA 01234

Dear Ms. Guardado,

I am writing to express my interest in the PC/LAN Support Associate position, which your organization posted with the job listings made available on LinkedIn. From my research on Glamtone Publishing, I know that you are a young, fast-growing publisher with a reputation for producing highly professional medical materials. After talking to Louise Shawerma in your Human Resources Department, I am confident I can perform this job effectively and would especially enjoy working in Glamtone's fast-paced environment.

As you can see on the enclosed resume, I have numerous skills and qualities that make me a great fit for this position. Despite challenging myself with a double concentration in MIS and Marketing, I have managed to maintain a 3.6 GPA at Northeastern University. I believe that my excellent academic record reflects my ability to learn quickly—a critical skill for any new hire in a technology-oriented position. In my previous job experience, I have an outstanding record of providing patient and effective customer service. This experience should prove invaluable when providing PC support to Glamtone's end users.

While I have not had the opportunity to work with Symantec Ghost or with Local Area Networks, I have done extensive reading on these areas since reviewing your job description. As a result, I have a good but basic sense of how to re-image a computer as well as an understanding of networking fundamentals.

I would be delighted to come in for an interview at your earliest convenience. Please feel free to contact me via e-mail or by phone to arrange an interview. For your convenience, I am also enclosing my references—I urge you to contact them to verify anything on my resume or to ask any questions about my work and academic history. I look forward to hearing from you soon.

Sincerely,

Meghan Brooke
617.555.0000
m.brooke@yahoo.com

WRITING A COVER LETTER AS A CO-OP STUDENT OR INTERN

In some instances, students also may write cover letters when attempting to find a co-op job—most often with a co-op employer who is not currently involved with a co-op program. When writing this kind of cover letter, you will need to provide a brief explanation of what you are seeking as well as why hiring a co-op student would be a good move for the employer.

With this in mind, let's revise the previous letter. In this case, let's assume that Meghan is a co-op student seeking an IT position for six months. We also will use this example to show how to write a more general cover letter. As noted earlier, you also want to write the cover letter with a specific job description in mind. If that is not possible, however, this might be a good approach. When writing a letter to investigate the possibility of a co-op position, always research the company and find a person to send your letter to, just as you would for regular employment.

Look at the following page to see this co-op job search cover letter in its entirety.

March 24, 2013

Human Resources Manager
Glamtone Publishing
145 West North Street
Southborough, MA 01234

To Whom It May Concern:

As a current student at Northeastern University, I am writing to express my interest in a computer-related co-op position (like an internship) with your company. In my academic program, I developed a variety of computer skills that would be put to good use in your organization. I am willing to consider any position that involves computers—some examples would include PC/LAN support, database design/development maintenance, Web page design and maintenance, QA testing, or positions that use computers to help other functional areas such as marketing and finance.

At Northeastern, co-op students are expected to attend classes full-time for the first half of the calendar year and then work full-time during the next six full months. I am available to begin working for you on Monday, July 5 and would continue through December. As a co-op student, I will be earning academic credit, which means I have an additional reason to perform to the best of my abilities.

From your perspective as an employer, there are many benefits to hiring a co-op student. In these economically uncertain times, co-op student workers represent a relatively short-term commitment. Co-ops are cost-effective and benefit-free. Co-op students are trying to build great resumes and references for future employment, so they are highly motivated workers as well. Lastly, co-op hires are a good way to keep a recruiting pipeline active in anticipation of brighter economic times in the future.

As you can see on the enclosed resume, I have numerous skills and qualities that make me a great fit for a computer-related position. Despite challenging myself with a double concentration in MIS and Marketing, I have managed to maintain a 3.6 GPA at Northeastern University. I believe that my excellent academic record reflects my ability to learn quickly—a critical soft skill for any new hire in a technology-oriented position. In my previous job experience, I have an outstanding record of providing patient and effective customer service. This experience would prove invaluable if your Network Administrator needs assistance in providing PC support to Glamtone's end users.

I would be delighted to come in for an interview at your earliest convenience. From my research on Glamtone Publishing, I know that you are a young, fast-growing publisher with a reputation for producing highly professional medical materials. After talking to Susan Shawerma in your Human Resources Department, I would say that I especially would enjoy working in the fast-paced environment at Glamtone.

Please feel free to contact me via e-mail or by phone to arrange an interview. For your convenience, I am also enclosing my references—I urge you to contact them to verify anything on my resume or to ask any questions about my work and academic history. I look forward to hearing from you soon.

Sincerely,

Meghan Brooke
617-555-0000
m.brooke@yahoo.com

FINAL THOUGHTS ON WRITING A COVER LETTER

You may never have to write a cover letter during your undergraduate career, but sooner or later you will have to know how to write one effectively. Even when you learn about job opportunities through friends, family, fellow students, or former employers, you frequently will be asked to write a cover letter when submitting your resume.

Given that cover letters are time consuming, there is nothing inherently wrong with having a few cover letters that you re-use to some degree—certain elements might remain the same across quite a few letters. I have created cover letters geared toward jobs in learning and development, instructional design, writing, experiential learning, and consulting that I used as a foundation before modifying to meet the specifics of a given position. However, as alluded to earlier in this section, don't EVER send out a cover letter without making sure that you have changed ANY customized references! Imagine how well it would go over if Meghan took her Glamtone cover letter and reworked it for another position—but accidentally left in the reference to Glamtone in the final paragraph!! All of a sudden, the first impression that the other employer has of Meghan is of someone who lacks attention to detail and who may indeed be flinging dozens of cover letters at jobs with only slight modifications.

Because organizations listing jobs may get tons of replies—especially in a tough economy—a little persistence can't hurt. If you hear nothing from an employer within a few weeks, you might try writing a brief, upbeat note to reaffirm your interest—particularly if you think the job is a great fit.

Several years ago, I replied to a *Boston Globe* ad listing a position that appeared to be an unusually good match for me at that time. Two weeks passed, and I heard nothing. I wrote a follow-up letter and politely acknowledged that I was sure that the company was very busy—particularly given that they were a small company listing a position emphasizing their need for a medical writer/project manager. In the letter, I reaffirmed my interest in the position and briefly recapitulated why I was a great match. Then I just said the honest truth—I was only a few weeks away from needing to make a commitment regarding a teaching position that was available to me. If the position was filled or if they were uninterested, I understood completely. If not, I urged them to arrange an interview as soon as possible.

Within three days of mailing the letter, I received a call to arrange the interview. Three interviews later, I got the offer and accepted it. I often wondered if that would have happened if I had simply waited however long it might have taken for them to acknowledge my first attempt. After the second letter, they definitely knew that I was seriously interested. I don't know any organization that wants to hire someone who only wants the job a little!

APPENDIX D
Bridging Exercise

Many individuals are strong job candidates, but they are hurt by failing to tailor their answers in an interview to the job for which they are applying. When they get asked general questions such as "Tell me about yourself," they always give the same generic response—not a strategic one. This exercise was created to help you come up with a strategy as well as supporting proof for that strategy.

Educators at University of Massachusetts Lowell improved upon an earlier version of this activity that I created, so almost all of what follows should be credited to them. All I've added is a few explanatory notes.

TWO-PART EXERCISE

There are two parts to the Lowell version of the Bridging Exercise. In the first part, you will be asked to name a specific time when you displayed quite a few different transferable skills, such as a "strong customer-focused attitude" and the "ability to solve problems." You probably will find that some are easier to think of than others. After you finish that activity, review the examples that came to mind. Based on those, what skills appear to be the ones that you can best support by talking about a specific experience? These are the ones you'll want to emphasize most frequently on your resume, at job fairs, and in interviews.

In the second part of the exercise, you'll tighten your focus. Here you'll need to look at a specific job description. This is where the bridging really comes through: You need to think about specific things that the employer is seeking and then come up with examples of when you've displayed those skills. This exercise will lead you to an interviewing strategy as well as stories and examples to prove that your strategy can be supported by evidence!

BRIDGING EXERCISE PART 1

Name _Victor Souza_   Date_____

ABOUT YOU:

EDUCATION: UNIVERSITY OR COLLEGE	
WHAT YOU LIKE(D) Learning Being involved meeting new people (Learning from them)	**WHAT YOU DISLIKE(D)** Lack of time for other things finals
EDUCATION: HIGH SCHOOL	
WHAT YOU LIKED Learning	**WHAT YOU DISLIKED** The amount of time spent there
PREVIOUS JOBS	
WHAT YOU LIKE(D) experiences people met money	**WHAT YOU DISLIKE(D)** time consumism

SKILL IDENTIFICATION EXERCISE: JOB-RELATED EXAMPLES

1. Review the list of job-related skills below.

2. Think about times or situations when you have used each skill, and note that example in the right-hand column.

3. Use this worksheet to develop content for your resume, and to prepare for career fairs and interviews.

Skill	Example (job, academic, and/or volunteer experience)
The ability to solve problems (related to your major or concentration if possible)	· Dunkin Donuts when things went wrong. · CCF. when experiences go wrong.
Strong hands-on mechanical skills; can take things apart and put them back together	· cleaning machines at DD

216

Strong analytical aptitude and attention to detail	Learning 250+ menu at CCF
The ability to apply sound professional judgment	When I have to decide on how to handle difficult situations w/ guest at the CCF
The ability to use laboratory equipment to generate data and process materials and/ or the ability to do research to generate data and credible insights	N/A
Professional communication (written and verbal)	Acct class and CWI + II projects.
Effective utilization of time and resources	my whole life
Working as part of an effective and collaborative team	Difference maker Capstone Biz cafe
Innovation and creativity; can think of new ways to make things work more efficiently	CCF with certain meals modifications
Strong customer-focused attitude	CCF when serving and DD serving
The ability to manage competing priorities	Sense of urgency at DD & CCF
The ability to quickly learn and apply new skills	DD & CCF Both had only one week to learn
Positive attitude / work ethic	DD & CCF
Dependability, reliability, and flexibility	Shift lead and trainer at both DD & CCF
Proven leadership skills	VP of DECA, member of MLC.
Critical thinking; using logic to identify alternative solutions or approaches to problems	When I analyze transactions and apply GAAP concepts in CFR I.
The ability to analyze needs and product requirements to create a design or idea for a product or service that addresses those needs or requirements	Reading guest, analyzing them and predicting their needs and what is required to meet it.
Naturally inquisitive; the ability to examine things and conceive of ways to make them better	growing up at the farm. Dealing with the crops and finding efficient ways to approach the cleaning tasks.

STRENGTHS	WEAKNESSES - List 3 of your weaknesses with how you might overcome/better prepare
communication	written communication. take more time and pay more attention to errors.
Sense of urgency	
qeick learner	
Interpersonal Skills	
Time Management	
Customer Service	

BRIDGING EXERCISE PART 2

Student Name: Victor Souza

Company Name: EY

Job Title: Accountant

Date: 1/24/19

For this part of the Bridging Exercise, you're going to tighten your focus. Instead of thinking about your skills in general, you're going to see how they apply to a specific job description. For this segment, you may find it helpful to print out your resume and job description, comparing them both side by side. This will help you "bridge" between what the company is seeking for that specific job and what skills YOU have that are most relevant to THAT job. This will help you complete the tables that follow.

You'll also notice a section in which you are asked to come up with PARK statements. This is something that UMass Lowell uses to help their students take one of the "related examples" below and then organize it into a brief story for a job interview. The "PARK" acronym reminds you to make sure that your story efficiently describes a Problem, Action, Resolution, and Knowledge Gained.

COMPANY SPECIFICS:

THREE interesting facts about the company	Why do you want the job?
Their work environment is outstanding	I worry about where I work and with who
They are one of the best acct firms out there.	The opportunity for growth is greater.
Great clients	a various of clients = more experiences.

RELATED EXAMPLES:

Desired skill, quality, experience, interest THAT IS RELEVANT TO THE THIS EMPLOYER FOR THIS JOB	Related example (DESCRIBE WHERE & HOW YOU HAVE DEMONSTRATED THESE SKILLS)
face-to-face client interaction	CCF serving guests. meeting their needs
acct. skills	acct classes
punctuality	CCF, never late always happy to work
willingness to learn	I have always wanted to learn more. At the CCF, I started as a busser and now I'm a server, for the fact that I learned everything
Excel	I've learned with my experiences with projects and Business Info. Systems class.
Being able to communicate	I literally communicate for a living. I talk all the time @ work with guests and co-workers It's in my DNA :)

PARK STATEMENTS:

- PROBLEM: What problem or challenge did you face in the situation?

- ACTION: What steps did you take to address that problem or challenge? What were you thinking and feeling, and, most importantly, what did you DO about the problem?

- RESOLUTION: What happened? How did the problem or challenge get resolved? What was the outcome for you and others affected by the problem?

- KNOWLEDGE GAINED: What did you learn from this experience? What did it teach you? What lessons did you take away here, and how do they apply to the job that you're seeking now?

Problem	wrong meal went out to guest.	I found myself doing all the work in a team I was in for a project.	
Action	I apologized and got another meal to be prepared I felt bad, for them	It was frustrating. They just didn't deserve the grade because I was doing all the work.	
Resolution	They got the right meal and were happy.	I tried talking to them. It didn't work, so I spoke to the professor. +	
Knowledge Gained	pay more attention to details!	The professor talked to the students and they all ended up working on the project Never try to carry the time. Communicate!	

Application Date: _____

Key Contacts: _____

Notes:

Follow-up:

APPENDIX E
Behavioral-Based Interviewing

In Chapter 3, I touched on Behavioral-Based Interviewing (BBI). However, I developed this more advanced material for my prep course in Fall 2004, and it turned out to be a favorite activity for the class. Since then, I've come to believe that being able to develop and deliver stories that prove that you have relevant skills and experiences is a crucial differentiator for job candidates of any age. So it's worth devoting time to create as many as five to ten stories you can share in a job interview—regardless of the interviewing method.

Behavioral-based interviewing is an increasingly common interviewing method. Many large companies use it, including Microsoft and many consulting firms. Johnson & Johnson had a new interviewer come to campus and ask students for stories as a major component of the interview—stories about making the transition from high school to college, stories about previous jobs, and so forth. Some interviewers almost exclusively use this approach, while others may ask one or two BBI questions as part of an otherwise conventional interview. Although all interview methods are far from perfect in predicting future job performance, behavioral-based interviews generally are considered the most valid tool available. Why would that be? Probably because BBI questions require that you use true stories instead of scripted answers that sound good. Unless you're a pathological liar, it's quite difficult to make up a vivid, believable story with considerable detail.

But what if your interviews prove to be entirely conventional? Well, I've come to believe that ALL interview candidates should be prepared for BBI questions. Even when interviewers use the conventional approach to questioning, it's always helpful to be able to tell a couple of specific and vivid stories. After all, anyone can start off an interview by touting their excellent interpersonal skills or ability to juggle multiple tasks: But just *saying* that is not proving that you really have those traits. You need to *show* what you really mean, and it needs to be a true story for it to be credible and believable. In any interview, your strategy is your foundation, but BBI stories are a great way to build on that foundation.

Characteristics of Behavioral-Based Interview Questions

BBI questions are pretty easy to spot. The interviewer will often start questions by saying "Tell me about a time when....," before going on to ask you about a specific instance in which you demonstrated one of any number of qualities: customer service skills; ability to multitask; organizational skills; ability to be a good team player; willingness to go the extra mile; ability to overcome adversity; passion for technology; etc. Here are some examples:

- Tell me about a specific time when you encountered adversity working in a group. Describe the group's goals, the nature of the adversity, what your role was in the group, and how the situation turned out.

- What would you say has been the greatest achievement of your life thus far? Walk me through how you accomplished it.

- Please give me an example of a time when you failed at something and how you handled that.

- Tell me about a time when you went above and beyond expectations in a school or work situation.

- Describe a specific situation in which you took an unpopular stand.

From these questions, you might imagine that the interviewee ends up doing most of the talking in these interviews. If so, you would be correct. After setting the stage with the question, the interviewer probably will listen and take notes, occasionally stepping in with a clarifying question.

When faced with a behavioral-based interview, most candidates find it difficult to come up with a great and relevant story off the top of their heads. Sometimes the first answer that comes to mind may not be the best one to illustrate a given quality. You need to think in advance about the situations that truly show you at your very best.

Answering Behavioral-Based Interviewing Questions

Many career professionals favor an approach called STAR (Situation, Task, Actions, Results) in answering these questions. While this is a memorable acronym, I think that it perhaps oversimplifies the approach to answering these questions. In the previous appendix on bridging, you can see that the University of Massachusetts, Lowell uses a different acronym: PARK, which stands for Problem, Action, Resolution, Knowledge Gained. I like that acronym much more for three reasons:

- Whether we're talking about a book, a movie, or a story used for a speech or an interview, it's helpful to think of starting off with a problem or conflict. This is what makes the listener interested: It's the tension in the story that creates curiosity.

- Just as when you're reading a book or movie, it's frustrating if that conflict or problem is not resolved by the end of the story. What happened? People want to know, and they want to feel satisfied that the problem was truly resolved.

- The "Knowledge Gained" piece is a great way to tie the story back to the interviewer's agenda. Here you can talk about what you learned from that experience and, most importantly, how it ties back to the interviewer's needs and interests.

Here are more of principles of effective behavioral interviewing:

1. *Think STORY, not EXAMPLE.* What's the difference between a story and an example? When asked to give an example, many interviewees fall into the trap of responding too generally: "When I worked at Papa Gino's, we always had to juggle multiple tasks. We usually had many tables to handle at once, and more often than not we had a packed restaurant...."

   Right away, this answer is off to a bad start. If you find yourself saying things like "always" or "usually" or similar words, you're being much too general. If you're asked a BBI question in an interview, and you respond with a general overview of a job or classroom experience, the interviewer often will follow up by saying, "Okay, but can you tell me about a *specific* time when you [had to handle conflict, overcome adversity in a team, etc.]?" Often the interviewer will keep pushing until you do.

   Here are some good questions to ask yourself when attempting to come up with the best possible stories:

   - What was my very best day in that job? What was the hardest day or week?

   - What was my most challenging task or customer or problem I had to overcome? What was the biggest crisis I faced?

   Unlike an example, a story starts at one moment in time—maybe it's Tuesday, July 19 at about 10:30 a.m. Think in terms of a good book or movie. Usually any good story starts at a moment of conflict or crisis or challenge. Sure, a very quick overview may be appropriate, but make sure to get to that moment of truth very soon. Next, remember that you are the protagonist. Therefore, we are most interested in YOUR actions, thoughts, and emotions—be sure to convey them. Lastly, many a good story has been spoiled by a dissatisfying end. Be sure to RESOLVE the conflict by briefly describing the outcome, impact, or aftermath of the story.

2. *When you use a really good story to prove you have one particular soft skill, you will end up proving that you have three or four other soft skills.* BBI stories are usually rich in material. You usually have to convey so much detail to prove that you have a given quality that you end up showcasing other positive traits as well. Therefore, it's always great to use BBI stories—even when you're not in a BBI interview.

   Here's a terrific example of this phenomenon. I did a practice interview many years ago with one student, and I used a mostly conventional style. Her interview was absolutely mediocre: I wasn't getting any sense of what made this woman unique or why I might have any interest in her as a potential employee. So in an attempt to see if I could pull more out of her, I asked her a BBI question: "What, specifically, would you say has been the greatest achievement of your life?"

225

She thought about it for several seconds, and then she blew me away with her reply. "When I was very young, there were some sudden deaths in my immediate family. As a result, I grew up feeling very terrified of death and of any possible medical emergency. But one day when I was in high school, I just got fed up with being that way. I decided to get CPR training, and then I joined a Rescue Squad in my hometown. Now I know that if anything were to happen to a loved one, I wouldn't be powerless to help."

Wow! All of a sudden I saw many admirable qualities in this woman. Here was someone who had self-awareness and who had the courage to tackle a weakness head-on. Here was someone who certainly was able and willing to learn and who had training in handling high-pressure situations. More than anything, though, I think I saw her as a multidimensional, sympathetic human being for the first time. At the end of the interview, I told her that I wanted her to push that story to the beginning of her interview—using it as soon as she was given any open-ended question, such as "Tell me about yourself" or "What are your strengths?" I also reminded her that she could tap into these experiences for any number of other BBI or "specific example" types of questions. It didn't take long for her to have a dynamic interview.

3. *Make sure to walk through the story step by step.* After you've identified a pretty specific day or week or job task, then walk through it step by step:

    A. Give a quick, brief overview of the job or situation. Ideally, use the overview to help the interviewer understand what is really "at stake" in the story.
    B. Pick a specific moment in time when something caused a problem or conflict.
    C. Walk through the situation step by step: What did you do in response? What were you thinking as you dealt with it? What were you feeling? What was the outcome?

    That's a good rule of thumb if you feel like your stories lack depth or meat: Dig deeper into your actions, thoughts, and feelings to help us understand HOW you got through this situation. Some interviewers will pull your thoughts and feelings and specific actions out of you, but it's much easier if you can just lay them out without being asked.

4. *Focus on YOUR role in the situation.* There's an old cliché that "There is no 'I' in TEAM." Well, that's not true in behavioral-based interviewing. In fact, there are FOUR "I"s in BEHAVIORAL-BASED INTERVIEWING! When you're telling a story about a work or school team, make sure to describe YOUR individual role on the team—not just the team as a collective. There are many ways to contribute to a team: describe what KIND of team player you are by spelling out roles in a team situation.

5. *Don't "use up" a job in just one story!* Another problem with the more general stories is that you can use up a job in just one story… and you may need more stories later in the interview. If it's a job you've done well, there should be MANY stories from various days, customers, tasks, projects, and so forth. Odds are that these stories can be used to highlight many, many transferable skills.

6. *Be sure to pick a high-stakes story if you have one.* Stories about doing something simple to turn around a slightly disgruntled customer or solving a fairly minor problem at work

or school aren't terrible, but they do make one wonder if this is really the individual's best achievement. If it isn't, the person made an error in judgment in picking that story. If it is, maybe the person just isn't all that impressive. Start off by thinking about some of the proudest moments in your life—overcoming a major weakness or fear or failure, or maybe just something where you blew away people's expectations in a situation. Dig deep and give this some thought in coming up with more great stories.

A few years ago Microsoft asked this question: "Tell me about a specific time when you failed at something and how you responded to that failure." A couple of students talked about getting a D or F on a first paper and then responding by working harder and getting, say, a C+ in the course. That's not too inspiring. Maybe it was the best story they had, but I have to think that with more planning they could have come up with something that would be more impressive. In contrast, another candidate talked about failing accounting despite going to office hours, getting tutoring, working harder, and so on. The interviewers were impressed because he was able to convey his emotions about all of this—what stood out was how much this failure upset him. They were even more impressed when he talked about taking his accounting textbook to work every day the following summer so he could study during breaks. He wrapped up by telling them that he finally retook the class and got a B+. That was a great story: He showed that he DID care about his grades, and he also showed the soft skills of persistence, initiative, and overcoming adversity. I might add that after he graduated he accepted a job at Microsoft.

7. *Vivid details make the stories come alive.* One good mnemonic device is ABC, as it helps remind you to inject *affective, behavioral, and cognitive* elements—emotions, actions, and thoughts—into your stories. Just like in a good novel, I want to get inside your head—especially when you get to that "moment of truth" in your story. For every major plot twist in your story, try telling me what was going through your mind at those critical moments. Quantitative details also make the story come alive.

8. *Be careful about too little information—or too much!* When there was a problem with story length, often the stories were too short. If it's something you can tell in three or four sentences and less than 30 seconds, the story probably lacks depth. Microsoft talks about interviewees failing to "drill down into the details."

One analogy that may be helpful is to think of your stories the way a novelist or film director would think of them. There are times in movies or novels where we skip over the action quickly... and there are times when we have that extreme close-up, that tight focus when we really see and hear everything that the protagonist is doing. Give us a quick overview, but be sure to have that extreme close-up, too.

Conversely, some stories are too long. Avoid any information that is not "need to know." Some details may be entertaining, but if they aren't really showcasing your skills or traits, they aren't helping you. Even in BBI, a good story can be told in about 60 seconds, maybe 90 at most... and remember that you don't want to speak too fast in an interview! If you're not sure if you've gone on too long, try timing yourself while speaking at a reasonable pace.

9. *Life lesson stories also can work.* In my days in fiction-writing workshops, I learned that there are rules... but sometimes they can be broken. This came home to me again a few years ago. As you'll see with one of the following stories, it is indeed possible to have a story in which you learned something not so much from something you *did* but from something that happened to you. You have to be careful with this kind of story, as you don't want to come off as a passive person as opposed to a change agent in life. But if you can frame the life lesson in a way that shows how that experience helped you learn, grow, and change as an individual, it CAN work!

10. *What have you done for me lately?* When one prominent interviewer came to class recently, he reported afterwards that his BBI questions yielded some good answers... but that some candidates had no stories at all from their college years. So while you may have accomplished something great as a child or back in junior high, you want to make sure that you have at least some stories that reflect accomplishments in the last year or two. If you don't believe that you *have* any great successes from your college years, you need to think harder... or to start working toward the kind of performances in the classroom or in jobs that will result in some great success stories!

Here's an assignment that I recommend: Write up three stories that show you at your best. Then, for each story, write up at least three soft skills or marketable qualities that each story could be used to illustrate.

Each story should incorporate the following steps: What challenge or problem or situation did you face? What did you think, say, and do in addressing that problem, step-by-step? What were the positive outcomes and results of your actions?

To give you some excellent examples of how to do this, here are some of the best stories that my students submitted in response to the bridging assignment in Appendix D. I've taken each story a step further by mentioning three or more additional soft skills that the story could be used to show.

GREAT STORIES – STUDENT EXAMPLES

1. *Ali Ciccariello wrote up this story to prove that she has analytical and multitasking skills:*

"During the time I worked at the Fruit Center Marketplace, I was eventually promoted to a managerial position in the front-end department. Being in a supervising position was a great experience for me, allowing me to recognize store priorities and multitask different problems. I consider myself to be very analytical, so when I came across a particular store problem I enjoyed finding a solution.

"I can remember one particular Saturday when everything in the store seemed to be going wrong. The Fruit Center had just received new cash registers, and my fellow bosses and I were still trying to figure out all the new "kinks" in the system. The registers had been working normally all day, until suddenly one register froze and wouldn't turn on. Believe it or not, it is a huge problem when even one register stops working on a high-volume day.

"Immediately, I tried to prioritize the problems I had to deal with. I knew customer satisfaction was the main goal of the Fruit Center, so I calmly and politely explained to the customers in that particular line what was occurring and suggested moving to another line for business. Because I had clearly explained the situation to the customers and apologized for it, they were willing to move to another line without incident. I then dealt with the cash register malfunction. I called the computer company that serviced the register, and their support staff walked me through the steps necessary to deal with the register problem. Although it was a stressful situation, I was able to work well under pressure and still manage to prioritize what needed to be done."

~ Alexandra Ciccariello, Northeastern University Class of 2008

Did Ali prove that she had strong multitasking and analytical skills? Absolutely! But there are several other skills that are displayed here: customer-service skills; problem-solving skills; ability to stay calm under pressure; and ability to prioritize. That's a pretty amazing assortment of skills!

I think that the power of this story is that it pinpoints the focus on one specific day while still giving a little background for that day. The more you tighten your focus on "one moment in time," the more likely you are to make the situation really come alive. When that happens, the interviewer can see all kinds of great qualities that you have—even ones that you're not trying to display!

The other bonus from a rich story is that Ali not only has a powerful story up her sleeve; she also has a story that can be used to showcase different qualities in different interviews. My students find that once they have done the heavy lifting of writing the story, they manage to find opportunities to work it into conventional interviews—not just BBIs.

2. *For her job description, Aimee Stupak needed to show dedication:*

"Last summer, I took a new position in the West Hartford Building Department as a temporary Office Assistant. I was eager to experience a new position with more responsibility. I quickly learned to dress in more businesslike attire and to wake up two hours earlier than I used to for my previous job. I learned to appreciate the office setting very quickly as well, and given the fact that initiative is the number one thing my boss was looking for, I excelled immediately.

"From the first day, I took the initiative to understand the filing system and to help organize the files in a new way, so as to simplify the process of finding files for anyone in the office who needed to. I set up new labels for the cabinets and was instantly shown appreciation from the secretaries that I was working for.

"After only a week, the head supervisor and main building inspector asked me if I'd be interested in attempting a job they had been trying to find someone to do for a while. He brought me into "the Vault" which is full of barrels that contain building plans for single-family homes, stores, and apartment complexes all over the Town of West Hartford. Unfortunately, the barrels were dated back so far that "the Vault" was becoming overfilled and impossible to work with. No one, however, was willing to do the "dirty work." My supervisor explained that I would need to search through each barrel, and weed out only the plans that applied to single-family homes. After collecting these plans, he asked me to send them back to the home to which they applied.

"I started the job immediately, completing my daily responsibilities and entering "the Vault" at any point in the day that there was some downtime. I made a lot of progress and ended up cleaning out a very large portion of the space. When my last day came at the job because of the upcoming semester, I was thanked by all and told that my motivation and intense dedication to the job would be greatly missed."

~ Aimee Stupak, Northeastern University Class of 2008

This story shows dedication but many other qualities as well: willingness to do whatever asked without complaint; positive attitude; persistence; and organizational skills. I'm fond of this story because it's a good reminder that most students have had high-school jobs that included a good amount of "grunt work." As a result, many students believe that they don't have interesting experiences to use for a BBI, as they haven't done anything "important" enough. Yet a story about taking on the task that nobody else wanted is a great way to show off some very attractive qualities in an entry-level professional.

3.   *Here's a story that Nat Stevens used in an attempt to prove that he has strong organizational skills:*

"As the day lagged on at TextHELP Systems, I thought about how it was already 3:30 p.m., and that I only had an hour and a half left to finish up the logs. Just then the phone rang. I picked it up to hear the lovely voice of one of our sales reps on the west coast. She started off by saying, 'You're going to hate me,' so I knew that something challenging was coming. She added, 'I need you to get a mailing out to about five counties in Texas, by tonight. I didn't realize it until now.' I thought to myself about how difficult this would be, but I told her it wouldn't be a problem and I would gladly get it done.

"I started my work. First, I had to pull the names of all the directors from these counties that she wanted me to mail information to. The final list came to about 441 people. Next I had to print all the labels. In the meantime, I used two copy machines to make sure the first page of two of the press releases for the mailing were on letterhead. Then I had to make sure that the following pages were correlated appropriately. Finally, I had to fill each envelope, stamp them, and label them. Needless to say, although I had intended to leave at 5:00 pm, I did not step out of the office until 8:00 pm. The sense of accomplishment for completing the job provided me with much more satisfaction than I had originally anticipated."

~ Nat Stevens, Northeastern University Class of 2008

Here Nat attempts to prove that he has strong organizational skills, and he succeeds. However, a good story always ends up showing much more than one skill or quality!

Nat could use this story to show many other valued traits: positive attitude, dedication, willingness to go above and beyond... maybe even customer-service skills if we think of the salesperson as an internal customer.

4. *Jared Yee's story below proves a useful point: Many first-time job seekers take their retail experiences for granted. If you reflect on them, you're bound to come up with an impressive incident. Note how he jumps right in the phrase "One time..."—a good hint that we're about to get a story of one especially challenging or interesting day or incident.*

"One time at BJ's Wholesale Club where I worked, it was incredibly busy. All the lines at the registers were filled almost to the middle of the store. My supervisors were busy helping customers and the managers were too busy to assist customers. My supervisor told me to take over some of her responsibilities. She told me one of the freezers with dairy products was broken and that I needed to find one of the managers to fix the problem. She told me afterwards to help a customer with a problem she was having. I went to the produce section but the manager was busy. He told me to get another manager to handle the situation. This manager however, was also unavailable to fix the freezer.

"I realized that the freezer would not get fixed for possibly hours. I took matters in to my own hands. I got three carriages from the parking lot, filled them with all the dairy products from the broken freezer, and brought them into the storage section of a nearby freezer. After that was resolved, I found the very frustrated customer who was trying to buy a computer and was in a rush because she had to pick up her daughter. The computer she wanted was not on the shelf but she wanted the one on display. I had dealt with a situation like this before but with a supervisor's help.

"However, due to the chaos within the store I was told to handle the situation on my own. I wrote down the codes of the computer she wanted, being unable to look it up on the system's computer because it was being used. I then went to the storage room and looked for the empty box with the same code. I found it, went back down to the display shelf, and packed it along with all its parts in the box. I then assisted the customer with bringing the computer to my register line, since all the others were filled and she was in a rush. The manager said this was alright to do because she had been waiting for a long time. After ringing up the customer's computer, she thanked me and said that I had "saved her from a terrible day."

~ Jared Yee, Northeastern University Class of 2009

Jared picked this story because he wanted to show the ability to handle multiple projects at one time—a qualification for a job with Deloitte. However, Deloitte also seeks an excellent team player who is highly organized—two other qualities that this story captures. It also could be used to show an ability to work independently, perseverance, and customer service—to name just a few qualities!

5. *The next story is by Rebecca Harkess. As you read it, remember that the ultimate goal is to be able to write a story FIRST, and then to list at least THREE soft skills that the*

story could be used to prove about yourself. So as you read this story, try to think of all the different soft skills or qualities that Rebecca could use this story to prove during an interview:

"At my high school they take their yearbook very seriously. The book is over 400 pages long, has an annual budget of over $200,000, and has won numerous national awards. There is typically an editorial staff of two editors-in-chief and eight section editors, along with a staff of 30. My senior year our advisor asked if I would be willing to take on the position of Editor-in-Chief by myself as she did not feel anyone else was qualified for the job. I agreed and spent the summer before preparing the layout of the book, setting up our office, and buying new equipment.

"Our first deadline of around 80 pages was due in mid-October. I decided to tell the staff the deadline was at the end of September so we would have adequate editing time. The due date I set came and I went to collect layouts from my staff and found that only half had completed their layouts and even those were only mediocre. I went home that night feeling that I had already failed. I had nothing to work with and yet in a few weeks I was responsible for turning in 80 pages. No one had listened to the revisions I had made and I felt powerless.

"I decided that I couldn't give up; I was going to get this book done and done right because I had been given the responsibility to do so. I stayed up almost the whole night and wrote a two-page speech to deliver to my staff the next morning. I knew I had to be careful to balance coming off as angry to get my point across that I was serious, but at the same time I did not want everyone to think that I was on a power trip, especially because a lot of these students were in my same grade and people I considered friends. On the way to class that day I stopped at the grocery store to buy some doughnuts for the staff as I knew this was a way to show that I really cared about them and that I wanted this to be an enjoyable experience.

"I then sat everyone down and explained to them how very disappointed I was with the results I had seen and that they were unacceptable. I outlined a plan of how I wanted the layouts to get done including showing them new forms that I had created so that each student could review his or her own work before turning it in to me. I stressed the fact that I believed in the ability of each one of them and that I truly believed we could have a lot of fun and produce a book that we would all be really proud of. I could tell when I was done that everyone seemed much more motivated, they really wanted to work hard as a team and get this done.

"Every deadline after that I almost always received layouts on time and in near perfect form. In addition, our staff really bonded throughout the year and we had a really great time. When the book came out at the end of the year we heard from countless students that of all the years this was their favorite yearbook. I felt so proud of the book and my staff."

~ Rebecca Harkess, Northeastern University Class of 2010

Rebecca's story is one of the best BBI stories that I've seen in a long time. Consider some of the elements: Even when she is giving background/overview to set up the critical moment of the story, we learn some things that are impressive about her. Due to the quantitative and qualitative details, we see that her editorial position was a high-stakes role.

The next great thing about this story is how well it conveys her thoughts, emotions, and actions as she encounters a major obstacle. We really know what it was like to be her in this role, and we have an appreciation for how seriously she took the failure that she faced. She proceeds to walk us through her thought process and actions in addressing the problem and carries it right through to the outcome. Just wonderful.

Better still, the story is one that Rebecca will have up her sleeve in case she needs to prove any number of qualities or soft skills: leadership, responsibility, conflict management, results orientation, and interpersonal skills to name just a few!

6. *The next story is from Cheyenne Olinde. This story is an almost fiendishly clever story for a Supply Chain Management (SCM) major to use in an interview. Cheyenne never worked in corporate SCM… but this story absolutely will resonate with SCM professionals: After all, it entails meeting a logistical challenge—one that required consideration of manpower, equipment capabilities, delivery time, and so forth. So while the story illustrates many soft skills—see if you can spy them as you read—it is particularly smart in showing that he has an appreciation for what a SCM interviewer may want to know.*

"As a combat photographer, I have been fortunate enough to document every aspect the Marine Corps has to offer. I have documented everything from aerial reconnaissance to autopsies. I have been deployed to Cuba, Spain, Seychelles, Malta, Greece, Italy, Puerto Rico, Djibouti Africa, and Wisconsin. The one thing that all my missions had in common was that I was serving a customer. Whether it was a Captain for a routine passport photo, or aerial photographs of a military base's security weakness for a General, I have always interacted with clients. Many times my customers would want certain photographs that were impractical and I would have to tactfully explain why their request would not work and offer a solution to solve their problem. Other times, I would get a call from an important client who needs an exceptional amount of work done in a very short window of time.

"When our Marines were preparing to go to Afghanistan, we had to provide them with the tools to help teach their Marines basic Arabic. Their request was for over 1,000 instructional Arabic CDs, needed in less than seven days on top of the other 30 jobs we currently had. My shop had neither the manpower nor the equipment to handle the request, and the customer did not have the funds to go elsewhere. I had to make it work.

"The original CDs were provided; we just needed to make the copies. We only had the capability to copy 20 CDs an hour, plus the work could not interfere with our other jobs requested by my other customers.

"I implemented a split schedule of three eight and a half-hour shifts, operating non-stop. This allowed for the constant copying of CDs, and the continuous work on other current productions. Not only did we meet the goal in less than three days, we made an extra 500 copies for future operations and completed all the current productions in house.

"I approached my commanding officer and requested time off for the team after the hard work and dedication my Marines showed. I then had them all come over to my house and treated them to a BBQ to thank them. After that, there was nothing my Marines would not do for me, and superiors knew that there was no challenge too large I couldn't handle."

~ Cheyenne Olinde, Northeastern University Class of 2010

If I remember correctly, Cheyenne used this story to prove that he had good customer-service skills. While it does so, it also could be rolled out to illustrate problem-solving skills, leadership, and time management skills.

7. *This story is from Jake Thaler, and it shows how a story about athletics can be very effective. Pay special attention to how he works his thoughts and emotions into the story.*

"Let me tell you of a time when I proved to be self-motivated. Upon being recruited for hockey at Northeastern, I received a packet for strength and conditioning. I was planning on showing up on campus in the best shape of my life. I had begun my first week of the workout when I experienced a great deal of pain in my left knee. I learned that I tore my meniscus and was forced to undergo surgery. Frustration overcame me as I learned that most of my hard work getting to the point of being recruited was going to waste. After repairing the torn cartilage, I was told that I had to slowly rehab my knee for a full three months without heavily working out. A feeling of bitterness took control of me, and I knew that this was going to be a huge setback for me in the long run. My dream of playing college hockey increased in difficulty but I knew I could come back from it.

"After a summer of tedious rehab sessions I was finally cleared to play by the school. My excitement took over and adrenaline flowed through my body before my first workout with the team. In a matter of seconds, my joy turned to a heart-stopping experience when I heard the same "pop" that indicated my knee was not fully repaired. The first thought that went through my head was that I completed three months of rehab for nothing. After this initial thought, my conscience took over and I realized that I had wanted to play at this level ever since I watched my first hockey game. Another surgery was necessary, and this time they partially removed the cartilage, letting me recover much faster. After not being able to skate and work out for months, I had been eagerly waiting to catch up. I felt aggravated from my hiatus as I needed to acclimate myself to the position again.

"As the season drew close to the end, I still had yet to play in a game although our team had been riding an unsuccessful year. I kept on thinking that the next game was going to be the one where I'd get my shot. The last weekend of the year we played two games against Boston University—the third-ranked team in the nation and two days before we played them my coach told me I had the start. All of the obstacles I had to overcome to get my shot and I finally had my chance to show what I could do. Our team battled hard and lost both games that weekend, but I surprised myself and a lot of other doubtful people that I could play at this level. Although we had lost, I had felt that I demonstrated a winning attitude that was driven by motivation."

--Jake Thaler, Northeastern University Class of 2010

In addition to self-motivation, this story could be used to show persistence, ability to handle frustration and adversity, being goal-oriented (literally!), and patience. That's a lot of mileage for one story!

Remember my rule: Use a specific, vivid story to prove that you have one great quality, and you'll wind up proving you have at least three other great qualities!

As described earlier in this appendix, write three stories showing you at your best. Then, read over your stories, and list three different transferable skills that each story could be used to prove.

As you look at a job description's qualifications, think of stories you might use to prove that you have those qualities. However, it's also worth your while to come up with situations that show you at your best, and THEN figure out various ways in which you could apply them in job interview situations. It's always smart to find opportunities to tell your best stories.

Something really fun happens when you've developed several of these stories: You'll find that once you have them down, you'll keep finding opportunities to plug them into interview situations! And it's hard to have too many of them. Years back, I had a student who interviewed for a job with The Boston Globe, the major newspaper in Boston. Afterward, she was excited to tell me what had happened: Much to her surprise, the whole interview was behavioral! She had to share eight stories. When she was done, she compared notes with another student, who looked exhausted: "That was so difficult!" the other student said to her.

"I know!" my student said. "I only had five stories ready to tell, so I had to think fast to come up with three more.

The other student stared at her. "You had five stories ready to tell?!"

"Well, yeah," my student said. "We were required to come up with them for our preparation class..."

Coming up with these stories can give you a big advantage in these situations, obviously. One thing I love about the stories is that they're an opportunity to show an employer what you really mean when you claim to have great customer-service skills, the ability to multitask, or whatever. Plus people know that you aren't just blowing smoke if you tell them you have some skills that they're seeking: You've got hard proof in the form of a story.

In my job at Bates Communications, we encourage business leaders to develop an "anthology" of stories that can be used for all sorts of purposes—making a sales presentation to a client, delivering a crucial speech, or convincing senior leadership to back one of your proposals, for example.   So your ability to develop and deliver concise, relevant, engaging stories is a skill that can benefit you throughout your career!

APPENDIX F

Special Guide for International Students: Understanding the World of Work in America

By Charlie Bognanni, Senior Coordinator of Cooperative Education, Northeastern University

If you're an international student getting ready to the work in the United States for the first time, then everything in the main part of this book applies to you. On top of that, though, there are some special considerations that you should keep in mind as you get ready for your first co-op job, internship, or full-time job in the US.

As an international student, you face all kinds of psychological transitions when first coming to the US for your education. For many of you, the classroom experience will be different: It's often easier to get individual attention from a professor here, and there may be more group projects than you would do back home. There are all sorts of extracurricular activities at most universities here as well, and this is good news for many international students.

In my experience, though, one of the most challenging adjustments can be to the process and practices of finding a job as well as understanding an employers' expectations once you are in a job. So in this appendix, I will address many of the issues that I have seen arise and offer some advice on how to avoid problems while getting the most out of your work experience.

First, let's talk about finding a job. In many countries, having a strong family connection is paramount in landing a job. Often, the resume is secondary to having the proper connection. Many of my international students will tell me "it's not *what* I know, it's *who* I—or my family—know(s)." I recall that a few years ago one of my Chinese students told me that because his father was so well-connected, professionally and politically in China, a few phone calls from his father to the "right" people would result in a job for him when he was back home. Furthermore, he told me that he could perform poorly but that he would never be terminated because of his father's connections. To the student's credit, he admitted that he would never intentionally perform poorly because it would be an embarrassment to his father.

This is in very stark contrast to the US system. There's no denying that personal or family connections in this country may have some value in finding a job, but the vast majority of students obtain their jobs without the benefit of a "connection."

As you learn more about the American attitude toward work, you might hear the word "meritocracy." A common definition of this word is:

> *A System Based on Ability – A social system that gives opportunities and advantages to people on the basis of their ability rather than, e.g., their wealth or seniority.*

In other words, students in the US obtain their jobs based on qualifications. Do they have the appropriate GPA that the employer requires? Do they have the necessary skills? Can they work well in teams, and can they communicate both verbally and in writing? Consider the difference between *that* system and the "family connections" system that is the rule in many other parts of the world.

Working in a meritocracy system can be good news or bad news for any student, regardless of where you're from. In a meritocracy, your individual effort matters much more. I have seen international students who overcame challenges with language and culture, becoming some of the best students in our program. They were the ones who quickly figured out that they could outwork other students when it came to putting together a great resume and being incredibly prepared for an interview. The US system rewards those that do that.

But if the good news is that individual effort matters, the bad news is... individual effort matters! If you don't put in the effort, you will miss out on opportunities—both during the job search process and on the job. The sooner you understand the meritocracy system, the easier it is to navigate the job search process in the US.

PROCESS USED IN THE US TO OBTAIN A JOB

1. Resume

   All candidates must have a completed, well-written, error-free resume in order to apply for a job. Please refer to Chapter Two of this book for detailed instructions on how to write a resume. It is especially important for international students to be cognizant of not making any mistakes on their resumes. Errors on any resumes are obviously a problem, but these errors are magnified for international students. Although it's not always a fair assumption, there tends to be a perception from some employers that international students have a difficult time writing. True or not, that perception is there. You do not want to perpetuate that perception. You need to proofread your resume, proof it again, and then proof it one more time. It's also a good idea to have someone else proof it as well.

   Let's discuss grades. As indicated in Chapter Two, if you have a 3.0 or above, please put your grade point average on your resume. Many international students have very limited work experience, so it becomes especially important to do well academically and list your GPA on your resume. It's your biggest marketing piece so you need to advertise it, assuming it's a 3.0 or higher. Although research has shown that there is no scientific correlation between good grades and good job performance, most employers don't know that or believe that. They will look at a strong GPA as evidence of your ability to learn as well as your work ethic. In fact, an employer may be even more impressed by an international student with a great GPA than a US-born student with the same GPA. If you can get excellent grades even though English is not your native language, this will impress an employer.

With respect to work experience, many international cultures do not encourage high school or college students to work part-time while they are high school students. This is pretty much the exact opposite of the American culture, and it may prove to be a disadvantage to you. Most American young people are highly encouraged to find part-time work as soon as they are legally allowed to work—usually at 16.

So you may be starting off at a real disadvantage with your resume. Given this, it's very important for you to become involved in community service, volunteer work, or an on-campus work experience in order to have some significant content on your resume. Many universities allow international students to work on campus—take advantage of that if you can. Any sort of work experience in this country will result in a resume that makes several subtle points with employers:

- You have already proven that you can work in a US organization, so that will ease concerns for the employer.

- You probably have a reference who can be called locally who can give the employer a better sense of your work ethic and other important soft skills.

- You are the kind of person who takes action to address their inexperience, which reflects positively on you as well.

Whether or not you work prior to your co-op or internship in the US, do try to get some work experience at home before coming to school here or during summer vacations. Take advantage of this: It really pays off.

2. Interview

All candidates will undergo an interview or two with the employer in order to be considered for employment. Please read Chapter Three of this book for detailed instructions on interviewing. Let's discuss some specific things that international students should be aware of when interviewing.

In preparing for the interview, many international students are understandably concerned about being able to understand interview questions and respond articulately. As a result, they attempt to memorize answers to "commonly asked questions." This is a huge mistake. Memorizing answers creates many problems. The first problem is that, simply, there is an almost infinite number of interview questions that an employer can ask. There is no possible way any candidate can anticipate which questions will be asked... so don't try it; it's wasted effort. Additionally, memorizing answers will cause candidates to respond to questions in a very prescribed and "scripted" manner. Employers will see right through that and these "rehearsed" answers are not what employers are looking for. Instead, it is best to prepare as is outlined in Chapter Three.

During the interview itself, make sure that you speak slowly and deliberately. Most international students experience some form of language hurdle, and many international students have an accent. Because of this, it is vitally important that employers can understand you during the interview. Unfortunately, most candidates have a tendency to speak fast during the interview due to nervousness. Do just the opposite. Speak slowly, make sure that you articulate and express your words so that you can be understood.

You do not want employers struggling to understand you. The immediate concern from the employer's perspective is that if they can't understand you during the interview, they will not understand you on the job. This is not good. I primarily work with accounting students, so they are usually great with numbers. Unfortunately, that is not enough. In any job, you need to be able to communicate well enough to interact with your manager and co-workers. Among other things, the interviewer will be trying to determine whether your English skills are good enough for you to be able to do the job. Speaking slowly will also calm you down and will give you a chance to think more clearly about what you want to say. Practice this and practice some more. Also, it's not a problem to have an accent or to have to ask to have a question repeated or an unusual word explained once or twice in an interview. However, you should look up any words or phrases in the job description that you don't understand before the interview. As an international student, you may have to put in more preparation time for an interview than US-born students—especially if your English skills are only okay. But one thing we always say is this: If you want a job a little, prepare a little... if you want a job a *lot*, prepare a lot!

3. Follow Up After the Interview

As mentioned in Chapter Three, make sure that you send the employer a thank-you note. As is discussed about the importance of not making any errors in your resume, the same holds true about the thank-you note. In a meritocracy, an employer views every bit of communication with you as additional evidence as to whether or not you can do the job. Please make sure that your note is grammatically correct and that you do not have any spelling errors or typos. Again, as we mentioned earlier, employers may dissect your note even more closely than the thank-you note of an American student because they want to ensure that your writing skills are good – make sure the note is good. A poor thank-you note can ruin a great interview. Not writing one at all is bad, but sending one that has several errors is even worse.

4. Accepting the Job

Don't forget that after you've accepted a job, you must meet with your university advisors to complete the appropriate paperwork. Be aware of all regulations regarding the Social Security Number application process and other work regulations that apply to you as an international l student. Prior to 9/11, many universities were more relaxed about authorizing students to work. These days, failing to complete the authorization process prior to starting work can have truly terrible consequences for an international student. Sadly, I have seen students who have lost their jobs and been forced to leave the country at least temporarily as a result. It's your responsibility to make sure that you are in touch regularly with your international student office and that you are aware of all rules and regulations about your eligibility to work in the United States.

PERFORMING ON THE JOB

Cultural differences also can be a big issue once you have started working. Here, too, the idea is that the workplace is a meritocracy. US employers usually expect all of their employees—even unpaid or low-paid interns—to show up on time, work hard, take direction well, and show that they are ready and willing to learn. If that doesn't happen, the student may face unpleasant consequences. This includes getting fired.

Scott, the author of this book, told me a story about an international student that may surprise you. Years ago, he worked with a young woman from Kuwait. In those days, unpaid internships were more common than they are now. To her credit, this woman managed to use family connections to obtain an unpaid job with a company that did a good amount of business in her home country. About two months into a six-month job, though, the student got fired. She was shocked. She couldn't understand how it was possible to get fired from an unpaid internship.

After talking it over with the employer to learn the facts, Scott explained it for her. "Employers let people go when the cost outweighs the benefits of having someone work there," he said. "In your case, there was no *financial* cost to having you there. But what your boss told me was that you were extremely unreliable: He expected you to be there for 35 to 40 hours per week, but you often told him that you had to miss work to meet with your academic advisor, take care of personal errands, and so on. And when you were there, the quality of your work was poor—people often had to redo it. So it became more trouble than it was worth to keep you on."

Performing well on your job is extremely important. Please refer to Chapter Four for detailed instructions on how to maximize your work performance. Let's discuss some specific things that international students need to be aware of when working.

International students will sometimes tell me that punctuality is not as stressed in their culture as it is in the American culture. This is a very important distinction. Punctuality (being to work on time) is highly stressed in the American culture. If a supervisor says you need to be at work at 8:30 a.m. it means 8:30 a.m., not 9:00 or even 8:45. Being late for work is not acceptable in the American workplace and reflects very poorly on the employee. There's an expression you sometimes hear in American organizations: "Early is on time.... and on time is late!" In fact, many American managers are pleased when an employee shows up 15 or 30 minutes earlier than what it required... or if someone stays later than required, especially if there is urgent work to be done.

This also applies to making sure that you adhere to lunch time schedules and do not abuse the amount of time given to you for lunch. Your overall work ethic is very significant also. As is mentioned in Chapter Four, you always want to invest 100% of your work effort in any job. Regardless of your assignments, you need to work hard and demonstrate an excellent attitude in every task assigned to you. You will need to do excellent work on your job to be able to leverage this to help you obtain your next co-op/internship job or a full time job. Doing great work is also how you prove to an employer that you're ready for more challenging—and maybe more interesting—assignments. That's another aspect of working in a meritocracy.

Co-ops/Internships versus Optional Practical Training

As you may know, any eligible international student in valid F-1 non-immigrant status typically has the opportunity to apply for a period of 12 months of full-time work for purpose of training in the United States after graduation. This is called "Post-Completion Optional Practical Training" or "OPT." If you're hoping to apply for a period of training in your field of study in the United States after getting your degree, this may sound interesting to you.

As long you do less than 12 months of full-time Curricular Practical Training—meaning co-op or internship work—*prior* to graduation, you are eligible to apply for OPT. If you do more than 12 months of co-op or internship work prior to graduation, then you are no longer eligible to apply for it. However, there are some tricky aspects to this:

- Generally, you must be enrolled as a full-time student for at least one academic year before applying. Exceptions may apply for transfer students.

- You're not allowed to work on campus while authorized to work on co-op.

These are just general guidelines: Check with your school's international student office regarding your status and eligibility. However, one more point: In some programs, students may struggle in deciding whether they should do a third six-month, full-time co-op because this means that you would sacrifice the opportunity to do OPT. For many, this is a judgment call. If a third co-op or internship is optional, it would be good to find out if you can get a job that will improve your experience significantly... or if an OPT training experience is possible and preferable. While you never know how things might turn out, you definitely can't count on a company hiring for OPT. And if they do, that doesn't necessarily mean that they would sponsor you for an H-1 visa. In some cases, doing a third full-time co-op job might work out better than OPT. Again, though, talk to your co-op or career professional about this.

Staying in the US After Graduation

There are many different factors to be aware of if you're seeking H-1 sponsorship by a US employer. One major issue is the US economy. When the economy is strong, the US government sometimes makes more H-1 visas available to companies, as employers are facing labor shortages. Obviously, the relatively weak economy in recent years has not helped those seeking H-1 visas.

It's hard to predict what will happen with H-1 visas. In an April 2013 article in the *Boston Business Journal*, there was speculation that immigration reform could result in the number of H-1 visas potentially doubling nationwide from 65,000 to anywhere from 110,000 to 180,000. If this were to become a reality, it would have a big impact. The article reported that the US Citizenship and Immigration Services received 120,000 requests for H-1 visas... and that was just in the first two weeks of the application period for 2014!

What does that really mean? The article's author believes that the main reason for this boom is that US companies—especially in areas like high tech and biotech—are thriving, and they need talented people with great technical skills and experience. So if there are more H-1 visas available, those students most likely to benefit will still be in fields such as computer science and engineering.

This leads us to our next point. After the economy, your field is the biggest factor. Students in science and engineering majors are going to have a better chance than liberal arts majors as a general rule, as not enough Americans are majoring in technical areas to meet the demands of industry. Still, there is no guarantee for any student seeking sponsorship.

Your region can make a difference, too. In general, cities and states with more technology or engineering-related jobs may hire international students more readily.

All of that said, this section is not intended to provide any legal advice on how to seek training opportunities after graduation. You should always consult with your school's international student office for immigration rules and regulations.

Our experience with international students does tell us that if your goal is to try to be sponsored by an employer and stay in the US after graduation, then it is enormously important that you perform not just well, but extremely well. In other words, a term that is sometimes used in the US is that, "It's not good enough to be good enough." You will have to perform above and beyond to prove to an employer that they should invest in you as a full-time employee. It is costly for employers to sponsor international students, and it also requires a ton of time-consuming paperwork. Your employer basically will have to prove to the government that they could not hire someone comparable to you who already has citizenship or a green card... so you will have to prove yourself to the employer first.

One note of caution: There are many companies who will charge you a considerable amount of money to help you find H-1 sponsorship. Scott has dealt with at least one of these companies, and his advice is to be wary of them. For a fee, they will write your resume for you, but the end product isn't likely to be any better than what you would get through working with your university. In fact, it may be worse. Beyond that, these companies send your resume out to employers... with no guarantee of results. You're probably better off saving your money.

In summary, it is not an exaggeration to say that international students have to work extra hard to obtain a good job and perform well on it. However, international students who do work very hard during the job search process often end up with outstanding jobs and improve their chances greatly of receiving a full-time job offer from an American employer after graduation.

APPENDIX G
Informational Interviewing

All of the information in this chapter was provided by the co-op and career services team at University of Massachusetts Lowell.

What is an informational interview?

An informational interview is an interview with someone currently working in a field of interest to you.

Why should I conduct an informational interview?

- To help you make informed choices about where you want to work and what kind of job you want.

- To get "inside information" about places of work.

- To create a network of contacts and make a favorable impression with someone who may be able to offer you a job or a job lead at some point in the future.

- To build your confidence for your job interviews by practicing asking questions and providing information about yourself—you can't be rejected after an informational interview!

How do I find people to interview?

Anyone can be part of your network. Here are some people you might consider asking for career-related information:

- Friends, family, neighbors, and acquaintances

- Professors, advisors, classmates (current and previous)

- Current and previous employers and co-workers

- People whose careers interest you or that you are curious about

- People employed at organizations where you think you might like to do an internship or work

- People to whom you have been referred by your contacts

How do I set up an informational interview?

You can set up your interview by phone, letter, or e-mail. If someone refers you, be sure to mention his or her name. Here are some things to include in your introduction:

- I'm currently a student at _____ (indicate your school, what you are studying, and when you are planning to graduate).

- I'm not looking for a job right now; I'm just collecting information about various fields.

- I'm really interested in the work that you do.

- I only need 20 minutes of your time to ask you some questions.

- When would it be convenient for you to talk? What is the best way to reach you (phone or e-mail)?

Informational Interview Guidelines

- Try to hold your informational interview in person rather than on the phone, if possible. You'll get a better understanding of what the company is like: how people interact, how they dress, what kinds of facilities are available for employees.

- You can write notes during the interview. Jot down key words to help you remember the conversation and questions asked.

- After 20 minutes, thank the person for spending time to meet with you. If the other person wants to continue beyond 20 minutes, you may.

- Bring your resume with you, just in case they offer to critique it.

- Before you leave, ask for a business card or write down the person's name and job title, and the company's complete name, address, telephone number and/or e-mail address.

- Write your interviewee a thank-you note as soon as possible (within 24 hours, ideally) after the interview. Remember to include your name, address, and phone number in the note. Be sure to proofread your note carefully for typos and professionalism.

What questions should I ask?

1. What do you do in a typical work-day?

2. How did you get started in this job? What experience, education, training, and skills did you need? What has your career path been like?

3. What do you like about your work? What do you dislike about your work?

4. How has the economy affected this industry?

5. What advice would you give me if I were interested in this field/industry/type of job? What classes should I take? What experiences should I get?

6. Who else do you know that I can talk to? (If the interviewee gives you a name, ask if you may use the interviewee's name when contacting the referral.)

Pointers

- Relax and enjoy yourself.

- Be well groomed and neatly dressed. Professional dress is appropriate. Just like any interview, first impressions count!

- Make eye contact with the person to whom you are talking and smile when it is appropriate.

- Extend your hand when you are being greeted and shake hands firmly.

- Do not sit down until you have been invited to do so.

- Look around and notice your surroundings. Notice what you like and don't like about what you see, and be sure to put these observations in your notes.

- Be aware that many informational interviews turn into employment interviews. Don't count on it, but it happens. Be prepared to talk about your background and why you are interested in learning more about this field.

- Gathering job-related information doesn't have to be a formal process—talk to people you meet on the bus, at the gym, waiting in line at the grocery store, or wherever. You never know who might know someone who knows someone you'd be interested in talking with!

INFORMATIONAL INTERVIEWING ASSIGNMENT

Informational interviewing is perhaps one of the most rewarding, yet most underused career development tools in everyone's career tool-box. As the name suggests, the goal of talking with people actually working in the career you're considering is to get *information*, not a job.

Informational interviews are great opportunities to help you determine whether you're in the right major for your career goals, learn more to make better choices about your career path, build a network of career contacts, gain confidence for job interviews by practicing asking questions and providing information about yourself, and help map out strategies for making yourself more marketable when you are looking for work.

Your Assignment

1. Find someone to interview

   There are lots of ways to connect with people in your field of interest:

   - From career expos, career fairs, career advisors, or alumni events

   - From professors, friends, colleagues, or classmates

   - From LinkedIn groups and/or contacts (including alumni groups)

   Once you've identified someone you'd like to talk to, make contact with that person either via phone, e-mail, or LinkedIn. If you are contacting this person in writing, try something like:

   "Dear Ms. Jones: I obtained your name from _____. I'm a _____ major at _____ and am in the process of defining my career goals following my graduation in June 20xx. My current area of interest is _____, so I thought you would be a great resource for information and advice about this career field. Would you be willing to meet with me for 30 minutes so I could ask you a few questions about the _____ field and how best to prepare for it? I could easily come to your office at a time that works for you, or we could talk over the phone if that would be easier. Please let me know by return e-mail or, if you prefer, call me at xxx-xxx-xxxx. Thank you for your consideration. Sincerely, [your name]"

   Remember to mention the 30-minute limit – a contact is more likely to say "yes" if you ask for a short amount of time. If you try to reach someone twice with no response, look for someone else to contact.

2. Prepare

   - Plan ahead so you appear professional and prepared.

   - Write down your questions and take them to the meeting. Make them open-ended questions that require more than a "yes or no" answer.

- Plan to dress as you would for a job interview.

- Bring a resume in case they ask for it, but don't volunteer it unless it feels appropriate.

- Know how to get to the interview and plan to arrive 10 minutes early.

3. Go on the interview

When interviewing people for information (versus them interviewing you for a job), there's less pressure to "sell" yourself, so you can ask honest questions about the person's job, industry, or organization.

Questions to ask include:

- What do you consider to be the best part of this job?

- Is there anything about this job (or field/industry) that doesn't appeal to you?

- What has your career path been?

- What was your college major? If you could do it over, would you change your major or do anything else differently?

- What recommendations would you have for a student interested in moving into this career?

- What pressing professional challenges do you see for this industry?

- What does a "typical" work day look like?

- Who else would you recommend I talk to as I explore this field? When I contact them, may I use your name?

Remember these important things:

- Try to relax and enjoy yourself, but always behave professionally.

- Introduce yourself and offer a firm handshake.

- Reiterate your promise to stay only 30 minutes.

- Ask your questions, but try to make it a conversation rather than an interrogation.

- Take brief notes if you like.

- After 30 minutes, offer to stop. Your interviewee may say it's fine to continue, but if he or she indicates that your time is up, say thank you, ask for a business card, shake hands, and leave.

4.   Follow up

Within 24 hours, send a thank you note (e-mail is fine). Express your appreciation for the time spent with you and mention your plan to follow through on any suggestions offered in the interview.

5.   Presentation

Prepare a 2-3 page paper demonstrating the following:

- Who you met with and brief information about their work experience/co-op

- The most significant thing you learned

- How (if at all) this meeting has impacted your career, co-op, or academic plan

- A brief reflection on the experience as a whole

APPENDIX H
Additional Resources

In this last section of the book, I have included a few different materials that I have found useful in teaching the Introduction to Co-op courses at Northeastern University as well as sheets that I developed for working with my graduate assistants and students over the years.

Fine-Tuning Your Resume may be useful for students wishing to do a spot-check of their resume or for instructors who want to tip off students to common errors. I developed **Common Interview Problems and How To Solve Them** after conducting over 250 practice interviews. It's easy to tell if an interview is good, bad, or somewhere in between, but it can be difficult to articulate exactly *why* an interview is lacking. I have given this to my graduate assistants when training them, but it also can be helpful for co-op and career services professionals in their efforts to get beyond *symptoms* of interview difficulties to identify the root problems. The problems are listed in approximate order of frequency, and each is paired with plausible solutions to the problem. The **Interviewing Scenarios, Job Search Scenarios,** and **On-The-Job Performance Scenarios** can be provocative for classroom discussion in small or large groups; I also use these as make-up assignments for students who miss classes. Lastly, **You Make the Call! Decide What to Do If YOU Were the Co-op Coordinator** is an exercise designed to make students walk in our shoes as career professionals. Understanding the roles of all constituencies—student, co-op/intern, co-worker, supervisor, internship/co-op coordinator, and career services professional—is critical to becoming successful as a developing student/employee. This exercise may help students appreciate the delicate balance that co-op and career professionals must maintain when providing services to numerous students and employers.

FINE-TUNING YOUR RESUME

Is your resume REALLY all set? Here are a few elements to double-check. They represent solutions to the most common mistakes on business co-op resumes!

1. Make sure to include your month and year of graduation (i.e., May 2015).

2. Add *References Provided Upon Request* as last line.

3. If appropriate, consider adding *Financing ___% of Education Through Part-Time and Cooperative Education Employment* to bottom of education section.

4. Write out your degree: Say "Bachelor of Science Degree in Business Administration" NOT "B.S. Degree in Marketing" (or "Studying Psychology," etc.).

5. Have start and end dates for all jobs.

6. Add computer skills section if missing.

7. Add interests section if missing.

8. Differentiate between majors, concentrations, and minors if necessary.

9. Make sure jobs are in reverse chronological order (with some exceptions).

10. Add GPA if at least 3.0.

11. At most, list GPA to two decimal places (3.25); it's okay to round up or down (i.e., 3.072 can be written as 3.1).

12. Write out all numbers that are ten or smaller. Unless beginning a sentence, write 11 or higher as a number (i.e., 15, not fifteen).

13. Use bold and italic fonts to improve aesthetic quality of resume and add variety. Consider using something other than Times New Roman to be different (i.e., Arial, Garamond, Century).

14. Make sure each sentence or bullet point has a verb—almost without exception.

15. Avoid passive phrases such as "Responsibilities included."

16. In job descriptions, don't just list transferable skills: each sentence/bullet point should include an aspect of what you actually did.

17. Add quantitative and qualitative details to bring your job description to life.

18. Go beyond summarizing your duties: What were your *accomplishments* in the job?

19. Follow a format from this guidebook: NOT a MS-Word template or the advice of your brother's girlfriend's cousin's friend who is really good at resumes!

20. Be consistent in font, capitalization of words, and bolding; be consistent in the use of periods at the end of sentences and with abbreviations—especially for months and street addresses.

21. Use a consistent format for city and state (e.g., San Diego, CA).

22. Spell-check **and** proofread!

COMMON INTERVIEW PROBLEMS AND HOW TO SOLVE THEM

	PROBLEM	SOLUTION
1.	Being "interviewer dependent" (Quality of your interview depends on quality of interviewer)	• Answer general questions with specifics. • Use specific stories and examples. • Make interview a "conversation with a purpose."
2.	Lacking a strategy	• Write down three reasons why YOU should be hired for THIS specific job. • Discuss these reasons ASAP in interview (i.e., when answering open-ended questions).
3.	Inadequate research	• Prepare as if your life depended on it! • Weave your research into answers and end-of-interview questions.
4.	Answers aren't helpful	• Always tie answers to company's needs according to the job description.
5.	Negative nervous energy	• Preparation. • Practice. • Put energy into presentation. • Maintain external focus.
6.	Weak opening and/or closing	• Don't rehash resume. • Articulate strategy early. • Prepare ten good questions. • Bridge to close of interview.
7.	Getting stuck; blanking out	• Ask clarifying question. • Don't be afraid to pause. • Use notes page (carefully).
8.	Raising flags for interviewer (making statements that raise concerns about whether you are appropriate for the job)	• Preparation • Focus on positives, always. • If negatives must be discussed, choose ones that won't hurt you.
9.	Insensitivity to interviewer --Talking too fast --Lack of "active listening" --Digressing from the point	• Practice speaking style. • Pause, especially after key points. • Respond to verbal/nonverbal cues. • Stick to what he or she needs to know.

INTERVIEWING SCENARIOS

Scenario 1

You're asked what pay rate you'd be seeking for a job. What would you say?

Scenario 2

A person from a company calls to invite you in for an interview. You set up an interview for 10:00 a.m. on Friday. "Oh, by the way," the interviewer says. "It's Casual Day here on Friday, so no need for you to get dressed up." How do you dress for the interview?

Scenario 3

You agree to have an interview at 11:45 a.m. on Tuesday. But then one of your professors announces that there will be a review session at the same time, and you know it will hurt you to miss it. What do you do?

Scenario 4

You don't have a car now, but you will have one in time for your co-op or internship. You have the opportunity to interview for a great job that's about 25 miles outside of the city. Describe three different ways you could get to the company for the interview.

Scenario 5

You arrive 15 minutes early for a 9:00 a.m. interview. You had to get up early to be there on time, so you are annoyed when the interviewer doesn't appear until 9:20. How would you pass the time while waiting? What do you say about the interviewer being late?

Scenario 6

You are an international student. At some point in the interview, you are asked: "Do you plan to stay in the US after graduation, or will you return home?" How do you respond?

Scenario 7

It is Monday, May 8, and you don't have a job lined up for the summer or fall. You are hoping to get an offer from Cornell Products but know you probably won't hear from them until early in the next week. The phone rings, and you get an offer from Carew Software. It's not a bad job but definitely one that you would turn down if you had an offer from Cornell. What do you say to the person from Carew Software?

Scenario 8

You accept a job offer from Pandolfo Hospital in mid-May and feel pleased that you lined up your co-op job so early. Two weeks later, though, you get a surprise offer from The Drury Rehabilitation Center that had interviewed you in early May; you had given up on getting an offer from them, but now they are offering you more money and a better job than the one at Pandolfo. What do you do?

JOB SEARCH SCENARIOS

1. You're looking for a job for January. You meet with your co-op or internship coordinator and agree on six jobs for which your resume will be sent. Two weeks later, you haven't heard anything at all, and there's a job with Boston Beer Company that you really wanted in that group. What do you do?

2. You come home and you get the following message from an employer: "This is [indecipherable name] from John Hancock, and we'd like to have you in for an interview. Can you contact us as soon as possible to arrange an interview for Monday?" You applied for three different jobs at Hancock and have no idea which job the employer is referring to. You call the number on your caller ID, but you get a message indicating that the number is not a working number; it's only used for outgoing calls. What do you do?

3. An employer calls you and wants to schedule you for an interview in two days: "What's your availability?" The problem is that you don't have your schedule handy. How do you handle the situation?

4. You know that resumes have already started going out, and you're freaking out because whenever you try to see your coordinator during her walk-in hours, there are impossibly long lines. There are no other times on her schedule for appointments or walk-ins that work for you, and you can't wait around because you have a class. What do you do?

5. You have an interview scheduled for Monday with RSA for their E-Commerce Analyst position. You know that you're a "reach candidate." What do you do to prepare in order to give yourself the best chance for an offer?

6. It's November 12, and you get an offer for a very entry-level position doing general office work. You are lukewarm about accepting the offer, but the fact is that you have no corporate experience, no other interviews scheduled, and no other possible offers at this point. You're supposed to start work on January 2. What do you do?

7. You have a friend who is currently on co-op for State Street Bank. He tells you to forward your resume to him; he will pass it along to his manager and put in a good word for you. It's a great job, and you're excited to hear that you may have an "in" with the company. What do you do?

8. You get two job offers, and you're struggling in attempting to decide which one to accept. Job A has really nice people and a great work environment, and it's also a very easy commute of about 15 minutes. However, the job itself is very easy. You're not sure if you would learn very much. In contrast, job B would be very stressful at first. It's in a very fast-paced environment, and it's obvious that you'll be thrown in at the deep end of the pool to sink or swim. It's also a 45-minute commute. But you know that you would learn much more in this job, as it's significantly more challenging. Which job would you accept? Would you change your mind if the other job paid significantly more than your first choice?

ON-THE-JOB PERFORMANCE SCENARIOS

Scenario 1

Jeff is interviewed by a large company for a finance job. The job description is vague and mentions little more than the need for a 2.0 GPA and dependability. The interviewer asks only one or two questions; at the end of the interview, Jeff asks a question about the hours. Jeff is surprised to receive an offer two days later. He accepts. After two weeks on the job, he finds he is very bored. Assisting the finance department, he spends most of his time filing and faxing and photocopying. He does a little data entry each day, but this is not difficult to master. Though he has agreed to work for six months, he thinks he will go crazy doing this kind of work for that long. What should he do now? Should he have done anything differently?

Scenario 2

Lucinda is feeling a little annoyed about her job. It seems like her boss is picking on her about everything she does. First, her boss complained that Lucinda would just sit at her desk when she ran out of work, instead of asking for more. Then the boss gave Lucinda a hard time because Lucinda thought she should double-check on how to do a bookkeeping procedure that she was trained to do a week before. Today, she is especially irritated because her boss gave her a hard time about being late a couple times this week. Lucinda had come in only five or ten minutes late: Several full-time employees did that, but she didn't see the boss talking to them about it! At 11:00 a.m., Lucinda puts aside the spreadsheet work that she has been asked to get done as soon as possible, and she calls her co-op coordinator to complain. What would you say to her if you were her co-op coordinator? Do you think Lucinda is being treated unfairly?

Scenario 3

Ya-hui is asked to back up all of the voice mail systems on the tape. It is a long and tedious job, and it is not her favorite thing to do. Yet her job for the most part is good: she is learning a lot about networks, databases, and hardware. Her boss comes in as she is finishing up with the voice mail back-up process. "Do you like doing this sort of work, Ya-hui?" the supervisor asks. How should she reply?

Scenario 4

Steven is an Arts and Sciences student studying communications. He lands an internship with an advertising agency. He is excited about the job. During the interview, the manager told him that he would be working on an important event and get to use his writing skills on developing some promotional materials. Three weeks into the job, he finds that all he ever does is clerical work such as faxing or sorting through file cabinets to throw out dated material. He feels that the employer hasn't kept their promise, and he is tempted to simply up and quit. How should he handle this situation?

Scenario 5

Oliver, a sophomore, is hired to do a fairly low-level job at an animal hospital. He knows it is not the best job, but he wants to get a good evaluation. What are some suggestions that you would give him?

Scenario 6

Sarah is feeling uncomfortable about a situation at work. As one of three co-ops working in an accounting group during tax season, Sarah has enjoyed her job—especially the opportunity to work overtime hours for good pay. However, she finds it odd that she is usually the only co-op asked to work overtime. A few days ago, her manager praised Sarah's work and offered to give her a ride home because it was dark. This morning he suggested taking her out to dinner to thank her for putting in all the overtime hours without complaint. Nothing has "happened," but she feels uncomfortable about being asked out to dinner by her boss. What should see do? If you were her co-op coordinator, and Sarah told you about the situation, what would your response be?

Scenario 7

Upon being hired for a co-op job, Max is told by an HR person that his hours are 8:45-5:00 Monday-Friday, including 45 minutes for lunch. His pay will be $12/hour, which multiplies out to $450/week before taxes. Max hits it off with a couple of full-time co-workers during the first few weeks of the job. One Friday they tell Max that they're going way across town for a long lunch—does he want to come? It's obvious that they'll be gone for a couple of hours. "Don't worry about it," one of the co-workers says. "The boss won't be back today, and HR will never know." Max isn't sure. At times it does seem like he's the only one who's usually taking just 45 minutes for lunch, and he's definitely the only one carefully tabulating his hours to submit on Monday morning. What should he do?

Scenario 8

Here is what one student wrote after being fired from a co-op job a few years ago: "I am currently a fourth-year student at Northeastern University. I recently was let go from a co-op position that I held for more than a year. The reason for my dismissal was because I received an e-mail that was deemed unacceptable by my employer. I was let go on the same day that I received this e-mail and forwarded it to my NU account.

"The purpose of e-mail in a co-op environment is as a way to conduct corporate communication—not for the social benefit of the co-op student. This is the lesson that I hope you take from this case. Actually, I think I was lucky—the situation could have been more serious. When I opened the e-mail, someone could have seen the letter and been offended—maybe offended enough to charge me with sexual harassment. Or I could have forwarded the e-mail to a co-worker by accident.

"Here are my suggestions for future co-ops: Use e-mail only for work purposes, and if you must send e-mail to friends, then keep it simple. Ask them what time they want to meet after work, for example. Also, you may want to make sure that your friends do not have access to your e-mail address at work. Additionally, don't check your other e-mail accounts while at work if at all possible: You never know what someone might send to your personal e-mail account."

QUESTIONS FOR DISCUSSION

1. Do you think the employer was ethically and/or legally right in choosing to terminate this student? More specifically, is it ethical and/or legal for an employer to read a co-op student's e-mail?

2. What would be some examples of an "inappropriate" e-mail?

3. Besides e-mail, list other examples of ways in which a student could be doing something "inappropriate" at work.

YOU MAKE THE CALL!

Decide What to Do If YOU Were the Co-op Coordinator

In the following scenarios, assume that you are the internship or co-op coordinator. As such, you are the go-between working with both students and employers, trying to do what is fair and right in all situations. You also are trying to ensure that your students are learning to become professionals, which includes being responsible for their actions. With all of this in mind, how would you handle the following scenarios?

Scenario 1

Co-op was scheduled to start on September 21, and Alex came to your office for the first time on September 17. When asked why he started so late, Alex said, "I was real busy, and then I had to drive to Florida." When you ask if he can get the guidebook today and bring in a resume tomorrow, he says, "I can buy the guidebook, but I have to go to Delaware tomorrow for the weekend. I can come in Tuesday." When he comes in Tuesday with a resume—two hours late for his 9:00 a.m. appointment—you go over it and make many corrections. Alex says, "Since it's so late, can I call you at home tonight to go over the revisions?" You say no, and he accepts this.

You help him get a job at Premium Life Insurance in the suburbs. He is pleased because it is near his house. But less than two weeks later, he calls you in an irate mood because he has been fired. "They screwed me over!" he says repeatedly. "I was late ONCE because I had a flat tire... what am I supposed to do about that? And they said I used the Internet too much, and I only went on it TWICE, when there was NOTHING to do. My supervisor thought I was great...It was HER boss that fired me. I think he doesn't like co-ops."

You call his immediate supervisor. She says that Alex was 1) on time twice during just eight days of employment—generally five to 15 minutes late; 2) using the Internet after being specifically warned not to do so until he had mastered all the basics of customer service, which he had not done; 3) accidentally hanging up on customers after keeping them on hold for a long time, then denying that he did it; and 4) coming in very tired, wearing wrinkled clothing, etc. She had tried to work with him but others had become fed up and demanded that he should be terminated. She found it hard to object.

The two versions of this story differ dramatically. Alex is coming to your office shortly. He

258

has already said he wants to talk to another of your employers about a co-op job, as they had wanted to interview him but had been unable to because he accepted the job with Premium Life. How would you deal with Alex? What would you say to him? Would you send his resume out to another employer?

Scenario 2

Tarek is a student looking for an internship starting in early January. It is early December, and you have not seen him for months. He comes into your office with a resume and says he wants to interview for a position at Raytheon that just became available. You look at the resume for the first time. It has several typos, and the format doesn't match the guidebook, but these are mistakes that could be fixed fairly quickly. And you see that he actually has much more experience than the seven or eight students who have been looking for jobs since referrals began in mid-October. There's a good chance he would get the Raytheon job. How would you handle the situation? Would you refer his resume to Raytheon? Whether you would or would not, what would you say to this student?

Scenario 3

It is mid-November, and you are incredibly busy with employers on campus, students making decisions on offers, and other students who are at various stages of the process. The phone has been ringing like crazy, maybe 40 to 50 times today alone. On top of everything, there is a long line of students waiting to see you this afternoon during walk-in hours. You are trying to deal with each student efficiently, but you also need to keeping things moving along.

Around 4:00 p.m., a student named Samantha from another coordinator comes into your office. As she sits down, she says, "I've been sitting here waiting to see you for over an hour." You tell her that you're sorry for the inconvenience and point out that it is an extremely busy time of day and time of year.

Samantha says, "You're never available. I've come in every afternoon this week, and you're either not in your office or there's a long line ahead of me. Everybody else is getting jobs, and you haven't even seen my resume yet. This isn't fair."

Checking your files, you see that Samantha contacted you just once this quarter. Three weeks ago, she left a message saying that she needed to see you as soon as possible. You left a voice mail for her indicating a few days and times that you were available. There has been no contact since then.

You have some good employers coming in over the next week or so to interview students. It would be easy enough to put Samantha on a few interview schedules. What would you say or do?

Scenario 4

A new employer has interviewed four of your students for a new position with a small company. "I don't know who to hire," the employer says. "Why don't you tell me who the best one is? I'll just offer the job to whoever you think."

You consider the candidates: **Carol** was in your Introduction to Co-op class last year and

259

came to all the classes but otherwise doesn't stand out in memory. **Henry** is a transfer student who has made a good impression on you so far in terms of his attitude and professionalism. **Mark** has the most relevant job experience on his resume, but he strikes you as being difficult: He made a stink over needing to revise his resume repeatedly. What would you say to the employer about whom to hire?

Scenario 5

You receive an evaluation for Nkeche Adebiyi, who recently completed a position with your second-largest employer. It's an extremely negative evaluation, giving her low rankings almost across the board. You ask Nkeche about it, and she says, "Oh, it's just because my immediate supervisor didn't like me for some reason. But her boss thought I was terrific, and we were great friends."

You call up her boss. The boss acknowledges that she thought Nkeche was okay for a while, but she now thinks that they just weren't aware of her shortcomings because the company admittedly did a poor job of giving her structured work in the first two months on the job. After that, though, the boss was amazed at how seemingly uninterested Nkeche was in doing the work. Nkeche apparently has told co-workers that she really doesn't like this type of work—she just does it because the pay is good. There also were issues with her making many personal phone calls, apparently to her boyfriend.

Nkeche basically denies all of this when you confront her with these new facts. She says that this manager now has it in for her because she received such negative information from her immediate supervisor. You tell Nkeche that you're concerned about referring her out to another employer; she pleads with you to give her another chance. You're not sure: It's a bad economy, and you can't afford to alienate any more employers. What do you do?

Scenario 6

A company in Florida calls you up in December looking for a co-op student to work for six months in their Florida office. It's a great job, and they are willing to hire up to four students to start in January.

You only have 12 students still available. While they all need jobs, some are stronger than others. There are only two candidates whom you are fairly positive would do a very good job in this situation. The others started looking late and/or have come across as having attitude problems, difficult personalities, and a questionable work ethic. If you send all 12 resumes, the chances are that three or four students will be hired, and that you will be very nervous about a couple of them. A highly successful performance by one or two co-ops likely will increase the number of jobs available in the future. But if even one student goes down to Florida and performs poorly, the company may never hire another student from your program. Would you send all the resumes?